FORM AND STYLE

HOUGHTON MIFFLIN COMPANY · **BOSTON**

Dallas   Geneva, Illinois   Palo Alto   Princeton, New Jersey

FORM AND STYLE

THESES, REPORTS, TERM PAPERS

EIGHTH EDITION

William Giles Campbell

Stephen Vaughan Ballou

Carole Slade *Columbia University*

Printed in the U.S.A.

Library of Congress Catalog Card Number: 89-80967

ISBN: 0-395-43204-9

ABCDEFGHIJ-SM-9543210/89

CONTENTS

PREFACE

The eighth edition of *Form and Style* provides guidance to writers of research papers and reports in college, graduate school, business, government, and the professions. The review of the fundamental processes of research makes *Form and Style* suitable as a text in courses of many kinds: basic and advanced writing courses, writing courses in the disciplines, and undergraduate and graduate courses in research and methods. At the same time, the book continues to serve experienced writers with its discussion of procedures for writing various types of theses, its thorough presentation of bibliographical forms and principles of documentation, and its comprehensive treatment of the conventions for presenting the results of research.

This book will serve as a reference work to help solve problems that arise during work on a paper. The index allows the reader to locate particular subjects quickly and easily; the glossary provides explanations of abbreviations. Writers may want to read through the entire book before beginning a project to attain some perspective on the entire process and to avoid learning by trial and error. Leaving out necessary reference information on working bibliography cards, for example, can necessitate a return trip to the library.

Chicago Manual, MLA, and APA Formats

Form and Style incorporates changes in bibliographical format made by the University of Chicago Press in *The Chicago Manual of Style*, 13th ed. (1982), and by the Modern Language Association of America in the *MLA Handbook for Writers of Research Papers*, 3rd ed. (1988), by Joseph Gibaldi and Walter S. Achtert. *Form and Style* continues to cover both formats, but in the interest of clarity it emphasizes one form, *Chicago Manual* style. In many instances, the *Chicago Manual* and MLA formats agree entirely; when MLA differs from *Chicago Manual*, directions for the alternative MLA entry appear in parentheses below the main entry.

An appendix describes the bibliographical format specified by the American Psychological Association (APA) in the *Publication Manual of the American Psychological Association*, 3rd ed. (1983).

Like previous editions, this new *Form and Style* provides complete instructions for using the note-bibliography format described in the *Chicago*

Acknowledgments

I wish to thank George E. Harlow for providing new figures for Chapter 6 and information on computers; Jeffrey C. Slade for reviewing the section on legal citation; and Marsha Z. Cummins, Bronx Community College of the City University of New York, for a continuing conversation on teaching writing. For their valuable suggestions on the preparation of the eighth edition of *Form and Style*, I am also indebted to Margaret Hilton Bahniuk, Cleveland State University; Laurel A. Briscoe, The University of Texas at Austin; Charles A. Guatney, Central Washington University; Margaret A. Kiley, Towson State University, Maryland; Alan Leftridge, Humboldt State University, California; Craig A. Newton, Bloomsburg University, Pennsylvania; Richard D. Nordstrom, California State University, Fresno; Kristine L. Olsen, California State University, Los Angeles; Joseph O. Pecenka, Northern Illinois University; Dean B. Roberts, Tennessee State University; Richard T. Ruetten, San Diego State University; Joseph C. Sommerville, The University of Toledo; Sandra Millon Underwood, University of Wisconsin-Milwaukee; and James Wolford, Joliet Junior College, Illinois.

C.S.

INTRODUCTION

Although this book has long been entitled *Form and Style,* it considers not only details of format and matters of style but also the essential processes of research and writing for research papers, reports, theses, and dissertations. These kinds of papers draw on information gathered systematically in the library or in the laboratory, research conducted either in collections of printed materials or through direct observation and experimentation. Although writers of such papers often work with materials compiled by others, they make an original contribution by organizing the information in a new way or by drawing a new conclusion on the basis of existing knowledge. The writer's creativity reveals itself in the choices made at every stage: selecting the topic, locating appropriate sources, organizing information, and presenting a clearly written and accurately documented paper.

The academic community designates research papers by a number of different names—research paper, term paper, report, thesis, dissertation—depending in part on the level, scope, and nature of the paper, as well as on individual and institutional preferences. Widely accepted definitions of these types of papers follow.

Research Paper

The library paper assigned in undergraduate courses is most often labeled a *research paper.* This name distinguishes a paper based on work in the library from an essay, which usually draws on common knowledge and the writer's personal experience. An essay on the situation facing the elderly today, for example, could derive from conversations with the writer's grandparents. A research paper on the same topic might be based on a thorough review of sources such as government statistics on Social Security benefits or on a critical reading of books such as Simone de Beauvoir's *The Coming of Age,* a study of society's attitudes toward the elderly. The writer of a research paper carefully documents the sources of information and conclusions presented in the paper. In general, the more advanced the course, the more extensive is the research required for the assigned paper.

Term Paper

The name *term paper* refers to a project that summarizes or demonstrates mastery of the work of a term or semester. Many instructors use this label interchangeably with *research paper*. Depending on the course, a term paper may or may not include formal research. A course that includes field work in teaching, for example, could require a term paper summarizing the development of teaching skills during the semester. A literature course could require a critical paper as evidence of the development of analytical techniques during the term. Similarly, a paper for either of these courses might require library research in secondary sources to substantiate the student's observations and conclusions.

Report

The word *report* generally refers to a thorough record or description of the results of firsthand experiences or reading in primary sources. A report might present the results of mixing particular chemicals under specified conditions, a compilation of observations of classes in a school for gifted children, or a summary of attitudes toward new business in a particular region. Although the writer of a report may evaluate or interpret the results of research, most often a report presents information as objectively as possible so that readers may make judgments or decisions for themselves.

Thesis

The word *thesis* commonly refers to a substantial research project. As the word (which also means a proposition or point of view defended through argument) implies, a thesis should draw an original conclusion based on information derived from research. Although the term can refer to the paper written for a doctoral degree, American usage generally reserves the name *thesis* for the master's or the undergraduate honors paper.

Dissertation

A *dissertation* is a research paper submitted by a candidate for the doctoral degree. This paper requires more research and more extensive development of ideas than a master's thesis. The word *thesis* can generally be used interchangeably with *dissertation*, depending on the field and on the preference of the institution.

Theses and dissertations are usually written under the supervision of a professor but outside of any particular course and after the completion of all course work and qualifying examinations. Most institutions require a thesis or dissertation to draw upon substantial research, to demonstrate mastery of research techniques, and to reveal an ability to communicate knowledge to the academic community. A doctoral dissertation should make an original contribution to knowledge in the field through presentation of new conclusions, previously undiscovered materials, or new methods of analysis. Theses and dissertations usually require the approval of a group of readers and an oral defense, or justification, of the procedures and conclusions before readers and other members of the department.

Most doctoral dissertations accepted by American universities are indexed in one of several bibliographies, such as *Dissertation Abstracts International (DAI)* and the *Comprehensive Dissertation Index*. Microfilm copies of dissertations can be purchased from University Microfilms, Ann Arbor, Michigan 48106.

1 WRITING RESEARCH PAPERS

Manual. A section of facing note and bibliography entries helps the writer to translate information about a work from bibliography form into note form, and vice versa. This edition includes full instructions for following the MLA policy of parenthetical references as well. The suggestions of an adviser, the personal taste of the writer, or the requirements of a college, office, or other institution will govern the choice between these two formats. Those who want to use the note-bibliography system of documentation and widely accepted, traditional bibliographical forms may choose the *Chicago Manual* style, the basic format presented consistently throughout *Form and Style.* Those who want to use parenthetical references and briefer bibliographic citations may select MLA style.

Organization and Coverage

Chapter 1 explains the process of writing a research paper from the initial steps of choosing a topic, preparing a working bibliography, and collecting information through outlining, drafting, and revising the paper. These explanations of fundamental principles make the book accessible and useful to undergraduates at all levels. Some graduate students may want to use this chapter to review the essential stages in writing a research paper. This edition includes a new section on writing with a word processor.

Chapter 2 presents the elements of a thesis or dissertation, along with requirements for research and writing of such projects. The chapter offers guidelines for preparing two types of graduate papers: theses based on the collection of empirical data and theses based on critical analysis or philosophical speculation.

Chapter 3 provides a full explanation of principles for attributing ideas and quotations to their sources. Because most plagiarism results from careless application of the rules for documentation, the chapter thoroughly discusses the documentation of direct and indirect quotations.

Chapter 4 explains the conventions for citation of sources, with reference to the note-bibliography format and MLA-style parenthetical references, and includes a section on legal citation.

Chapter 5 begins with an explanation of the format of bibliographical entries for a wide range of sources and concludes with the convenient layout of facing pages of note and bibliography forms. The sections on unpublished sources, documents, and computer materials have been considerably expanded for this edition.

Chapter 6 offers full instructions for preparing tables and figures, as well as for including figures, graphs, plates, and computer-generated materials. An expanded Chapter 7 presents the principles of grammar and mechanics most often needed in writing and revising research papers. Chapter 8 discusses in detail the process of preparing the finished copy and presents new information on using a word processor and computer printer.

Sample pages in chapters 1, 2, 5, and 6 illustrate the formats for research papers and systems of documentation described in *Form and Style.* These pages have been designed to resemble pages typed on a typewriter or printed by a computer so that they can serve as models for research papers, theses, and dissertations. The format of any printed book necessarily differs from that of a typescript, particularly in its spacing, margins, and typefaces; therefore, the printed text of *Form and Style* may vary slightly from the format recommended here for typescripts.

The principles discussed in this chapter apply to all types of research projects, reports, theses, and dissertations. Whatever the subject and scope of the project, the processes involved are quite similar. The usual steps in preparing a research paper are (1) choosing a topic, (2) preparing a working bibliography, (3) collecting information, (4) outlining the paper, (5) drafting the paper, and (6) preparing the final copy. The process of writing a research paper does not necessarily proceed sequentially; you may find yourself going back and forth or working on two or three steps at once.

CHOOSING A TOPIC

The choice of a topic involves identifying a general subject area, limiting and defining the topic, and stating the topic as a question or hypothesis.

General Subject Area

Choice of topic

The instructor or adviser sometimes specifies a broad area of study. The instructor may assign a particular topic, provide a list of possible topics, or give the writer a free choice of topics within a broad range. You should begin to consider possible topics for a research paper as soon as the assignment is announced. Graduate students can begin to compile a list of possible thesis or dissertation topics early in their academic careers, perhaps trying out some of their ideas in papers for seminars.

Possibilities for research

Even in fields that seem to have been well covered by other scholars, possibilities for further research can often be found. Scholars frequently suggest new or undiscussed areas of inquiry in their studies. Also, commonly held but unsubstantiated conclusions or new ways of testing some basic assumptions in a field can provide subjects for research papers. Recently published books or new developments in current events can afford new insight into existing ideas and thus lead to opportunities for research. As you make decisions leading to a topic, you should also consider such factors as your interest in the subject; your ability to be objective (especially if the topic is controversial); and the time available for completing the assignment.

Definition of the Topic

As you begin to focus on a specific topic within the general subject area, you should evaluate the possibilities according to the following criteria: importance and interest, manageability, and availability of resources. You do not want to begin working on a topic that will not hold your interest, that is not practical under the circumstances, or that cannot be completed within the time allowed for the assignment.

IMPORTANCE AND INTEREST Naturally you will want to devote your time to a topic of considerable importance and interest to your readers. To a certain extent, importance and interest are subjective judgments that depend on the nature of the assignment and the requirements of the instructor. A topic that seems trivial to persons in one field of study might hold great significance for specialists in another. However, a clearly important topic, such as gun control, may not make a good topic if the extensive public debate hampers your ability to make an original contribution or if your strong feelings prevent you from at least examining opposing viewpoints. Your instructor or adviser should confirm the importance of your topic, and your paper should convince readers of its significance.

MANAGEABILITY   Careful limiting of a topic will help you conduct research successfully. Topics that are too vague or broad, too narrow, or too specialized prevent you from finding suitable material. A topic that is too broad will not give sufficient direction to research and probably will necessitate superficial treatment of the subject. A topic that is too narrow will yield inadequate information, limiting your ability to reach a valid conclusion. If a topic is too specialized or too technical, it may demand knowledge you cannot acquire in the time allotted for your project. For example, you probably would not want to choose a topic that requires statistics unless you have some background in mathematics or can consult with a statistician. Ultimately, of course, readers will judge the manageability of your topic by the treatment you give it because a good paper defends not only its content but also its scope.

AVAILABILITY OF RESOURCES   Even if a topic is worthwhile and manageable, it may not be suitable if the necessary research materials are not available. The holdings of the library or libraries in which you are working should influence your choice of topic. While trying to avoid areas in which your library's holdings are weak, you may discover a subject in which it is particularly strong. If your research paper entails a survey or an experiment, you need to determine whether you can collect the required data within the time limits of the assignment.

Statement of the Topic

For most undergraduate research papers in the humanities and social sciences, you should formulate your topic as a question:

Topics stated as questions

- What are the psychological effects of computer-assisted instruction?
- How have E. D. Hirsch's ideas of "cultural literacy" been received?
- How has the Vietnam War affected Americans' view of themselves?

You will then conduct your research by exploring a full range of possible answers to your question.

As you gather information, you may discover that you have asked the wrong question or that you are more interested in answering a related question. If so, you can revise your question. Probably you will also narrow your question as you work. A question about the psychological effects of computer-assisted instruction might be narrowed to focus on instruction in foreign languages, perhaps even on one specific language. You may want to narrow your questions about the reception of the concept of "cultural literacy" to the reactions of college professors, elementary school teachers, or the general public.

Your answer to the question will become the *thesis statement,* or *controlling idea,* of your paper.

PREPARING A WORKING BIBLIOGRAPHY

After selecting the broad subject of your paper, you should begin to work in the library to determine how to shape and limit the topic with the materials available. This effort should result in a *working bibliography,* a list of sources that appear to be relevant at the initial stage of your research. Developing the working bibliography requires knowledge of library resources, the use of reference systems to locate sources, and a consistent method of preparing bibliography cards (see page 12).

During the first phase of your research, you will want to write down information about every source you encounter that might be relevant to your study, even if you are not certain you will be able to use it. You are likely to regret ignoring potential sources at this early stage. As your thinking develops, you will wish that you had made bibliography cards for works that seemed irrelevant at the time but later proved essential. Instructions and suggestions from your instructor, as well as the nature and scope of your topic, should indicate the appropriate number of sources for your working bibliography.

Library resources Even before you begin to work on a particular assignment, you should become familiar with the resources and services offered by your library: the information desk, the reference area, the card catalog (in card form or online), indexes to periodicals, reading rooms, the reserve reference area, government documents, and special collections. Your library may also provide services such as interlibrary loan, computerized searches, and database services, as well as equipment such as computer terminals, typewriters, copy machines, and microform readers. Some libraries distribute printed guides and conduct tours of their facilities. If your library does not, you should spend some time locating library resources on your own. You should also investigate all the different libraries that you may be able to use, such as the libraries of other public and private universities and colleges, museums, art galleries, and businesses in your area.

Reference room Your work in the library will probably begin in the reference room, where general and specialized indexes, bibliographies, and the card catalog can help you develop a list of relevant works. In many libraries you can use these materials in computerized form. Whether you use them in book, card, or computerized form, however, the principles remain the same. If you have trouble locating information, you should consult a librarian, who will have not only knowledge about the library but experience and expertise in the use of reference materials.

General and Specialized Indexes

The word *index* means an alphabetized list of names or topics. An index of topics covered appears at the end of most nonfiction books. *Index* also designates a kind of reference work that can be valuable in formulating a working bibliography. Such indexes are useful for locating journal and newspaper articles, which are not entered in the card catalog. Some indexes contain abstracts, or brief summaries, of articles and book reviews. Certain indexes also list books and other materials.

General indexes cover a wide range of subjects because they list every article, editorial, or review in each issue of the periodicals they survey. Specialized indexes focus on specific fields and subject areas, often collecting material from a wide range of periodicals and books. As you work in a particular field, you will accumulate a list of relevant indexes. To find out whether your library owns an index on a particular subject, consult the card catalog under the heading *Indexes,* or look up *Indexes* as a subdivision of a specific subject (as in *Spanish-American History—Indexes*). A reference librarian can identify suitable indexes for you.

An index usually includes a key to its organizational format and lists the abbreviations it uses. Brief study of this material will help you decipher the numbers and abbreviations used in a particular index.

A list of widely used general and specialized indexes appears below. The first date indicates the beginning of the series; a second date indicates the end of coverage.

JOURNAL INDEXES

Readers' Guide to Periodical Literature, 1901–
Public Affairs Information Service (PAIS), 1915–
New Periodicals Index, 1977–
Popular Periodicals Index, 1973–
Poole's Index to Periodicals, 1802–1907
Nineteenth-Century Readers' Guide, 1890–1922

NEWSPAPER INDEXES

Christian Science Monitor Index, 1960–
New York Times Index, 1851–
The Times Index (London), 1906–
Wall Street Journal Index, 1958–
Chicago Tribune Index, 1972–
Los Angeles Times Index, 1972–
Washington Post Index, 1972–

INDEXES TO GOVERNMENT PUBLICATIONS

American Statistics Index, 1973–
The Monthly Catalog of the United States Government, 1898–
Congressional Information Service Index to Publications of the United States Congress, 1970–

INDEXES TO PARTS OF BOOKS

Biography Index, 1946–
Essay and General Literature Index, 1900–

INDEXES TO BOOK REVIEWS

Book Review Digest, 1906–
Book Review Index, 1965–
International Bibliography of Book Reviews, 1971–

INDEXES IN THE HUMANITIES

America: History and Life, 1974–
Art Index, 1929–
British Humanities Index, 1962–
Guide to the Performing Arts, 1957–
Humanities Index, 1974–. With *Social Sciences Index*, 1974–. Preceded
    by *Social Sciences and Humanities Index*, 1967–73, and by *International
    Index*, 1907–66
Index to Religious Periodical Literature, 1949–
International Bibliography of Historical Sciences, 1926–
Library Literature, 1933–
Music Index, 1949–
Philosopher's Index, 1967–
*MLA International Bibliography of Books and Articles on the Modern
    Languages and Literatures*, 1921–
World Literature Today, 1960–
Guide to the Performing Arts, 1957–
Year's Work in Modern Language Studies, 1929–

INDEXES IN THE SCIENCES

Applied Science and Technology Index, 1958–
Biological and Agricultural Index, 1964–
Energy Index, 1973–
General Science Index, 1978–
Science Citation Index, 1964–

INDEXES IN THE SOCIAL SCIENCES

Business Periodicals Index, 1958–
Current Index to Journals in Education (CIJE), 1969–
Education Index, 1929–61; 1969–
Educational Studies, 1973–
International Bibliography of Economics, 1952–
International Bibliography of Political Science, 1952–
International Bibliography of Social and Cultural Anthropology, 1955–
International Bibliography of Sociology, 1952–
LLBA: Language and Language Behavior Abstracts, 1967–
Resources in Education, 1966–
Social Sciences Index, 1974–. See the listing above for accompanying
    Humanities Index.
Writings in American History, 1902–

For an exhaustive listing of reference works in the above categories as well
as in numerous others, see *Guide to Reference Books*, 10th ed., edited by
Eugene P. Sheehy et al. (Chicago: American Library Association, 1986).

Bibliographies

The word *bibliography*, which means a systematic and comprehensive
listing of works, refers not only to the section within a book that lists works
cited or consulted for the study, but also to book-length compilations of bibliographical entries on a given subject. These reference works can be very

helpful for the development of a working bibliography. To determine whether a bibliography on your subject exists, refer to the *Bibliographic Index: A Cumulative Bibliography of Bibliographies* (1937–) or to *A World Bibliography of Bibliographies* by Theodore Besterman. These works provide subject indexes to bibliographies of both types, those published separately as books and those included within other works.

After looking at these bibliographies, consult the card catalog under the heading *Bibliographies* alone, or look up *Bibliographies* as a subdivision of a specific subject. In addition, *union catalogs*, which list the holdings of books and/or periodicals in one or more libraries, as well as *trade bibliographies*, guides to books currently in print, can help you locate books relevant to your subject.

The Card Catalog

A catalog is an index of materials owned by a library. This catalog may take two forms: (1) a set of cards arranged in drawers, a *card catalog*, or (2) entries in an electronic database that may be retrieved at computer terminals, an *on-line catalog* (see page 10). Even if your library has a computerized catalog, you need to understand some of the principles governing the creation of a card catalog.

Library materials are classified by means of letters and numbers and are listed alphabetically in three ways—by author, by title, and by subject. Each work, then, has at least three cards, or entries in the catalog. More than three cards may exist for some works: a book with two authors will have author cards for both authors; a book cataloged in more than one subject area will have more than one subject card.

Author listing   The *main entry card* is the author listing. Included in the category of authors are writers, editors, compilers, and translators. When you want to know which works by an author can be found in a library, you should consult the *author cards*.

Author card

```
Ref
CB        Schrecker, Paul, 1889-
19          Work and history : an essay on the
.S39      structure of civilization / Paul
1967      Schrecker. Gloucester, Mass. : P.
          Smith, 1967 [c1948]
            xviii, 322 p. : 21 cm.
            Bibliographical footnotes.




          1. Civilization--Philosophy.
          I. Title

     13 MAY 81      1094656    HMCCat      67-5472
```

Title listing

The *title card* can lead you to a work when you know the title but not the name of the author. Libraries usually interfile title cards alphabetically with author cards according to the first word of the title, excluding *A, An,* and *The.* (For information about how to alphabetize entries in a bibliography, see page 137 in Chapter 5.)

Title card

```
                    Work and history

Ref
CB          Schrecker, Paul, 1889-
19             Work and history : an essay on  the
.S39        structure of civilization / Paul
1967        Schrecker. Gloucester, Mass. : P.
            Smith, 1967 [c1948]
               xviii, 322 p. : 21 cm.




               1. Civilization--Philosophy.
            I. Title

            13 MAY 81      1094656    HMCCat        67-5472
```

Subject listing

Subject cards are important tools for locating sources relevant to your topic; they indicate all the works in the library dealing with one subject. It is useful to note the subject areas under which the books for your topic are cataloged; those subject headings can lead you to related headings and additional sources of information. You can also find subject headings by looking up a general subject area, such as art, history, literature, linguistics, or physics, and noting the subdivisions and cross-references for the subject.

Subject card

```
            CIVILIZATION--PHILOSOPHY.

Ref
CB          Schrecker, Paul, 1889-
19             Work and history : an essay on  the
.S39        structure of civilization / Paul
1967        Schrecker. Gloucester, Mass. : P.
            Smith, 1967 [c1948]
               xviii, 322 p. : 21 cm.




               1. Civilization--Philosophy.
            I. Title

            13 MAY 81      1094656    HMCCsc        67-5472
```

Related subjects

When you search through subject headings, you should be open-minded about subjects that seem peripheral to your topic: thoughtful and inventive use of subject listings can yield original approaches and materials.

Lists of subject headings

To use subject cards efficiently, you should first study the category headings, subheadings, and cross-references in the cataloging system used by your library. The two cataloging systems you may encounter are the Library of Congress and the Dewey Decimal systems. The Dewey Decimal system is older, and many libraries no longer use it to catalog new books. Many libraries have books shelved under both systems, so you may have to look in two places for books in the same category. Knowing the major categories and subcategories of each system will help you locate sources, especially in a library with open stacks (shelves of books accessible to library users).

For a card catalog with headings based on the Library of Congress system, see either *Subject Headings Used in the Dictionary Catalogs of the Library of Congress* (with supplements), edited by Marguerite V. Quattlebaum, or *Outline of the Library of Congress Classification*. The latter is organized under the following major categories, which serve as the basis for Library of Congress call numbers (found in the upper left-hand corner of the cards):

Library of Congress system

A	General Works—Polygraphy	N	Fine Arts
B	Philosophy—Religion	P	Language and Literature
C	History—Auxiliary Sciences	Q	Science
D	History and Topography (except America)	R	Medicine
E-F	America	S	Agriculture—Plant and Animal Husbandry
G	Geography—Anthropology	T	Technology
H	Social Sciences	U	Military Science
J	Political Science	V	Naval Science
K	Law	Z	Bibliography and Library Science
L	Education		
M	Music		

For a card catalog with headings based on the Dewey Decimal system, see *Sears List of Subject Headings* by Minnie Earl Sears. The major categories are as follows:

Dewey Decimal system

000–099	General Works	500–599	Pure Science
100–199	Philosophy	600–699	Technology
200–299	Religion	700–799	The Arts
300–399	Social Sciences	800–899	Literature
400–499	Language	900–999	History

You should use these lists of subject headings when you cannot find your topic in the card catalog. For example, *Equal Rights Amendment* does not appear in the card catalog. By consulting a work on subject headings, you would discover that material on the ERA is filed under *Women's Rights—United States*.

Alphabetization

Some familiarity with the rules of alphabetization can prevent confusion in locating materials. Most abbreviations are alphabetized as if they were fully spelled out (*Mr.* is filed as *Mister*). Names beginning with *Mc* or *M'* are listed as if they were spelled *Mac* (*McHenry* is alphabetized as *MacHenry*, for example). The articles *A, An,* and *The* are disregarded in the alphabetization of titles.

Word-by-word order

A library may use one of two systems of alphabetization: word by word or letter by letter. The word-by-word system is the most common. With this system, complete words precede longer words containing them. *Hard Times* would come before *The Harder They Come*, because *Hard* precedes *Harder* under this rule. Entries with the same spelling are ordered as person, place, thing: *Reading, Thomas* comes before *Reading, Pennsylvania*, which comes before *Reading is Fun*. In the letter-by-letter system, every letter is considered. *The Harder They Come* precedes *Hard Times* because the *e* in *Harder* comes before the *t* in *Times*. Librarians will have information concerning the alphabetizing and cataloging rules followed in their library.

Letter-by-letter order

Library Information On-Line

Many libraries have begun to catalog new books on electronic databases and to replace card catalogs with computerized listings that can be retrieved at computer terminals in the library. Such a computerized listing is known as a *card catalog on-line*. Libraries with computerized catalogs provide printed instructions and the assistance of librarians. You may be able to make arrangements to retrieve library information with your personal computer by using a modem, a device that enables computers to communicate with each other over the telephone lines.

Most libraries have individualized on-line systems, but all systems operate on the same principle as a card catalog. Entries for works available in the library are organized by author, title, and subject. Some on-line systems allow you to browse through a series of call numbers; some include materials that have been ordered or are being bound. Most libraries now have acquisitions from only a few years on-line. The statement that a library has works from 1980 on-line means that all books cataloged from 1980 on are included even though they may have been published in previous years. A book published in 1970 but not purchased until 1978 and not cataloged until 1980 would thus appear in the on-line catalog; alternatively, a book published in 1978 and cataloged in 1979 would appear only in the card catalog. Eventually, the entire catalogs of most libraries will be on-line, but in the meantime you will have to use both card and computer systems.

To use an on-line catalog, you will have to follow directions for entering the system. Once you have entered the system, you will be asked to request a work by author, title, or subject. If you want either a specific work by a particular author or a list of an author's works, you will type in the name of the author (last name first) at the appropriate place with whatever punctuation and commands the instructions request. If you know only the title of a work, you will type in the title, also at the appropriate place, again following instructions about punctuation and commands. If you have a general subject in mind, you will type in that subject. The only subjects you can use in an on-line system are the standard headings and subheadings found in the card catalog and fully listed in *Subject Headings Used in the Dictionary Catalogs of the Library of Congress* (with supplements), edited by Marguerite V. Quattlebaum, and *Outline of the Library of Congress Classification*.

Many systems have printers that produce a paper copy of the entry as it appears on the screen. This service allows you to have complete bibliographical information without copying it by hand, a time-consuming and sometimes inaccurate process. You should remember, however, to verify the information in the entry when you consult the book itself. A sample printout of an entry from an on-line catalog appears on page 11.

Print-out of an on-line catalog entry

```
                              (1)
    Personal author:  Jones, Emrys.                    (2)
(3) Names:    1. Eyles, John, joint author.
   →Title:  An introduction to social geography / Emrys Jones and John Eyles.
(6) Publication facts:  Oxford (Eng.) ; New York : Oxford University Press,
     → 1977.        (4)      (7)    (8)      (9)       (10)                    (5)
(11) Physical description:  xi, 273 p. : ill. ; 23 cm.
   →Subjects:    1. Anthropo-geography.   2. Sociology, Urban.

    Library, Item Location Code (call number) and Holdings:
      1. BURGESS  GF41.J66
                (12)
```

(1) Author of book	(7) Number of pages in introduction
(2) Co-author of book	(8) Number of pages in book
(3) Title	(9) Indication of illustrations
(4) Places of publication	(10) Height of book
(5) Publisher	(11) Subject entries for book
(6) Date of publication	(12) Call number

Database Services

Many libraries provide computer searches that allow you to retrieve bibliographical entries from numerous electronic databases, collections of information available on a computer terminal. Many indexes and bibliographies, including *Arts and Humanities Citation Index, Biological Abstracts, Chemical Abstracts, Dissertation Abstracts, ERIC, Legal Resource Index, MLA Bibliography, Physics Abstracts, Psychology Abstracts,* and *Sociological Abstracts,* are available through computers as well as in print form.

Use of descriptors

To use a database, you must enter a *descriptor,* a key word that the computer looks for as it searches its lists of titles. Some database systems have a list of descriptors from which you can select the words most likely to yield relevant entries. Other systems allow you to search for any word that appears in a title, abstract, or article. You may also enter a series of descriptors or words to narrow the focus of your search. For a study of Saint Augustine's interpretations of Genesis, you might ask the computer to retrieve titles that contain two or more of the following words: *Saint Augustine, Genesis, Scripture, interpretation.*

Charges for database searches

Libraries that own database services may not charge for the use of them. However, when a library must contact a database off-campus, you may have to pay for each computer search and for each title located. Because the cost of such searches can be considerable, you should not use them until you have precisely defined your descriptors.

For information on database services, see the *Directory of Online Databases,* published quarterly with two additional updates a year by Cuadra/ Elsevier.

Some large databases, such as encyclopedias, dictionaries, and complete works of major authors, are sold in the form of CD-ROM (Compact Disk–Read Only Memory), the type of disk that is used in compact-disk stereo systems. To read these disks with a personal computer, you need a special drive unit. For information on materials available in CD-ROM form, see Jean-Paul Emard, *CD-ROMs in Print, 1988–89: An International Guide* (Westport: Micklin, 1988).

COLLECTING INFORMATION

To gather information for your paper, you need to develop a bibliography, evaluate sources for their dependability and authority, and take accurate, useful notes.

Bibliography Cards

Books and articles that appear to be relevant to your topic should be listed systematically, one to a card and in the bibliographic format that you will use for your final draft.

For ease of revision and alphabetization, you should list each source on a separate card. Most researchers prefer three-by-five-inch cards, but other

Bibliography card for a book

McPherson, James M. <u>Battle Cry of Freedom: The Civil War Era.</u> New York: Ballantine, 1988.

> Oates, Joyce Carol. " Soul at White
> Heat: The Romance of Emily Dickinson's
> Poetry." <u>Critical Inquiry</u> 13.4 (1987):
> 806 - 24.

sizes may be used. It is important, however, to use consistently whatever size you choose.

Each entry on a bibliography card should follow the format specified by the style sheet governing your final paper. (See pages 146 through 179 for the various bibliographic formats used by the University of Chicago Press and the Modern Language Association.)

Even though you may not find all the information you need for a particular bibliographic form in the index you consult, you will save a good deal of time by recording the entry as the style sheet indicates, leaving spaces for the missing elements as a reminder to locate them when you consult the source itself. If the entries on your cards follow the specified format, you will be able to prepare your final bibliography by simply transferring the information from the cards.

Critical Evaluation of Sources

As you select works to read and sources to use in your paper, you should continually evaluate the materials with regard to the primary or secondary nature of the source, the objectivity of the source, the qualifications of the author, and the level of the source.

PRIMARY AND SECONDARY SOURCES You should consider whether a particular work is a primary or a secondary source for your purposes. *Primary sources* are basic materials with little or no annotation or editorial alteration, such as manuscripts, diaries, letters, interviews, and laboratory reports. *Secondary sources* derive from primary materials and include analysis, interpretation, and commentary on primary materials.

Depending on the point of view of your research paper, a set of materials may be considered either primary or secondary. A research paper on the contribution of E. B. White, a writer and editor, to *The New Yorker* magazine would treat White's articles in the magazine as primary materials. It would treat as a secondary source Brendan Gill's book *Here at the New Yorker*, an account of the editorial leadership of the magazine during the years White worked there. The writer of a paper on Brendan Gill, however, would consider *Here at the New Yorker* a primary source. Your topic may require you to emphasize either primary or secondary sources or to use a combination of the two.

OBJECTIVITY   The objectivity of a source is its lack of bias or prejudice. Total objectivity is not humanly possible, but the most valuable sources identify any biases that might be caused by the author's affiliations or allegiances—whether economic, political, philosophical, or religious—and any limitations inherent in the author's approach or the materials used. A writer with investments in farms that produce soybeans, for example, should indicate the possibility of bias for economic reasons in a study on the relative advantage of soybeans and seaweed as bases for new foods. Similarly, the writer of a study of the automotive industry based on information obtained from executives at Chrysler or Ford should make readers aware that the nature of the sources may have influenced his or her conclusions. Even if a writer does not reveal possible reasons for bias, you should try to discern the writer's point of view and evaluate the work accordingly.

Bias and prejudice in sources

QUALIFICATIONS OF THE AUTHOR   An author's qualifications for writing a work, such as academic degrees, professional credentials, and experience and status in the field, may influence your choice of a source. Information about an author's qualifications may be found in preliminary or appendix materials in the source itself, in a biographical dictionary or directory such as *Who's Who*, or in an encyclopedia. The information may provide clues to the quality, nature, and objectivity of a source.

LEVEL   The intended audience determines the level of a work in areas such as diction, sentence structure, complexity, and assumed background knowledge. You may find sources that are too technical and advanced. When you do, you should either seek guidance in understanding them or not use them. On the other hand, you may encounter works written for a wide audience that are too general or simplistic for your paper. You should not use these works either.

Note Taking

An effective system for recording information requires you to select cards of a convenient size, a system of notation for relating the note cards to the bibliography cards and the outline, and a form for recording information. Even though you will probably want to photocopy some materials in the library, you will still need to take notes on the works that you find useful for your paper. Having a photocopy of a work does not substitute for having a set of note cards on which you organize selected information from the work.

NOTE CARDS The size of card you choose (three-by-five, four-by-six, or five-by-eight inches) should depend on the anticipated length of your notes. Some researchers prefer the discipline of using the small three-by-five cards, which preclude placing too much material on one card. The four-by-six size provides more space for notes without being too large to use for bibliography cards. The five-by-eight size is convenient if you wish to make substantial comments or attach photocopied materials. Half-sheets of paper can substitute for five-by-eight cards, but papers tend to stick together and become rumpled. The temptation to take notes on large sheets of notebook paper or on both sides of a page should be avoided because this kind of note taking makes rearranging the material difficult. You will find that you are likely to follow the logic and development of each source rather than to impose your own organization on the material. Whatever size of card you choose, use it consistently.

SYSTEM FOR NOTE TAKING Before you begin to take notes, enter on the card the information you will need to link the note card to the appropriate bibliography card. The last name of the author (and, if you have more than one entry for an author, the title) usually suffices. Some researchers number each bibliography card and put the corresponding number on each note card. Using the author's name, however, is more likely to be accurate than using numbers. You should check to be certain that you have recorded accurately the page number from which you are transcribing information. If you turn a page in the middle of a note, indicate precisely the point of division between the pages so that if you use only part of the note in the paper, you will know to which page in the source the note should refer. Also, before you put the note card aside, enter either the section of your outline or the area of your subject to which the information is relevant. Some researchers pencil in this comment so that they can make changes as their thinking develops.

Identification of sources on note cards

Subject headings on note cards

FORM You may choose to record information in one of two basic forms: direct quotation or summary. A *direct quotation* is an exact copy of a portion of the original text (see note card 1 on page 16). The quotation may encompass one or more words, phrases, clauses, complete sentences, or paragraphs. It is a good idea to take down a direct quotation when you feel there is a chance you will want to quote the passage or when the material meets one of the criteria for direct quotation discussed in Chapter 3 (see page 67). You should also write down a quotation when you wish to have the material on your note cards precisely as the author wrote it so that you can reread or verify it later. Before leaving the source, check direct quotations carefully so that you can be confident of their accuracy.

Direct quotation

Note card 1: direct quotation

Musical Settings – Novels
III. A.

Smith, Grover, ed.
p. 821
 Aldous Huxley to Leonard Bernstein, 4 Apr. 1957

"... I am writing to ask if you would be at all interested in reading a dramatic version of my novel <u>Brave New World</u>, which I have recently made, with a view to a musical setting."

The use of direct quotation in note taking helps ensure accuracy, but direct quotation can be a waste of time if you do not plan to use the quotations in the paper or if you merely copy information without understanding or digesting it. The use of summary or paraphrase rather than direct quotation

Summary or paraphrase

forces you to comprehend as you read and leads naturally into the process of writing the paper. A *summary* is a brief restatement of the original material in your own words. A restatement of the author's ideas in about the same number of words as in the original is a *paraphrase*. The terms are commonly used interchangeably.

When you write a summary during note taking, you must be careful to avoid using the author's wording. Changing an occasional word or reversing

Precision in note taking

the order of phrases or sentences does not result in an adequate summary. A good method is to try to write a summary without looking at the source. After writing a summary, look at the original and make a critical comparison, checking for duplication of wording and accuracy in the statement of ideas (see note card 2). If you find that you have used more than two consecutive words from the original (with the exception of articles and prepositions), place them in quotation marks. Carelessness in writing a summary can result

Unintentional plagiarism

in unintentional plagiarism. (See pages 65 through 67 in Chapter 3 for advice on avoiding plagiarism.) Even though the summary contains your own words, you will want to give credit for the ideas if you use them in your paper. Be as careful about recording the author's name and page numbers for a summary or a paraphrase as you would be for a direct quotation.

Note card 2 is a summary of the contents of a letter. If you have large amounts of material to summarize, you might want to write your summary notes in outline form (see note card 3), either in an informal way or in a de-

Outlines in notes

tailed, formal manner following the specific rules for outlining presented later in this chapter. Even when you outline, you should distinguish carefully between your own words and the words of the author.

Whatever form you choose for taking notes, you will want to strike a balance between taking enough notes to avoid having to return to your

Note card 2:
summary

> Musical Settings – Novels
> III. A.
>
> Smith, Grover, ed.
> p. 821 Aldous Huxley wrote to Leonard
> Bernstein on April 4, 1957, to ask him to
> consider setting a "dramatic version" of
> <u>Brave</u> <u>New</u> <u>World</u> to music.

Note card 3:
outline form

> Smith, Grover, ed.
> Aldous Huxley's letters on liberty
> Threats to liberty
>   1. Applied psychology (p.539) letter of 18 March 1946
>   to Julian Huxley
>   2. bureaucracy (p.451) letter of 19 March 1940
>   to E.S.P. Haynes
>   3. conditioning and mind control (p.837)
>   letter of 12 December 1957 to
>   Julian Huxley
>   4. "urge for tidiness" (p.847) letter of
>
>   cont.

sources and taking repetitious or irrelevant notes. Judgment in this matter develops naturally as you learn more about your topic and as you master the process of writing a research paper.

OUTLINING THE PAPER

Some researchers begin with a tentative or working outline that guides the choice of research materials; others let the outline grow from their research. If you develop an outline in advance, it should remain open to change as you read and take notes. Formulating and revising an outline will help you arrive at a logical and meaningful structure for your paper.

Creating an outline involves making decisions about the thesis statement, the principle of organization, the type of outline, and the format of the outline.

The Thesis Statement

The answer to the question with which you began your research or the substantiated hypothetical statement will eventually become the thesis statement, or controlling idea, for the paper. As your outline evolves and your research leads you in new directions, your thesis statement may change, and you should frequently consider revising it as your work progresses. The statement you make will depend on the nature and amount of material you find. Your final thesis statement should cover all the points made in the paper. It need not necessarily enumerate each point, but your reader should not be disconcerted by encountering an area of inquiry not suggested by the thesis statement.

Principles of Organization

The organization of a paper often develops naturally in the course of research and during the writing of early drafts. Nevertheless, it is often instructive to try out various principles or patterns of organization with your material. Experimentation can help you to find the pattern most appropriate to your material or can lead you to new insights. Among the most useful principles for structuring a research paper are chronology, comparison and contrast, spatial pattern, cause and effect, and analysis. These patterns of development are often used in combination, and they can be applied to individual paragraphs as well as to an entire paper.

CHRONOLOGY   The chronological pattern explains each of the steps in a sequentially ordered process. The basic plan of this chapter, for instance, is chronological: the suggestions for writing a research paper begin with selecting a topic and progress step by step to proofreading the final copy. The chronological pattern is often appropriate for a paper describing a series of historical, political, or sociological processes or events.

COMPARISON AND CONTRAST   The pattern of comparison and contrast presents the similarities and/or differences between two or more persons, places, or things. A logical development by comparison and contrast entails discussion of the same qualities of both subjects. For example, the statement that one politician was a poor public speaker and another had a good understanding of the legislative system does not provide a basis for comparison and contrast. The speaking ability of both politicians, as well as their understanding of political institutions, should be discussed.

Comparison and contrast are appropriate when a subject can best be understood by distinguishing it from others in its class.

SPATIAL PATTERN   The spatial pattern develops the physical layout or geographical dimensions of a topic. It can guide the reader through a topic that includes several locations, such as the seasonal habitats of various animals, the movement of troops in the Vietnam War, or the concentration of heavy industry in the United States.

CAUSE AND EFFECT   A cause-and-effect paper presents the events or forces that produced certain results, speculates about how things might have turned out if conditions had been different, or reports controlled experimentation to determine the factors important to a particular outcome. Cause and effect are difficult to determine, particularly in the social sciences, and valid work in this area should either control or take into account as many factors as possible. Topics such as possible explanations for the decline in students' reading scores in the United States in the past decade or reasons for population shifts away from inner cities lend themselves to development by cause and effect.

ANALYSIS   Some subjects can best be understood by an examination of their component parts. Analysis is the process of dividing a subject into its parts and classifying them. A research paper on the responsibilities of a hospital administrator might proceed by grouping the duties by types and discussing each type.

Major divisions of a paper   Your outline will develop naturally from the principle of organization you select. A paper involving comparison and contrast or cause and effect, for example, will usually have two major divisions. A paper organized chronologically, spatially, or analytically may have a number of major divisions. After you have identified the large segments of the paper, you can fill in the points to be made in each part.

Types of Outlines

Your working outline may consist of casual jottings, but the outline you present to your instructor either in the middle of your research or with your final paper should be formal and consistently developed. You may choose either a topic outline or a sentence outline, depending on your preference and that of your instructor.

TOPIC OUTLINE   The entries in a topic outline are words, phrases, or clauses: they are not complete sentences. The entries should be parallel; they all should take the same grammatical form. If you use a noun phrase for one entry, you should continue using noun phrases consistently. You may have to rework some of your entries to make them parallel, but paying attention to grammatical form often leads to clear and logical thinking. (See the sample topic outline on page 27 and the discussion of parallelism that begins on page 216 in Chapter 7.)

SENTENCE OUTLINE   The entries in a sentence outline are complete sentences. The process of writing a research paper involves writing sentences from the topics in the topic outline, in effect producing a sentence outline. A sentence outline therefore serves as a beginning for the paper and as a test of the logic of the outline. (See the sample sentence outline in Chapter 7 on page 217.)

Outline Formats

The two basic formats for an outline are the number-letter sequence and the decimal pattern. The number-letter sequence is shown in the following example:

Number-letter sequence

```
I. The two reasons for . . .

    A. The first reason . . .

        1. The women . . .

            a. They could . . .

                (1) The time . . .

                    (a) The technology . . .

                        i) The latest development . . .

                        ii) The plans for . . .

                    (b) The receptive public . . .

                (2) The place . . .

            b. They could . . .

        2. The men . . .

    B. The second reason . . .

II. The reasons against . . .
```

Decimal outline

The sequence for a decimal outline proceeds as follows:

```
1. The two reasons for . . .

    1.1 The first reason . . .
```

```
1.1.1 The women . . .

    1.1.1.1 They could . . .

        1.1.1.1.1 The time . . .

        1.1.1.1.2 The receptive public . . .

    1.1.1.2 They could . . .

1.1.2 The men . . .

1.2 The second reason . . .

2. The reasons against . . .
```

With either format, logic requires that there be at least two items at each level or subdivision; that is, an A must not appear without a B, a 1.1.1 must not appear without a 1.1.2 because nothing can be divided into fewer than two parts. When you find that you have only one subdivision for a section, you should either restate the major heading to include the subdivision or search for another logical division for the heading. (See the sample outline on page 27.)

WRITING THE PAPER

Writing a research paper involves preparing a first draft, revising the draft as often as necessary, editing the draft, preparing the documentation and attending to other elements of the format, and proofreading.

Although to some extent you will approach these tasks in the order they are listed here, you should not expect to complete any of them until you have a finished copy. Each activity proceeds both linearly and recursively. Even as you proceed with writing your first draft, you will constantly be thinking back to the sentences and paragraphs you have already written and thinking ahead to the projected design of your entire paper. Similarly, throughout the writing process you may be preparing parts of the final format such as the notes and bibliography.

The First Draft

Exploratory writing
As you do your research, you may want to write brief, exploratory pieces to develop your thinking. You may eventually incorporate them into your paper, or you may set them aside. Either way, because writing not only reflects thought but generates it, writing during all stages of research will help you refine your thesis statement and outline.

When you write short papers or portions of a long paper, you may not need an outline in advance. For a lengthy research paper, however, you probably will want to have a relatively complete outline, with your notes organized by topics and subtopics, before you begin to write. As you write, you may find that you will need to rework your outline or that you will need to do additional research.

Even if they plan to use a word processor to type their papers, many writers prefer to draft their papers by hand. Some find that they choose their words more carefully and that they write more varied and complex sentences that way. Others prefer to write the first and other drafts on a typewriter or a word processor. Whichever equipment you choose, you should be aware that your choice may affect your writing.

Writing on a word processor

One of the advantages of a word processor is that it allows you to write as fast as your fingers can press the keys. This capacity to produce a great deal of prose quickly may allay your fear of the blank page and help you cut short the slow process of writing in longhand. Many people who use a word processor, however, tend to produce prose that is repetitive and loosely structured, that contains many superficial errors, some of which may be typographical, and that resembles spoken rather than written language. Such writers may overcome the initial impediments to writing, but they must develop the ability to correct for any deficiencies fostered by the machine. Other writers derive pleasure from writing with their favorite pen and on paper of a particular size or color and then typing their draft into a word processor or on a typewriter. Whatever your preference, you should constantly monitor your writing process and scrutinize your writing, making changes in your tools and techniques to best serve your work.

Revision

Writers often resist revising because they do not want to mess up a clean handwritten or typed copy. Writing, however, is a craft; and writers, like other craftspeople, should be prepared to cut, discard, and reshape their materials. Most workshops contain a clutter of scraps. Some of the scraps can be collected and reused; others are eventually swept away. Most artisans cherish such evidence of the progress of their work. Experienced writers have generally learned to do likewise. Rather than seeing a draft with insertions and deletions marked in pencil as a mess, they see it as a work in progress. This is not to deny that revision is a sometimes painful, though natural, part of the creative process.

If you use a word processor, your printed copy will give you a view of your drafts that is different from the view that appears on the screen. Seeing your writing in different formats will help you to revise, which means to re-envision. You also give yourself the opportunity to have this double perspective on your work if you type a handwritten draft (or have someone else type it).

Revising on a word processor

Although word processors facilitate revision, most writers who use them tend to make the small changes, of words and individual sentences, more readily than they rearrange paragraphs and sections. Working on a screen that allows you to see only twenty-four lines at a time makes it difficult to keep the structure of the entire paper in mind. Often it is easier to print out several pages and make your revisions on paper. It is quite common for writers to rework a sentence or paragraph on the computer screen, only to find that it no longer fits logically into the paper.

The computer also allows you to shift entire paragraphs and sections by pressing only a few keys. Any change in the position of a paragraph nearly always requires other revisions, such as changes in transitions and the re-ordering of sentences elsewhere in the paper. As you revise, you would be wise to keep all versions of your draft because you may find that you want to restore something you had deleted. Some writers keep each draft in a separate, dated file; others keep a file of deleted paragraphs, sentences, or even single words for possible use in another part of the paper.

Questions for revision

The following questions can help you notice passages in your work that need revision:

- Does the thesis statement govern everything in the paper?
- Does the introduction prepare the reader for the paper?
- Are the paragraphs developed logically and arranged in a sequence that is coherent?
- Do any sections repeat or contradict other sections?
- Does the entire paper read smoothly, with transitions that carry the reader from one idea to the next?

After you have answered all these questions affirmatively, you can begin your editing.

Editing

When you have a thoroughly revised draft ready for final typing, you should read through it at least once more, paying attention to every detail. Once again you should evaluate every sentence for clarity, check every paragraph for coherence, think about every choice of diction and sentence structure. In addition, you should look for mechanical errors in spelling and punctuation as well as for typographical errors. Chapter 7 discusses the problems that most often arise in the editing of a research paper.

Editing on a word processor

Many word-processing programs have features that you can use to help identify and correct errors. When you find an error, you can use the search command to retrieve other instances of it and to replace it automatically with the correct form. An adjunct to most word-processing programs is the spell checker, which identifies the misspelling of any word in its dictionary and allows you to add to the dictionary any words that you tend to misspell. Other programs, such as Grammatik and Workbench, can be used to check for some grammatical and mechanical errors.

When you use any of those features or programs, you should remember that the computer does not think; it only simulates thinking. The only misspellings that a spell checker can identify are errors in words that are in its dictionary. If you type the wrong word but spell it correctly—if you type *thee* when you meant to type *three*—the spell checker will not find the error. Other error identification programs may point out problems, but they cannot help you find the most effective way to revise.

Format

Instructors in different disciplines have different requirements for the format of research papers. Most undergraduate papers, however, include the following parts in addition to the body, or text: a title page, an outline page, documentation (through parenthetical references in the text or through endnotes or footnotes), and a bibliography. Any given paper or instructor may require only some of these elements. (See Chapter 2 for the elements of a thesis or dissertation and for complete typing instructions for research papers, theses, and dissertations.)

TITLE PAGE   The title page of a research paper should include the title of the paper, the student's name, the course and section, the instructor's name, and the date. (See the sample title page on page 26.) If your instructor does not require a title page, you should include this information on the first page of the text. (See page 28 for a sample paper without a title page.)

OUTLINE PAGE   The outline page of a research paper presents a topic or sentence outline and sometimes includes the thesis statement. The numbers and headings on the outline page should not appear within the text of your paper. (See the sample outline on page 27.)

DOCUMENTATION   Each fact or opinion obtained from a source, whether quoted directly or summarized, must be documented with a parenthetical reference or with a note. Notes may be in one of two forms: footnotes or endnotes. Footnotes are placed at the bottom of the page that contains the material they refer to. Endnotes are grouped together in a separate section at the end of the paper. (See the sample endnotes page on page 30.) Chapter 4 discusses the documentation of first and subsequent references in two formats: the note-bibliography format described in *The Chicago Manual of Style* (13th ed.) and the parenthetical-reference format favored by the Modern Language Association and described in the *MLA Handbook for Writers of Research Papers* (3rd ed.).

BIBLIOGRAPHY   The type of bibliography most often requested for an undergraduate research paper is a list of the works that are referred to in the paper. If you read a work but did not cite it, that work is not included in your list. Chapter 5 presents information on preparing bibliographies and lists of works cited. (See the sample bibliography page for a short research paper on page 31.)

Proofreading

Rereading the finished copy, or proofreading, can make the difference between a mediocre paper and an excellent one. You should read your paper just one more time, even though you may be tired of it. Better yet, if possible, you should allow yourself enough time to set the paper aside for at least one day so that you can read it with a fresh perspective. Speed-reading techniques are not appropriate for proofreading. You need to read almost letter for letter. Careful proofreading will help ensure that the paper you submit does justice to the time, energy, and thought you invested in its creation.

ELEMENTS OF
RESEARCH PAPERS

Sample Pages

On the following pages are sample pages from research papers illustrating principles of layout and format described in Chapter 1.

[5 inches]

Euthanasia: Mercy or Murder?

[quadruple space]

Beth Ganter

Professor Slade

English 1304.7

College Composition

19 May 1990

[1 inch]

Title page for a research paper (optional)

[double space]
                             Outline
[double space]
Controlling Idea: With the advancement of medical technology,

              euthanasia has become increasingly common, and

              society now must decide whether euthanasia is an

              act of mercy or murder.

    I. Background of the Controversy

       A. Definitions of Euthanasia, Active and Passive

       B. Causes of Controversy

   II. Euthanasia as Murder

       A. Right to Life--Medical Argument

       B. God's Decision--Religious Argument

       C. Killing and Murder--Legal Argument

  III. Euthanasia as Mercy

       A. Unnecessary Suffering and Burden

       B. Right to Die

       C. Moral Justification

   IV. Court Decisions

       A. Quinlan Case

       B. Haemmerli and Montemarrano

       C. Other Cases

    V. Possible Solutions

       A. Resolution of Court Cases

       B. Proposed Legislation

Outline page for a research paper (optional)

Beth Ganter } [double space]

English 1304.7

Professor Slade

19 May 1990 } [double space]

[5 spaces] Euthanasia: Mercy or Murder? [double space]

→ Euthanasia literally means "good death," but we now use the word to mean the deliberate ending of the life of a person suffering from a painful or fatal condition.[1] This act may be committed with or without the person's consent, and euthanasia may be described as active or passive. Active euthanasia refers to withdrawing treatment already in progress, whereas passive euthanasia involves withholding treatment before it begins. As the law now stands, active euthanasia is criminal homicide, but passive euthanasia is a legal action. However, enormous advances in medicine, which have made it possible to keep a terminally ill person alive almost indefinitely, have blurred the distinction somewhat. At the same time, they have complicated the decisions about whether to prolong a patient's life by artificial means or whether to let him or her die naturally.

[5 spaces]
→ In the past two decades, euthanasia has been hotly debated by those who believe it is murder and those who believe it is mercy. Many people believe that a human life must be preserved at any cost and that any decision that shortens a life is murder. Others believe that it is wrong to prolong the life or the suffering of a terminally ill patient or one kept alive solely by artificial

First page of a research paper with endnotes and no title page

The law gives capable patients the right to refuse treatment before it is started,[17] but it does not give them the right to end treatment once it has been started. The right to die with dignity is a statement heard more and more, for many people fear deterioration of their minds and bodies more than they fear death. Olive Ruth Russell, author of <u>Freedom to Die: Moral and Legal Aspects of Euthanasia</u>, asks this thought-provoking question:

[10 spaces]   [double space]

> Does society or an individual have the right to deny
>
> him [the patient] the freedom to choose death to
>
> avoid hopeless suffering, provided that by so doing he
>
> neither harms another nor deprives society of useful
>
> services?[18]

[double space]

The advocates of euthanasia emphatically answer no, since the right to die with dignity is a basic human right. In the case of Karen Ann Quinlan, the Quinlans held that denying the family the right to end the use of extraordinary medical measures was a denial of constitutional rights.[19] The First Amendment states that Congress cannot pass a law prohibiting the practice of any religion. The Quinlans maintain that the discontinuance of extraordinary means is a part of the belief of Roman Catholics and that therefore denying the family the right to end treatment violated their First Amendment rights. This principle was supported in <u>Meyers</u> v. <u>Nebraska</u>, which established the right of a family to make basic decisions affecting the lives of its members.[20]

Page of text using endnotes

[1 inch]

Ganter 11

[double space]
Notes
[double space]

1 *In the Matter of Karen Quinlan: The Complete Legal Briefs, Court Proceedings, and Decision in the Superior Court of New Jersey* (N.p.: Univ. Publications of America, 1975), 93.

2 "Physician Notes Euthanasia Shift," *New York Times*, 7 Dec. 1975, late ed., sec. 1, 11.

3 G. Cant, "Deciding When Death Is Better Than Life," *Time*, 16 July 1973, 36.

4 "Euthanasia: The Deadly Dilemma," *Family Health* 10 (Sept. 1978): 39.

5 Frederic Grumberg, "Who Lives and Dies?" *New York Times*, 22 Apr. 1974, late ed., sec. 1, 35.

6 Cant, 36.

7 Olive Ruth Russell, *Freedom to Die: Moral and Legal Aspects of Euthanasia* (New York: Human Sciences Press, 1975), 218.

8 *In the Matter of Karen Quinlan*, 93.

9 David W. Meyers, *The Human Body and the Law: A Medico-Legal Study* (Chicago: Aldine, 1972), 144.

10 *In the Matter of Karen Quinlan*, 160.

11 Meyers, 143.

12 R. F. Morison, "Death: Process or Event?" *Death Inside Out*, ed. Peter Steinfels and Robert M. Veatch (New York: Harper & Row, 1975), 67.

Endnotes page

[double space]
Bibliography
[double space]

Cant, G.　"Deciding When Death Is Better Than Life."　Time,

　　　16 July 1973, 36—37.

"Euthanasia and the Law."　Newsweek, 28 Jan. 1974, 45.

"Euthanasia Pact Described."　New York Times, 14 March 1978, late

　　　ed., sec. 1, 41.

"Euthanasia: The Deadly Dilemma."　Family Health 10 (Sept. 1978):

　　　39—46.

Grumberg, Frederic.　"Who Lives and Dies?"　New York Times,

　　　22 Apr. 1974, late ed., sec. 1, 35.

Henson, R. G.　"Utilitarianism and the Wrongness of Killing."

　　　Philosophy Review 80 (1971): 320—27.

"Implications of Mercy: Case in the Netherlands."　Time,

　　　5 March 1973, 70.

In the Matter of Karen Quinlan: The Complete Legal Briefs, Court

　　　Proceedings, and Decision in the Superior Court of New Jersey.

　　　N.p.: Univ. Publications of America, 1975.

"Israelis Sentence Woman in Mercy Killing of Son."　New York Times,

　　　24 Oct. 1975, late ed., sec. 1, 4.

"'Mercy Killing' Trial Opens Tomorrow."　New York Times,

　　　13 Jan. 1974, late ed., sec. 1, 44.

Meyers, David W.　The Human Body and the Law: A Medico—Legal Study.

　　　Chicago: Aldine, 1972.

Bibliography page

By the time Williams began Paterson in the 1940s, he had already made most of his technical innovations, the consequences of which he would work out in this epic. In 1947, he wrote to Kenneth Burke, "I am trying in Paterson to work out the problems of a new prosody" (Selected Letters 257–58), and in his Autobiography he wrote of the composition of Paterson that "it was the 'line' that was the key——a study of the line itself, which challenged me" (60).

The development of a new poetic form is an essential theme in Paterson. Book I defines the poet's task as the rearrangement of reality so that its inherent meanings may be revealed: "a mass of detail / to interrelate on a new ground, difficultly" (30). At present, however, poetry is deformed, being "subverted by thought" (13) and "bent, forked by preconception and accident" (15). The first book ends with a prose passage from John Addington Symonds' Studies of the Greek Poets, which stresses the accommodation of subject and form: "Deformed verse was suited to deformed morality" (53). The introduction of prose into Paterson was not an "antipoetic" device for Williams, as it was for Wallace Stevens, but rather a demonstration that prose is the undigested source of poetry, the function of which is to organize and compress reality: "It [poetry] is life——but transmuted to another tighter form" (198). The word "line" in Paterson has multi-layered meanings and

Page of text with MLA-style parenthetical references

[1 inch]

Carmichael 17

[double space]

Works Cited

[double space]

Brinnin, John Malcolm. William Carlos Williams. Minneapolis: U of

Minnesota P, 1963.

Cambon, Glauco. The Inclusive Flame: Studies in American Poetry.

Bloomington: Indiana UP, 1963.

Guimond, James. The Art of William Carlos Williams: A Discovery and

Possession of America. Urbana: U of Illinois P, 1968.

Heal, Edith, ed. I Wanted to Write a Poem. Boston: Beacon, 1958.

Koch, Vivienne. William Carlos Williams. New York: New Directions,

1950.

Koehler, Stanley. "The Art of Poetry VI: William Carlos Williams."

Paris Review 32 (1964): 110–51.

Martz, Louis L. The Poem of the Mind. New York: Oxford UP, 1966.

Miller, J. Hillis, ed. William Carlos Williams: A Collection of

Critical Essays. Englewood Cliffs: Prentice, 1966.

Ostrom, Alan. The Poetic World of William Carlos Williams.

Carbondale: Southern Illinois UP, 1966.

Pearce, Roy Harvey. The Continuity of American Poetry. Princeton:

Princeton UP, 1961.

Peterson, Walter Scott. An Approach to Paterson. New Haven: Yale

UP, 1967.

Solt, Mary Ellen. "William Carlos Williams: Idiom and Structure,"

Massachusetts Review 3 (1962): 277–81.

Works cited page showing MLA shortened forms of publishers' names

2 ELEMENTS OF THESES AND DISSERTATIONS

A thesis or a dissertation contains three categories of materials: the preliminaries (front matter), the text (body) of the paper, and the reference materials (back matter or end matter). When the thesis or dissertation is bound in book form for library use or reproduced on microfilm, these elements are included.

This chapter presents descriptions and models of the parts of a thesis or dissertation along with procedures for preparing the entire typescript. A university graduate office usually provides information on required format. Consult university regulations before you begin to prepare final copy.

THE PRELIMINARIES (FRONT MATTER)

The preliminaries, or front matter, of a thesis or dissertation consist of any or all of the following elements: abstract; approval sheet; title page; copyright page; table of contents; lists of tables, figures, and plates; clearance forms; acknowledgments; preface. Not every thesis will include all these elements. They usually appear in this order, but a dissertation adviser or university regulations may require another arrangement. All the preliminaries, with the exception of the abstract and the approval sheet, are counted as pages of the paper. The title page and the copyright page, though counted, remain unnumbered. All other pages of front matter are given lowercase roman numerals centered at the bottom of the page.

Abstract

Most universities require that a doctoral candidate submit an *abstract*, a brief descriptive summary, of the dissertation. The abstract should include a statement of the problem or issue, a brief description of the research method and design, major findings and their significance, and the conclusions. A reader should be able to decide from the abstract whether to read the entire dissertation. Because the abstract is not part of the dissertation, it is neither numbered nor counted as a page. (See the sample abstract on page 55.)

To fulfill the requirement that the doctoral dissertation be available to other scholars, the graduate office generally sends a copy of the abstract to University Microfilms, which prints an abstract in *Dissertation Abstracts International (DAI)* for each dissertation available on microfilm. Abstracts published in *DAI* are limited to a maximum of 350 words.

Universities or individual departments may require an abstract for theses and other types of reports. An abstract for a short paper is usually limited to one page.

Approval Sheet

The approval sheet provides space for the signatures of the adviser, readers, department chairperson, graduate deans, and others indicating their acceptance of the work. Most institutions have a model or form printed for this purpose, and local requirements should always determine the format of this page. Approvals are sometimes incorporated into the title page. Many institutions do not bind the separate approval sheet into the dissertation.

Title Page

The first page of a thesis or dissertation is the title page. The graduate school office usually prescribes the form of the title page (see pages 52 and 53 for typical examples). The title page presents the title, the full name of the writer, and the submission statement, which includes the faculty or school, such as the Graduate School of Arts and Sciences or the School of Business Administration, and the institution, the degree sought (or granted), and the month and year in which the degree is to be (or was) granted. A particular institution may require different combinations of the elements shown in the samples, or it may require additional information, such as the writer's previous academic degrees.

The title should be concise as well as descriptive and comprehensive. Its wording should indicate the content of the paper so that scholars encountering mention of it in a bibliography will know whether it relates to their research. A title like "The Marriage of Poetry and Drama," for example, does not adequately describe a thesis on the poetic drama of T. S. Eliot. "T. S. Eliot's Poetic Drama" or "The Marriage of Poetry and Drama in the Plays of T. S. Eliot" would be more descriptive. Phrases like "A Critical Analysis and Evaluation of . . ." or "An Investigation of . . ." should be avoided when they are redundant. Subtitles should be used only when they contribute to the descriptive nature of the title. Humorous or catchy titles are not appropriate for research papers. The following excessively long titles have been shortened yet adequately identify the topic:

Wordy title   AN INVESTIGATION OF THE ACADEMIC STUDY OF OPERA IN

COLLEGES AND CONSERVATORIES BETWEEN 1965 AND 1985,

WITH SUGGESTIONS FOR DEVELOPING A PROGRAM OF OPERA

IN COLLEGES

Revision   THE STUDY OF OPERA

IN COLLEGES AND CONSERVATORIES BETWEEN 1965 AND 1985

Wordy title   A STUDY TO DETERMINE THE RELATIONSHIP BETWEEN THE

POSITIONS OF TEACHERS ON THE CALIFORNIA F. SCALE

AND THEIR ATTITUDES TOWARD TEAM TEACHING

Revision

THE RELATIONSHIP BETWEEN TEACHERS' POSITIONS

ON THE CALIFORNIA F. SCALE

AND ATTITUDES TOWARD TEAM TEACHING

Copyright Page

The microfilming of a dissertation is a form of publication. Thus you need to follow the law regarding copyright, both to protect your own work and to ensure that your use of other people's work meets legal requirements.

According to federal law, you own the copyright for your thesis or dissertation from the time you write the work until you formally transfer the copyright to a publisher or to some other organization or individual. Before such transfer takes place, you control all the rights to your work, including the right to make and distribute copies of it (that is, to publish it).

Whether or not you put a copyright notice on the second page of your unpublished thesis or dissertation (see the sample copyright page on page 54), you are legally protected against the unauthorized use of your work. Depositing a thesis or dissertation in a library and microfilming it, however, are equivalent to publication, and the law requires a copyright notice in any published work in which a copyright is claimed. You are not obliged to register your copyright with the Library of Congress, but you should consider doing so. Registering is a public record of copyright ownership and a prerequisite for legal action in the event of inappropriate use of your material.

If your thesis or dissertation is to be microfilmed, University Microfilms will register the copyright for a fee. If your paper is not to be microfilmed, you can register the copyright with the Library of Congress by writing directly to the Copyright Office, Library of Congress, Washington, DC 20559.

Just as federal law safeguards your copyright in your thesis or dissertation, it safeguards the rights of other writers in their work. In using material from other sources, you must follow the guidelines of *fair use*, a legal concept interpreted in various ways. According to one rule of thumb, you may quote up to 150 words from a source, or two lines of poetry, for critical or evaluative purposes without obtaining permission from the copyright holder. In most cases the copyright holder is the publisher (because the author has transferred the copyright to the publisher). Some publishers allow the quotation of 250 words without written permission; others allow up to 500 words.

When a quotation, even of fewer than 150 words, constitutes a substantial proportion of the source, you need to write to the copyright holder and request permission to quote. If you are in any doubt about whether the direct quotations in your thesis or dissertation qualify as fair use, consult your graduate school office or contact the publisher of the work you are quoting. Any permissions you receive should be acknowledged on the copyright page or in the acknowledgments section.

Table of Contents

In a thesis or dissertation the table of contents precedes all the sections it lists. The table of contents should list all elements of the preliminaries—the chapter (part or section) titles, the main headings and subheadings in the text, and the reference materials. The beginning page number for each section is indicated along the right-hand margin. The numbering of chapters and the wording, capitalization, and punctuation of titles and headings should be exactly the same as they are in the text. (See the sample table of contents on page 57 and the typing instructions on page 45.)

Lists of Tables, Figures, and Plates

Lists of tables, figures, and plates should follow the table of contents. Each type of illustrative matter should be listed on a separate page. Charts, graphs, maps, and illustrations of other kinds are usually grouped as figures, but they may be designated by their more descriptive names, as in "Chart 3" or "Map 7." Full-page illustrations, including photographs, are usually called *plates* and are listed after the list of figures. When there are only two or three tables or figures in a thesis or dissertation, local policy may permit omission of a listing in the front matter. All captions should appear in the listing exactly as they are in the text.

Capitalization of captions
The traditional form for listing titles or captions of tables, figures, and plates calls for capitalization of the first letter of the first and last words and of all nouns, pronouns, adjectives, adverbs, and verbs. Plates are sometimes listed in capital letters.

Numbering of captions
Tables, figures, and plates should be numbered consecutively in arabic numerals throughout the paper. (See the sample listings of tables, figures, and plates on pages 58 through 61.) If tables, figures, and plates are especially numerous, they should be double-numbered by chapter. Table 1.1 would be the first table in Chapter 1; Table 1.2, the second, and so on. Figure 2.1 would be the first figure in Chapter 2; Figure 2.2, the second. A period should separate the chapter from the item number. Chapter 6 contains a full discussion of the presentation of tables, figures, and plates with explanations and examples.

Clearance Forms

When human beings are the subjects of experimental study or when the facilities of an institution are used, clearance forms may be necessary. If the forms are short, they can be placed in the preliminaries. Any long or complex information on clearance should be placed in an appendix. Design of the experiment and requirements of the institution dictate the nature of the clearance forms.

Acknowledgments

The acknowledgments section contains expressions of appreciation for assistance and guidance. The help given by advisers and readers does not require written acknowledgment, but the recognition of generosity with time and knowledge is a courtesy that is widely appreciated. Acknowledgments should be expressed simply and tactfully.

Permissions that you have obtained for quotations may be presented in the Acknowledgments or on the copyright page. When permissions are granted as a special favor, they are best placed in the Acknowledgments.

Preface

The preface, usually an optional section for a dissertation or thesis, might include brief comment on subjects such as the motivation for the study or methods of research. Substantial development of these issues and significant historical or background information belong in the text of the paper. The preface should be an adjunct to the paper rather than an essential part of it.

THE TEXT (BODY)

The text, or body, of a thesis or dissertation begins with the first page of Chapter 1, which follows the preliminaries discussed above. Numbering in arabic numerals starts on this page with number 1; all pages are numbered, including chapter and section title pages. Position all page numbers one inch from the top of the page, flush with the right margin.

Organization of Chapters

Each topic calls for an organization appropriate to its own logic and to the discipline or field. Your research will determine the nature of the text, and your adviser will have suggestions concerning the design of your paper. Formats for the body of the paper differ for the two general types of theses: (1) theses based on the collection of empirical data and (2) theses derived from critical analysis or philosophical inquiry.

THESES BASED ON THE COLLECTION OF EMPIRICAL DATA   A standard format is often followed in theses based on the collection of empirical data, information derived from direct observation or experience. The chapters are usually divided into five categories corresponding to the stages of research. Although these parts may be variously labeled, essentially they consist of an introduction, a review of the literature, a presentation of the method, a report of the findings, and a summary and discussion.

Introductory chapter(s)

The introductory chapter(s) should contain the following:

1. An introduction to the subject area indicating the importance and validity of the problem chosen for study. The potential contribution of the study, the need for the research, and background information may also be included here.
2. A clear and concise statement of the problem, together with an analysis of its delimitation or scope. An experimental study should be stated as

one or more hypotheses and, particularly in the case of a statistical study of variables, an accompanying null hypothesis (a statement of the absence of the hypothesized correlation). Other kinds of research problems may be posed in the form of questions. The schedule and procedures for gathering data should be explained.

3. A section that establishes the theoretical framework within which the investigation was conducted. This section usually includes basic assumptions of the study and definitions of terms.

Review of the literature   The review of related research and literature, usually a separate chapter, should give readers the context for the present study. The review should not merely summarize a series of books and articles; rather, it should call attention to the most important previous work, identify the place of your study in relation to other research, and delineate areas of agreement and disagreement in the field. The review should evaluate and interpret existing research rather than simply repeat it. Organizing the review by topic rather than by author and avoiding unnecessary direct quotation can help you focus the review of research.

Design of the investigation   The chapter(s) devoted to the design of the investigation should discuss such matters as the method of research, the nature of the sample and any control groups, the data needed to test the hypotheses or to answer the questions, the sources of data, and the procedures followed in gathering and analyzing the data.

Analysis of the data   The analysis chapter(s) presents the results of the investigation, usually without interpretation or evaluation. This nonevaluative analysis of data constitutes the heart of a thesis based on the collection of empirical data. You will want to decide on the most effective method for presenting the data. Explanations of the information should be written in clear, coherent prose. You may wish to accompany your analyses with charts or tables, but these should supplement the text rather than substitute for it. The body of the paper should be comprehensible even if the reader chooses not to consult the tables. (See Chapter 6 for information on presenting tables, figures, charts, and computer data.)

Summary and interpretation   The chapter(s) of summary and discussion should be devoted to evaluation and interpretation of the data and formulation of conclusions. Also covered here, as appropriate, are implications of the findings for revising the existing body of knowledge, possible contributions of the thesis to research methodology, the relation of the results to previously published studies, limitations of the study, and unexpected conclusions. Practical applications of the findings or speculation about further studies might conclude this section.

THESES BASED ON CRITICAL ANALYSIS OR PHILOSOPHICAL SPECULATION

No specified format governs theses based on critical analysis or philosophical speculation. Rather, they contain a number of common elements either developed in separate chapters or interwoven in each chapter.

The introductory section usually places the study against the background of previous work in the field. The importance of the topic, its role in current controversy or developments, and the scholarly tradition in which the thesis belongs might be developed here. Although you want to acknowledge any studies that have influenced or guided your work as well as those you may have reacted against, this section should not turn into a summary of the works in question. Rather, discussion of these works should always demonstrate their relationship to your topic. Although you will probably be critically evaluating theories advanced by other writers, your comments should remain fair and evenhanded. You need not demolish previous studies to give your own work validity.

The central chapters of such a thesis should present the results of your research and analysis. These results should be set forth clearly and systematically in order to convince readers that you have considered every facet of the topic and that the material uncovered by your research confirms your thesis statement. One of the challenges of writing these chapters is to present a good deal of information while continually keeping the central point of the thesis before the reader.

The interpretation or statement of the significance of the thesis may be integrated with the exposition of the findings or may be presented in the concluding chapter(s). The conclusion might include the implications of the work for the revision of previous interpretations, proof or disproof of assumptions or theories in the field, or new areas of inquiry opened by the study.

Parenthetical Documentation

If you use parenthetical references, your documentation will appear in the body of the text within parentheses. See Chapter 4 for a full explanation of the principles of MLA-style parenthetical documentation. See Appendix B for a discussion of the parenthetical-reference style favored by the American Psychological Association (APA). See Appendix C for a brief account of the author-number style of parenthetical referencing.

Chapter Titles and Headings

The way in which a thesis or dissertation is divided is determined by its length and complexity. Papers under twenty-five pages do not require division of any kind; in fact, dividing a short paper can be distracting rather than helpful. Longer research papers may benefit from the insertion of headings, centered or flush with the left margin; organization into chapters; and grouping of chapters into parts.

Chapter titles   A title should indicate clearly and concisely the contents of a chapter and its relationship to the paper as a whole.

Headings   Headings may be used to divide a long or complicated chapter. The same principles of parallelism and logic of division that govern outlining are applicable here. Every division of a subject must yield at least two subdivisions. All headings at the same level should be parallel grammatically and logically.

Levels of headings   The number of levels of headings may vary from chapter to chapter, depending on the logic of organization in each. The first level of heading should be centered, the second level placed at the left-hand margin, and the third level indented into the paragraph. Underline all headings. (See illustrations of the three levels of headings on page 48.) Divisions beyond the third level should be avoided. If fourth-level headings are necessary, they should take the form of enumerated paragraphs. At least one paragraph of text should be placed between a heading and its first subheading.

Use of titles and headings

Chapter titles and headings should be used to clarify the organization of the thesis or dissertation. They should never be used to cover up inadequate organization, incoherent development, or insufficient transitions. A chapter should be clear and complete without its subheadings.

REFERENCE MATERIALS (BACK MATTER, OR END MATTER)

The reference materials for a thesis or dissertation may include an appendix or appendixes, a glossary, endnotes, a bibliography, and an index.

Appendix

Materials for appendixes

An appendix should be used for materials that supplement the text but are not appropriate for inclusion in it. Original data, summary tabulations, tables containing data of lesser importance (as distinguished from those presenting major data in the text), very lengthy quotations, supporting legal decisions or laws, computer print-outs, and pertinent documents not readily available to the reader belong in an appendix. Questionnaires with their letters of transmittal and the verbatim comments of respondents belong in an appendix. Supplementary illustrative materials, such as forms and documents, may also be included. Placing lengthy tables and other matter in the appendix prevents the text from becoming unduly bulky.

The material in the appendix may be subdivided according to logical classifications. List each appendix by letter and title, if any, in the table of contents.

Glossary

A *glossary* (a list of definitions of terms and concepts) is usually not necessary for a dissertation because it is directed toward a professional audience. For other types of papers, a glossary may be desirable when the typical reader might not be familiar with the terminology. See the glossary at the end of this book for a sample format.

Notes

If you use the note-bibliography format, you will have footnotes appearing throughout the paper or you will have a section of endnotes. Even if you use parenthetical documentation, you are likely to want to include some informational or bibliographical notes in a section at the end of the paper.

A thesis or dissertation to be microfilmed should use footnotes rather than endnotes so that the reader of the film will not have to turn the film back and forth to follow the notes. Notes should be numbered consecutively throughout each chapter, beginning with 1 for the first note in each chapter. A research paper or report that is not to be microfilmed may use endnotes. (See page 30 in Chapter 1 for a sample endnotes page.)

Bibliography or List of Works Cited

Papers based on research should have a bibliography or works cited section, listing the sources of information. See Chapter 5 for a discussion of the various types of bibliographies and forms for entries in these sections.

Index

A dissertation or unpublished report rarely includes an *index* (an alphabetical listing with page numbers of subjects treated in the work). If an index is required, it follows all the other reference material. (See the index at the conclusion of this book.)

TYPING AND PRINTING INSTRUCTIONS

This section contains instructions for typing the elements of a thesis, dissertation, research paper, or report, whether the typist uses a typewriter or a word processor. Instructions for typing quotations, footnotes and endnotes, bibliographies, and illustrations in the form of tables and figures can be found at the ends of chapters 3, 4, 5, and 6. Chapter 8 contains numerous suggestions for preparing the finished copy of a research paper.

One page of typescript should contain approximately twenty-seven double-spaced lines or their equivalent. A page should run no more than a single line long or short. You may continue a long footnote on the next page (see "Continued Footnotes," in Chapter 4, page 109). Most word-processing programs arrange notes automatically to keep pages more or less equal in length.

Margins

Margins should measure at least one and one-half inches on the left and one inch on the right and at the top and bottom. The wider left margin provides room for binding. If the completion of a word or syllable will take you more than two or three letters into the right margin, place the complete word on the next line. Most word-processing programs hyphenate words automatically.

Because precision in the spacing of note and bibliographical entries is important, right-hand margins should not be justified—that is, lines should not be spaced out so that the right margin is even. Justification on a typewriter or printer often leaves irregular, unattractive spacing that interferes with reading and distorts the spacing of the documentation. To avoid large gaps at the end of some lines, you should follow the rules for hyphenation (see Chapter 7, page 219).

Indention

Indent the first line of a paragraph five spaces. Bring all subsequent lines to the left margin.

Indent all lines of set-off quotations, whether single- or double-spaced, ten spaces from the left margin. (See the sample pages at the end of Chapter 1 and at the end of this chapter.) Indentions *within* set-off quotations are three spaces.

Numbering of Pages

All pages of the text of a thesis, dissertation, research paper, or report should be numbered, including the first page. Position numerals in the upper right-hand corner one inch from the top of the page, flush with the right margin. The name of the writer precedes the numeral without intervening punctuation, as in Ganter 2 (optional in a dissertation). Double-space to the first line of the text.

In a research paper, the title page and outline should not be numbered or counted as pages. The first page of the text of a research paper is page one.

In a thesis or dissertation, front matter, such as the abstract and approval sheet, should not be numbered or counted as part of the thesis or dissertation. The title page and copyright page should be counted but not numbered. Use lowercase roman numerals for front matter and arabic numerals running consecutively for the text and the back matter.

Front-matter page numbers are placed one inch from the bottom of the page, centered between the margins. Leave at least a double space between the last line of the front-matter text and the page number. If your word-processing program does not allow you to paginate according to these requirements, you may want to consult with your adviser about another format.

Table of Contents

Words designating elements of the paper, such as the preface and bibliography, should be typed in uppercase and lowercase (Table of Contents), following the rules for capitalization of titles. An alternative format places such titles entirely in capital letters (TABLE OF CONTENTS).

Type Table of Contents (*or* TABLE OF CONTENTS) one inch from the top of the page, centered between the margins. No terminal punctuation follows the heading of any line of the table of contents. Type Chapter flush with the left-hand margin and Page flush with the right-hand margin. Position Page a double space below the heading and place Chapter after the listing of the preliminaries. See Chapter 8 for the alignment of *period leaders* (spaced periods leading from the chapter title or heading on the left to the page number on the right).

Indent one-digit chapter numbers five spaces, and position numbers of two digits or more by aligning the numerals in the right-hand column. The wording, capitalization, and punctuation of titles and headings should be typed exactly as they appear in the text. Headings and subheadings underlined in the text should not be underlined in the table of contents. Use a two-space hanging indention (that is, the first line at the margin and subsequent lines indented) within headings and between successive levels. Type the names for the reference materials (Bibliography, Appendix, etc.) flush with the left margin; place the page number of the first page of each section in the column at the right. With separate appendixes, list each by letter (A, B, C, etc.) and title, if any.

For a partially condensed version of the above, single-space between the second- and third-level headings.

For an even more condensed version, you may run in second- and third-level headings, use period leaders only with chapter titles, and double-space only between chapters.

Acknowledgments or Preface

Type Acknowledgments *or* Preface (ACKNOWLEDGMENTS *or* PREFACE) one inch from the top of the page. The title should be centered between the margins and should have no terminal punctuation. Double-space to the first line of the text.

List of Tables

Type Tables *or* List of Tables (TABLES *or* LIST OF TABLES) one inch from the top of the page, centered between the margins and without terminal punctuation. Double-space to the labels Table and Page, which should be placed flush with the left and right margins, respectively. Indent and space captions for tables, following the guidelines for the table of contents on page 45.

List of Figures

Type Figures *or* List of Figures (FIGURES *or* LIST OF FIGURES) one inch from the top of the page, centered between the margins and without terminal punctuation. Place column headings, captions, and page numbers as in a list of tables.

List of Plates

Type Plates *or* List of Plates (PLATES *or* LIST OF PLATES) one inch from the top of the page, centered between the margins and without terminal punctuation. Place column headings, captions, and page numbers as in a list of tables.

Chapter Numbers and Titles

Type the word CHAPTER in full caps, use an arabic numeral (CHAPTER 1; CHAPTER 5), and position these one inch from the top of the page, centered between the margins. Type the title in uppercase and lowercase letters one double space below the chapter number. Center the title between the margins. Double-space titles of two or more lines, using an inverted-pyramid style. The title should not have terminal punctuation unless it ends with a question mark or an exclamation point. Double-space below the title to the first line of the text.

Headings within Chapters

The facsimile of typed manuscript below illustrates subdivision headings and their relationships.

Centered Heading

First-level headings

Double-space above and below centered headings. Capitalize the first letter of each word except articles, conjunctions, and prepositions; underscore with a solid line. Do not number unless local guidelines so specify, in which case use arabic numerals. If a heading is more than four inches long (forty-eight elite or forty pica spaces), use a double-spaced inverted-pyramid format. The title should not have terminal punctuation, unless it ends with a question mark or an exclamation point.

Second-level headings

Side Heading, Too Long to Put

on One Line

Leave a double space above and below freestanding side headings; align with the left margin. Capitalize and punctuate the same as centered headings. If a side heading is more than about two and one-half inches long (thirty elite or twenty-five pica spaces), divide the heading, placing the second line a double space below with a two-space hanging indention.

Third-level headings

Paragraph heading. Double-space to paragraph headings, indent five spaces, and underscore each heading with a solid line. Capitalize the first word and proper nouns and adjectives only; end with a period and begin the text on the same line.

Part-title Pages

If a work is divided into parts, each part may be introduced with a part-title page, which should be numbered and counted like any other page of the text. Type the part number and title slightly above the center of the page with double-spacing as follows:

```
PART 2

From the Renaissance to Hume
```

When a chapter title follows the part title without intervening text, the chapter title should be placed on the following page. When text follows the part title, it should begin one double space below the title.

Abstract

Type the word Abstract (*or* ABSTRACT) one inch from the top of the page, centered between the margins. Double-space to the full title of your thesis or dissertation as it appears on the title page, either in uppercase or in uppercase and lowercase letters. Double-space to your full legal name, which should be centered in uppercase and lowercase letters. Double-space to the text of the abstract, which should be double-spaced. The abstract page(s) are neither counted nor numbered.

Because requirements for the format and placement of the abstract vary greatly among institutions, be certain to consult your graduate office about its requirements.

Title Page

Use an approved title-page format, either selected from the examples on pages 52 and 53 or as specified by local policy. The title may appear entirely in capital letters or in uppercase and lowercase letters. The title page is counted but not numbered.

Copyright Page

The copyright notice, if any, appears on a separate page following the title page. Center the notice, and position the last line one inch from the bottom of the page. Circle a lowercase c next to the year; type your full legal name a double space below; center the words ALL RIGHTS RESERVED a double space below your name. (See the sample copyright page on page 54.) The copyright page is counted but not numbered.

Appendix

Type `Appendix` (*or* `APPENDIX`) along with its appropriate letter one inch from the top of the page, centered between the margins. Double-space to the text of the appendix, which should be double-spaced.

Glossary

Type `Glossary` (*or* `GLOSSARY`) one inch from the top of the page, centered between the margins. Double-space to the glossary. Double-space any preliminary explanation of the glossary, and arrange the words along the left margin and their definitions along the right margin. Your spacing should allow readers to find the meanings readily. The format for the glossary will vary with the length and type of terms.

Endnotes

Type `Notes` (*or* `NOTES`) (not *endnotes* because their position indicates that they are endnotes rather than footnotes) one inch from the top of the page, centered between the margins. Double-space to the first note, and double-space throughout the notes, both within a note and between notes. (Footnotes should be single-spaced.)

Bibliography or List of Works Cited

For a paper with notes, type `Bibliography` (*or* `BIBLIOGRAPHY`) one inch from the top of the page, centered between the margins; for a paper with parenthetical documentation, type `Works Cited` (*or* `WORKS CITED`). In both cases entries should be arranged alphabetically. Double-space to the first entry and double-space throughout the bibliography, both within an entry and between entries.

Index

Type `Index` (*or* `INDEX`) one inch from the top of the page, centered between the margins. The index should be double-spaced, one column to a page. Indent subheadings five spaces. Entries are followed by a comma and the page number(s) on which the reference to the subject appears.

ELEMENTS OF THESES AND DISSERTATIONS

Sample Pages

On the following pages are sample pages showing various formats and layouts for the different elements of theses and dissertations.

[2 inches]

EFFECTS OF SITUATIONAL AND SUBJECT VARIABLES

ON MMPI RESPONSES OF ALCOHOLICS

[3 inches]

by

[double space]

Jeanette Marie Hatch

A dissertation

[double space]

submitted in partial fulfillment

of the requirements for the degree of

Doctor of Philosophy in the Department of Psychology

The Catholic University of America

June 1990

Title page, Form A

[1 inch]

[2 inches]

A DISCRIMINATIVE STUDY OF METHODS OF THE QUANTITATIVE

DETERMINATION OF FLUORINE

[2 inches]

A Dissertation

Presented to

the Faculty of the Graduate School

Stanford University

[3 inohcs]

In Partial Fulfillment

of the Requirements for the Degree

Doctor of Philosophy

by

William Harold Robert

June 1990

[1 inch]

Title page, Form B

Copyright page

⎫
⎬ [1 inch]
⎭

[1 inch]

Abstract [or ABSTRACT]

[double space]

The Plays and Architecture of Sir John Vanbrugh

[double space]

by

[double space]

Emilia Field Cresswell Marsh

[double space]

As an artist Sir John Vanbrugh is distinguished for his work in two apparently only distantly related fields, comic drama and architecture. This essay is an analysis and evaluation of his nine original plays and adaptations, using as a primary tool his achievement in domestic architecture of the English baroque period. An examination in Chapter 1 of representative great houses (including Castle Howard, Blenheim Castle, and Seaton Delaval) and smaller private dwellings enables hypotheses to be drawn about Vanbrugh's general aesthetics: his fundamental artistic intentions, his methods of organization of materials, and his special taste for certain effects in both disciplines.

Vanbrugh's dramatic and innovative domestic architecture was, in Sir Uvedale Price's words, "designed to affect the imagination" by a combination of "what is striking, with what is simply pleasing," rather than to conform to any conventionally accepted rules of "decorum." The same intention can be found in his original plays and the modifications of the five plays which he adapted from Boursault, Dancourt, Fletcher, Le Sage, and Molière. Thus an analysis of the comedies is made within the framework of a psychologically oriented aesthetics which reflects a contemporary shift of emphasis, developing among a number of artists and critics, from formal questions about rules of construction to a concern with the nature of the audience's relation to the art in general or the specific work at hand.

Significant examples of Vanbrugh's psychological orientation in the plays are found in his posing of serious human problems in a comic context and his insistence upon the primacy of character over plot. Therefore Chapters 2 and 3 are devoted to the conflicts of his pivotal characters in the original plays, profiles of important secondary characters, and modifications of character and conflict in the adaptations. Chapter 4 deals with other technical questions: what Vanbrugh described as "the Business and the Event" and the peculiar nature of his comic effect. In Chapter 5 comparisons are drawn with some contemporary plays––representative not only of the older "hard" comedy of manners but also of "sentimental" comedy and the currently evolving "humane" subgenre––whose authors gave differing degrees of attention to those topics in which Vanbrugh was especially interested.

[1 inch]

Table of Contents [or TABLE OF CONTENTS]
[double space]

Table of contents page (only chapter titles and first-level heads are included here; see pages 45 and 46 for contents format showing first-, second-, and third-level heads)

[1 inch]

Tables [**or** TABLES]
[double space]

Table   Page

List of tables

[1 inch]

[1 inch]

Figures [or FIGURES]
[double space]

Figure   Page

vii

[1 inch]

List of figures

60 · **H**

[1 inch]

Graphs [**or** GRAPHS]

[double space]

viii

List of graphs

[1 inch]

[1 inch]

Plates [**or** PLATES]
[double space]

[1 inch]

List of plates (fully
capitalized format is optional)

[double space]
CHAPTER 2
[double space]
The Relationship of Writing and Reading Abilities
[double space]
E. D. Hirsch's concept of cultural literacy developed in part
from his study of writing abilities. In The Philosophy of
Composition Hirsch argued that writing is a skill and that
successful teaching of writing requires only isolating the
principles that allow students to master the skill. In that utopian
book he suggested that the literacy problem might be solved within
ten years if teachers and researchers could agree upon the right set
of principles:

> The maxims should be sound ones, having a wide
> application. They should be explained persuasively, and
> in a form the student can apply directly to his own prose.
> They should be limited in number, and grouped according to
> their relative importance for their typical audience. The
> book should encourage the student to believe that he can
> master the elements of the craft and make future progress
> on his own.[1]

Hirsch abandoned this formalistic approach when his numerous studies
of high school students convinced him that their writing revealed a
lack of common knowledge rather than ignorance of such maxims.[2]
Convinced of the need for a shared reading background, Hirsch
[double space]
———————————————— [1½ inch rule]
[double space]
    [1] E. D. Hirsch, The Philosophy of Composition (Chicago: Univ. of
Chicago Press, 1977), 168.
        [double space]
    [2] E. D. Hirsch, "Cultural Literacy," American Scholar 52 (Spring
1983): 159–69.

Chapter title page (dissertation text with footnotes)

the first indication she notices that she might not forever be able

to count on his affection, plunges her into a self-analysis that

results in perception of the "dangers" of her situation:

> How to understand the deception she had been thus
> practising on herself, and living under!--The blunders,
> the blindness of her own head and heart! . . . she
> perceived that she had acted most weakly . . . that she
> was wretched, and should probably find this day but the
> beginning of wretchedness. (283)

As the opening of the novel predicts, these "dangers," once

perceived, begin to "rank as misfortunes with her" (1).

Emma's recognition of blindness and blunders should make her

more sympathetic, or likable, yet at no point is her appeal more in

question. Critics divide over the question of Emma's change. Wayne

Booth, for example, attributes to her "genuine reform" that will

allow for a satisfactory marriage (258), while Marvin Mudrick finds

her still a "confirmed exploiter" (129), who might, in the words of

Edmund Wilson, "worry and exasperate Knightley" (39). Many feminist

critics seem to side with those like Booth who find her

transformation complete. Sandra Gilbert and Susan Gubar, for

example, find in her recognition scene "a realization of her own

powerlessness," an exposure of "vulnerable delusions," the defeat of

a "female artist" (159-60). Emma seems yet another depressing

instance of a woman's failure. Mudrick's view, however, provides

not only a more accurate portrait of Emma, but also a more

**Dissertation text page with MLA-style parenthetical references.
A paper with parenthetical documentation would be accompanied
by a list of works cited, a sample of which appears on page 33.**

3 QUOTATION

Quotations in a research paper, thesis, or dissertation are of two types: indirect (paraphrased or summarized) and direct (verbatim). You must document both types—that is, you must indicate the source of indirect and direct quotations either with parenthetical documentation accompanied by a list of works cited or with a superscript (raised number) in the text and a corresponding footnote or endnote containing bibliographic information. (See Chapter 4 for a detailed discussion of both styles of documentation.)

Plagiarism

Plagiarism (the use of another person's ideas or wording without giving appropriate credit) results from inaccurate or incomplete attribution of material to its source. Ideas and the expression of ideas are considered to belong to the individual who first puts them forward. Therefore, when you incorporate in your paper either ideas or phrasing from another writer, whether you quote directly or indirectly, you need to indicate your source accurately and completely. Whether intentional or unintentional, plagiarism can bring serious consequences, not only academic, in the form of failure or expulsion, but also legal, in the form of lawsuits. People take plagiarism seriously because it violates the ethics of the academic community.

Documentation to avoid plagiarism

You should document in your paper any fact or opinion that you read in one of your sources, whether you first discovered the idea there or you have assimilated it so thoroughly that it seems to be your own. Some exceptions to this rule are facts that are common knowledge (for example, that John Hancock signed the Declaration of Independence), facts that can be verified easily and do not differ from one source to another (for example, that the headquarters of the Common Market is in Brussels, Belgium), and well-known sayings or proverbs (for example, that Theodore Roosevelt said, "Speak softly and carry a big stick"). Under most circumstances, these kinds of materials do not need to be documented. In contrast, material available in one source or in a limited number of sources (for example, a fact about changes in the birthrate in China) should usually be documented. Statistics other than those you have compiled yourself should be attributed to the source. Such attribution not only gives appropriate credit but also protects you in the event that the information is erroneous.

Purpose of documentation

Acknowledgment of credit through documentation does not diminish the originality of your work. Your contribution consists of imposing your own order on your materials and drawing an original conclusion from them. Documentation allows your reader to see the materials you used to reach your conclusions, to check your interpretations of sources, to place your work in a tradition of inquiry, and to locate further information on your topic.

INDIRECT QUOTATION (PARAPHRASE OR SUMMARY)

You should choose indirect quotation whenever you do not have a compelling reason for using direct quotation (see page 67 for guidelines for choosing direct quotation). Indirect quotation calls less attention to itself than does direct quotation and thus concentrates the reader's attention on the development of your argument.

Paraphrase

The words *paraphrase* and *summary* are sometimes used as synonyms, but a paraphrase can be differentiated from a summary on the basis of

Summary

length. A paraphrase restates the original source in approximately the same number of words. A summary condenses the original. When you paraphrase or summarize, you should use your own words and sentence structure. Imitating syntax, rearranging words and phrases, and borrowing phrases even as brief as two or three words do not change the original sufficiently to avoid plagiarism. If you find that you cannot avoid using a phrase from the original, place the words in quotation marks. Paraphrases and summaries should represent the original source accurately and completely, avoiding distortion through imprecise or mistaken restatement, altered emphasis, or significant omissions.

Documentation of paraphrase or summary

Even when you have restated a passage completely in your own words, you must indicate that you encountered the information in your reading. In some cases you may wish to attribute the statement within your text by citing the author (by first and last name for the first reference and thereafter by last name only) and, if necessary or desirable, the title of the work. Even if you choose not to name the author in your text, you must document the source of the idea in a note.

The versions of the passage below demonstrate adequate and inadequate paraphrasing.

Original

I have said that science is impossible without faith. By this I do not mean that the faith on which science depends is religious in nature or involves the acceptance of any of the dogmas of the ordinary religious creeds, yet without faith that nature is subject to law there can be no science. No amount of demonstration can ever prove that nature is subject to law.[1]

Plagiarism

Science is impossible without faith that nature is

subject to law.
(Borrowed wording without quotation marks.)

Plagiarism

Faith makes science possible. This does not mean that

science rests on religious faith or the acceptance of

religious dogmas, but without the faith that nature

functions according to laws, science cannot exist.
(Imitated sentence structure.)

Correct paraphrase

The belief that nature functions in accordance with

laws makes science possible.[1]
(Documentation used to give credit for the idea even though the passage has been restated.)

---

[1] Norbert Wiener, *The Human Use of Human Beings: Cybernetics and Society* (New York: Avon, 1967), 262–63.

Correct paraphrase   `Science depends on faith, not religious faith, but`

`the faith that "nature is subject to law."`[1]
(A summary with a phrase quoted to preserve the tone of the original.)

DIRECT QUOTATION

Direct quotation presents material from a source verbatim (word for word). It is appropriate when you need to provide an authority, preserve the integrity of the source author's original wording, or ensure the accuracy of your borrowing from the source.

Authority   Direct quotation lends authority for controversial positions or statements requiring expertise in fields other than your own. For example, if in a thesis in higher education, you wish to substantiate a conclusion about the implications of a university's open-admissions policy for the region's economy, a quotation from a leading economist or a local businessperson could be effective.

When an author has stated an idea so inventively or forcefully that you cannot do it justice in a paraphrase, you should quote directly to lend color and power to your work. It would be difficult to improve on J. H. Plumb's way of stating the contrast between thriving, artistic Florence and declining, war-torn Milan: "If Florence belonged to Minerva, Milan belonged to Mars."[2] Direct quotation is also appropriate when you want to give your reader the flavor of the original. Malcolm X's sentence concerning the black nationalist Marcus Garvey communicates the importance of the leader to the community better than a paraphrase might: "I remember seeing the big, shiny photographs of Marcus Garvey that were passed from hand to hand."[3]

Accuracy   For statements in which accuracy is extremely important, such as laws, mathematical formulas, and complex theoretical formulations, direct quotation ensures precise presentation of the material.

Length of direct quotations   When you use a direct quotation in your text for whatever reason, you must reproduce the language of the source exactly, following the internal punctuation, spelling, emphasis, and even the errors, found in the original.

Direct quotations should be kept as short as possible; long quotations may be distracting to readers. It can be tempting to insert a quotation and thereby let someone else do some of your writing, but if you do so, you evade some of your responsibility. Direct quotations should be pared down to the absolutely essential portions. Long direct quotations are likely to contain some material irrelevant to your focus. When very long quotations, more than one-half page of text, seem out of place in the body of your paper yet are essential to the paper as a whole, place them in an appendix and refer the reader to this appendix.

---

[2] J. H. Plumb, *The Italian Renaissance: A Concise Survey of Its History and Culture* (1961; reprint, New York: Harper Torchbooks, 1965), 63.

[3] Malcolm X with Alex Haley, *The Autobiography of Malcolm X* (New York: Grove, 1966), 6.

Fair use   When deciding how much direct quotation to use in a dissertation that will be microfilmed or a thesis that will be deposited in a library (both considered published materials), you need to consider the concept of *fair use*, and you may need to secure the permission of the publisher or the copyright holder for some quotations. (See page 37 in Chapter 2 for more information on fair use.)

Quotations Run into Text

Brief quotations of prose   Direct quotations of prose that are shorter than five typewritten lines should be run into the text and enclosed in double quotation marks, as in the following example:

Ernst Robert Curtius's term "the Latin Middle Ages"

includes a range of Roman legacies, including "the share

of Rome, of the Roman idea of the state, of the Roman

church, and of Roman culture."4

Brief quotations of poetry   Direct quotations of poetry that run fewer than two full lines should be run into the text. Use a slanted line (called a virgule) with a space on each side between lines of the poem. Retain the capitalization of the original, even though the excerpt combines with the surrounding text to form a grammatical whole.

In his "Hymn to Intellectual Beauty" Shelley personifies

the immaterial, spiritual world: "The awful shadow of some

unseen Power / Floats though unseen amongst us."

You may, however, set off brief passages of prose or poetry that you particularly wish to emphasize.

Quotations Set Off from Text

A direct quotation of five or more typewritten lines of prose or more than two lines of poetry should be set off from the text by indention. Nearly all publishers prefer the double-spacing of indented quotations because it facilitates editing. For dissertations and theses, however, single-spacing is

---

4 E. R. Curtius, *European Literature and the Latin Middle Ages,* trans. Willard R. Trask (New York: Harper and Row, 1953), 27.

generally preferred because it more closely resembles a printed format. Set-off quotations are not enclosed in quotation marks. (See the sample pages at the end of chapters 1 and 2.)

Prose

Indention of set-off paragraphs

The paragraphing of the original source should be retained. If the quotation spans two or more paragraphs in the original, your set-off quotation should indicate paragraph breaks with additional three-space indentions.

```
William Barrett gives one explanation of the flattening of

space found in modern art.

          When mankind no longer lives spontaneously
     turned toward God or the supersensible
     world--when, to echo the words of Yeats, the
     ladder is gone by which we would climb to a
     higher reality--the artist too must stand face
     to face with a flat and inexplicable world.5
```

When the quotation begins in the middle of a paragraph, the first line begins at the ten-space indention.

```
Raymond Williams defends the use of jargon in appropriate

contexts.

          Every known general position, in matters of art
     and belief, has its defining terms, and the
     difference between these and the terms
     identified as jargon is often no more than one
     of relative date and familiarity.  To run
     together the senses of jargon as specialized,
     unfamiliar, belonging to a hostile position, and
     unintelligible chatter is then at times indeed a
     jargon.6
```

Letters

Quotations from letters should be treated like any other long prose quotation—that is, set off and double-spaced or single-spaced. If the salutation and date are quoted, they should be positioned as they appear in the original.

---

5 William Barrett, *Irrational Man: A Study in Existential Philosophy* (Garden City: Doubleday, Anchor, 1962), 49.
6 Raymond Williams, *Keywords: A Vocabulary of Culture and Society*, rev. ed. (New York: Oxford Univ. Press, n.d.), 176.

Oral Sources Quotations from oral sources, such as conversations and speeches, should also be treated like long prose quotations. You will need to obtain approval from the speaker for statements you quote unless the material was recorded with the speaker's permission.

Poetry

Quotations of poetry set off Set off quotations of three or more lines from the text, introducing them as the syntax of your sentence requires. Indent poetry ten spaces from the left margin; indention may be five spaces when the line would otherwise

Run-over lines have to be broken. Lines of poetry extending beyond one typescript line should be indented five spaces, broken, and indented ten spaces on the next line. Alignment, spacing, and punctuation within the set-off quotation should follow the original as closely as possible.

```
In "Song of Myself" Walt Whitman uses the diction and

rhythm of natural speech:

    A child said What is the grass? fetching it to me with
        full hands;
    How could I answer the child?  I do not know what it
        is any more than he.
    I guess it must be the flag of my disposition, out of
        hopeful green stuff woven.
```

Placement of partial lines When a quotation from a poem begins in the middle of a line, place the first word approximately where it appears on the page in the original, as the placement of the following lines from Keats's "Endymion" illustrates:

```
                        When yet a child
    I oft have dried my tears when thou has smil'd.
    Thou seem'dst my sister: hand in hand we went
    From eve to morn across the firmament.
```

Alignment Align quotations marks at the beginning of a line under the capital letter of the preceding line, as indicated in this quotation from Wordsworth's "Anecdote for Fathers":

```
    At this my boy hung down his head,
    He blushed with shame, nor made reply;
    And three times to the child I said,
    "Why·, Edward, tell me why?"
```

Original spacing Reproduce the spacing of a poem as accurately as possible, as in this typed version of the beginning of Robert Herrick's "The Pillar of Fame."

```
Fame's pillar here, at last, we set,
Out-during Marble, Brass, or Jet,
    Charmed and enchanted so,
    As to withstand the blow
        Of    overthrow:
```

Epigraphs

An *epigraph* is an apt quotation that precedes the text of a chapter or of a book. Epigraphs should be indented twenty spaces from the left margin. Such indention eliminates the need for quotation marks (see page 68). Cite the author and the title of the source below the quotation. Further bibliographical information is optional for widely known authors and works. If you wish to supply such information, do so in a note.

```
          The last years of the eighteenth
          century are broken by a discontinuity
          similar to that which destroyed
          Renaissance thought at the beginning
          of the seventeenth.
             Michel Foucault, The Order of Things:
                An Archaeology of the Human Sciences
```

Direct Quotations in Notes

Informational notes may contain direct quotations. All quotations should be run in with the text of the note and enclosed in quotation marks. If the quotation runs more than one paragraph, begin each paragraph at the left margin without indention. Place quotation marks at the beginning of each paragraph and at the beginning and end of the entire selection. Quoted material in notes should follow the spacing used throughout.

WAYS OF INTRODUCING DIRECT QUOTATIONS

Introductions to quotations should be varied, although you should not strain for novel effects for their own sake. Each introduction you select should indicate accurately the content and context of the source.

The introduction to a direct quotation should provide a smooth transition between your writing and the quotation. The introduction should also indicate your reason for using the source. The name of the author (the full name the first time; the last name only thereafter) and the author's profession or affiliation (the first time you quote; thereafter only if significant) should accompany the quotation. Your introduction should specify the relationship between your argument or ideas and those of the source. It should indicate, for example, whether you disagree or agree with the source or whether the source differs from another source that you have cited. Further, your introduction should reflect accurately the context and sense of the original. Notice how an introduction can affect the meaning of a quotation:

George Orwell, the English political activist, complains

that "Dickens's criticism of society is almost exclusively

moral."7

(The introductory word *complains* and the characterization of Orwell's career as political suggests that Orwell condemns Dickens's neglect of political analyses and solutions.)

George Orwell, the English essayist and novelist, explains

that "Dickens's criticism of society is almost exclusively

moral."7

(The introductory word *explains* and the characterization of Orwell's career as literary suggest that Orwell analyzes Dickens's attitudes toward society with the empathy of a writer rather than as a critic of his politics.)

Introductions to quotations should be unobtrusive. They need not include the word *quotation* because quotation marks or indention indicate that you are copying word for word. They need not use the word *said*; as the list on page 73 indicates, there are dozens of other introductory words.

Introductions to Run-in Quotations

You may choose to introduce a run-in quotation in a variety of ways, depending on the style of surrounding sentences and the effect you wish to achieve. The following examples of run-in quotations indicate only a few of the many stylistic possibilities. Each sentence is punctuated as it would be if the quoted phrase or clause were part of the report or thesis writer's own work. The only necessary punctuation is that required by each particular grammatical structure.

Jean-Jacques Rousseau admits, "I felt before I thought."8

"I felt before I thought," Rousseau explains.8

"It is not alone by the rapidity, or extent of the conquest," Edward Gibbon observes, "that we should estimate the greatness of Rome."9

---

7 George Orwell, "Charles Dickens," in *A Collection of Essays* (New York: Harcourt Brace), 51.
8 Jean-Jacques Rousseau, *The Confessions*, trans. J. M. Cohen (Harmondsworth: Penguin, 1953), 19.
9 Edward Gibbon, *The Decline and Fall of the Roman Empire*, vol. 1 (New York: Modern Library, 1961), 25.

Words for Introduction of Quotations

This list of alternatives to the word *said* suggests the possibilities for indicating the context of a quotation, the attitude of the source, and your own point of view. Each word gives a quotation a slightly different meaning or emphasis; the words cannot be used interchangeably.

acknowledged	contended	inquired	recognized
acquiesced	contested	insinuated	recounted
added	continued	insisted	refuted
addressed	contradicted	interjected	regretted
admitted	counseled	interrogated	reiterated
advised	countered	intimated	rejoined
advocated	debated	lamented	related
affirmed	decided	lectured	remarked
agreed	declared	lied	reminded
alleged	decreed	maintained	remonstrated
announced	demanded	mentioned	repeated
answered	denied	narrated	replied
argued	denounced	noted	reported
articulated	described	objected	reprimanded
asked	dictated	observed	requested
assented	directed	ordered	responded
asserted	disclosed	petitioned	revealed
assured	divulged	pleaded	ruled
attested	elaborated	pointed out	stated
avowed	enjoined	preached	stipulated
begged	entreated	proclaimed	suggested
boasted	enunciated	pronounced	supplicated
bragged	equivocated	proposed	supposed
called	exclaimed	protested	swore
charged	exhorted	proved	talked
chided	explained	queried	testified
claimed	granted	questioned	thought
commanded	held	quibbled	told
commented	hesitated	quipped	translated
complained	hinted	quoted	urged
conceded	imparted	ranted	uttered
concluded	implored	read	vowed
concurred	indicated	reasoned	warned
confessed	inferred	rebutted	
confided	informed	recited	

Gibbon concludes that "it is not by the rapidity, or extent of the conquest, that we should estimate the greatness of Rome."9

In his history of the Civil War, Bruce Catton describes Colonel Solomon J. Meredith as "a breezy giant of a man."10

According to Catton, Colonel Solomon J. Meredith was "a breezy giant of a man."10

Theodore Roosevelt counseled, "Speak softly and carry a big stick."

Theodore Roosevelt is the president who advised that leaders "speak softly and carry a big stick."
(When considered as a well-known saying, this quotation does not require a note.)

Introductions to Set-off Quotations

Formal
introduction with
colon

Introductions to set-off, or block, quotations should be punctuated according to their grammatical form. An introduction that is a complete sentence containing a formal introductory word or phrase, such as *following, thus*, or *in this way*, usually ends with a colon.

Basil Bernstein summarizes his argument as follows:

> I shall go on to suggest that restricted codes have their basis in condensed symbols, whereas elaborated codes have their basis in articulated symbols; that restricted codes draw upon metaphor, whereas elaborated codes draw upon rationality; that these codes constrain the contextual use of language in critical socializing contexts and in this way regulate the orders of relevance and relation.11

Informal
introduction

An informal introduction that does not contain a formal introductory word and that is a complete sentence may close with either a period or a

[10] Bruce Catton, *Bruce Catton's Civil War*, 3 vols. in 1 (New York: Fairfax, 1984), 225.
[11] Basil Bernstein, *Class, Codes and Control*, vol. 1 (London: Routledge and Kegan Paul, 1971), 175.

colon. The Bernstein quotation on the previous page might also be introduced as follows:

Basil Bernstein begins with a summary of his argument.

        I shall go on to suggest . . .

An introduction that is an incomplete sentence—a phrase or a clause—should end with the punctuation that would be necessary if the introduction and quotation were run together as one sentence:

James Moffett finds that when people try to talk about

abstraction,

        they resort finally to talking about how people,
        especially children, learn. It is hard to avoid
        an analogy between stages of information
        processing that go on in all of us all the time,
        and developmental stages of growth. A
        curriculum sequence based on such an analogy,
        however, needs to be carefully qualified.[12]

In some cases, punctuation may not be needed.

These tasks differ considerably because

        constructing a grammar of a simple text is not
        exactly the same as constructing the grammar of
        a language. Grammars of languages have to
        account not just for the available data in a
        language, but also for the potentially available
        data, the infinite number of sentences that
        could be produced in a language.[13]

PUNCTUATION OF DIRECT QUOTATIONS

Quotations should combine logically and grammatically with your own sentences and paragraphs. To incorporate a direct quotation in a research paper, introduce it with an attribution and with an indication of its importance for your arguments. You also need to punctuate it properly, using

---

[12] James Moffett, *Teaching the Universe of Discourse* (Boston: Houghton Mifflin, 1968), 23.
[13] Elizabeth Closs Traugott and Mary Louise Pratt, *Linguistics for Students of Literature* (New York: Harcourt Brace Jovanovich, 1980), 28.

internal capitalization, quotation marks, ellipses, brackets, and so on, to show the nature of the original source material.

Capitalization

You may alter the capitalization of a direct quotation to conform to the requirements of your own sentence. You may change a capital letter to lowercase or a lowercase letter to a capital.

Use lowercase for the first letter, regardless of the way it appears in the original, if the quotation forms a grammatical whole with the sentence that encompasses or introduces it, as in this example:

```
Harrison E. Salisbury has observed that "every war propels

some obscure city or town into the limelight," pointing

out that the identities of Guernica, Coventry, and

Stalingrad emerged largely in connection with wars.14
```
(In the original, *every* is the first word in the sentence.)

Capitalize the first letter, regardless of how it appears in the original, if the quotation is treated as a grammatical whole—that is, if the quotation is formally introduced as a direct quotation or is set by itself as a complete sentence.

```
William James asks, "How can things so insecure as the

successful experiences of this world afford a stable

anchorage?"15
```
(The original sentence reads, "To begin with, how *can* things so insecure as the successful experiences of this world afford a stable anchorage?")

You may use lowercase for the first letter of either a run-in or a set-off quotation, even when it is capitalized in the original, as the grammar of your sentence requires.

```
In the words of H. D. F. Kitto,

          a sense of the wholeness of things is perhaps
          the most typical feature of the Greek mind. . . .
          The modern mind divides, specializes, thinks in
          categories: the Greek instinct was the opposite,
          to take the widest view, to see things as an
```

---

[14] Harrison E. Salisbury, *Behind the Lines—Hanoi* (New York: Bantam, 1967), 84.
[15] William James, *The Varieties of Religious Experience* (New York: Collier, 1961), 120.

```
                    organic whole.  The speeches of Cleon and
                    Diodotus showed precisely the same thing: the
                    particular issue must be generalized.16
```
(The sentence in the original begins with *A*. The ellipsis points indicate the omission of a sentence.)

```
In the words of H. D. F. Kitto, "a sense of the wholeness

of things is perhaps the most typical feature of the Greek

mind."16
```

Alternate form:
MLA
The *MLA Handbook* recommends indicating the capital letter in the original source by enclosing the lowercase letter in brackets.

```
Harrison E. Salisbury has observed that "[e]very war

propels some obscure city or town into the limelight,"

pointing out . . .
```

Quotation Marks

Enclose direct quotations run into the text in double quotation marks. Quotation marks should be placed outside a comma or period and inside a colon or semicolon.

```
Oscar Wilde wrote that "unselfish people are colourless";

however, most would agree with William Gladstone that

"selfishness is the greatest curse of the human race."17
```

In the case of an exclamation point or question mark, the quotation marks are placed outside when the mark belongs with the quoted material and inside when the mark belongs with the text.

```
What does Hamlet mean when he tells the players "to hold

as 'twere the mirror up to nature"?18
```
(The question mark belongs with the writer's sentence.)

---

16 H. D. F. Kitto, *The Greeks* (Baltimore: Penguin, 1951), 169.

17 Oscar Wilde, *The Picture of Dorian Gray* (New York: Harper and Row, 1965), 68; William Gladstone, speech delivered at Hawarden, 28 May 1890.

18 William Shakespeare, *Hamlet*, in *The Riverside Shakespeare*, ed. G. Blakemore Evans (Boston: Houghton Mifflin, 1974), act 3, sc. 2, lines 21–22.

But:

```
Hamlet asks himself, "Am I a coward?"19
```
(The question mark belongs with the quotation.)

Quotations within run-in quotations

If a portion of the original was enclosed in double quotation marks, change them to single quotation marks in a run-in quotation, as in the following example:

```
Because the French vetoed the European Defense Community,

"the United States was no longer 'pushing on open doors,'

and afterwards Washington conducted itself far more

cautiously."20
```

When quotation marks within single marks are needed, use double marks, and so on, alternating the marks as necessary. This complication is best avoided, however.

Quotations within set-off quotations

When a set-off quotation contains an excerpt that was enclosed in double quotation marks in the original, retain the double quotation marks, as shown below.

```
Marshall McLuhan points out that the development of print

led to the concept of perspective.
```

> ```
> As the literal or "the letter" later became
> identified with light on rather than light
> through the text, there was also the equivalent
> stress on "point of view" or the fixed position
> of the reader: "from where I am sitting."21
> ```

End Punctuation

End punctuation that may be changed

The punctuation used at the end of a quotation depends on the context into which the quotation is placed. A period in the original, for example, may be changed to a comma or omitted to produce a grammatically correct sentence.

---

[19] *Hamlet* 2.2.571.

[20] William Diebold, Jr., *The United States and the Industrial World: American Foreign Economic Policy in the 1970's* (New York: Praeger, 1972), 26.

[21] Marshall McLuhan, *The Gutenberg Galaxy: The Making of Typographic Man* (1962; reprint, New York: Signet, 1969), 138.

Original   Every man bears the entire form of human nature.[22]

When Montaigne wrote, "Every man bears the entire form of

human nature," he advocated studying the self rather than

others.[22]

Montaigne asserted that "every man bears the entire form

of human nature": thus he defended his study of a common

life, his own.[22]

End punctuation that must be retained   Question marks and exclamation marks must accompany the quotations in which they appear. Either of these strong marks of punctuation can take the place of a period. The exclamation mark cannot be excluded even when a colon or a semicolon indicates the end of an independent clause or a complete thought.

"Give me liberty, or give me death!": Patrick Henry thus

stated his challenge to British rule.

The following sentence, though not exclamatory, ends with the exclamation mark of the quotation.

It was Patrick Henry who proclaimed, "Give me liberty or

give me death!"
(When considered as a well-known saying, this quotation does not require a note.)

For variations in end punctuation with parenthetical documentation and placement of superscripts after quotations, see Chapter 4.

Omissions from Quoted Material

You should indicate all omissions from quoted material. To show an ellipsis, use three ellipsis points (periods with one space on either side). The quoted material should read clearly and grammatically without the deleted portion, and the deletion should not alter the meaning or logic of the sentence. Punctuation may be added or deleted if necessary. The following guidelines apply to the use of ellipsis points.

---

[22] Michel de Montaigne, "Of Repentance," in *Selected Essays*, trans. Blanchard Bates (New York: Modern Library, 1949), 285.

Internal omission

Indicate omission of an internal part of a direct quotation with ellipsis points, separated from the text and from each other by one space. Note the following example:

Original

In the western farm states the Granger movement, organized in 1869 as The Patrons of Husbandry, was able to force regulatory legislation through some state legislatures.[23]

Cut version

According to Margaret G. Myers, "In the western

farm states the Granger movement . . . was able to

force regulatory legislation through some state

legislatures."[23]

(The original commas are not necessary when the phrase is omitted.)

Omission at beginning of sentence

Ellipsis points are not needed at the beginning of a run-in quotation, regardless of whether it is an incomplete or a complete sentence:

Original

As a reactor operates, the fissioning of the uranium nuclei results in the accumulation of radioactive waste—nuclear ashes, so to speak—inside the reactor core.[24]

Cut version

Daniel Ford explains that "the fissioning of the uranium

nuclei results in the accumulation of radioactive waste

. . . inside the reactor core."[24]

When you omit the beginning of the quoted sentence and use the rest of the quotation in a construction requiring a capital letter, the letter may be changed from lowercase to uppercase:

Daniel Ford explains, "The fissioning of the uranium

nuclei results in the accumulation of radioactive

waste."[24]

In MLA style the change from lowercase to uppercase is indicated by brackets. A lowercase *t* in brackets [t] would indicate that the original *T* was capitalized; an uppercase *T* in brackets [T] would indicate that the original *t* was lowercase.

Alternate form: MLA

Daniel Ford explains, "[T]he fissioning of the . . .

---

[23] Margaret G. Myers, *A Financial History of the United States* (New York: Columbia Univ. Press, 1970), 226.

[24] Daniel Ford, "Three Mile Island—Part 1: Class Nine Accident," A Reporter at Large, *New Yorker*, 6 Apr. 1981, 73.

Omission at end of sentence

Ellipsis points indicate the omission of the end of a sentence only when another sentence of quotation follows immediately. An ellipsis is not necessary in the cut quotation below:

Original

A foolish consistency is the hobgoblin of little minds, adored by little statesmen, philosophers and divines.[25]

Cut version

```
Emerson advocated the courage to change one's mind when he

said that "a foolish consistency is the hobgoblin of

little minds."25
```

Ellipsis with original end punctuation

When you wish to retain the original punctuation at the end of either a cut or a full sentence, the appropriate mark of punctuation substitutes for the period preceding the ellipsis points.

Original

Ilse smiled scornfully. "What's it to you? Just because Papa Kremer put us in the same row? You're not jealous of him?"[26]

Cut version

```
Then Ilse taunts Hans: "What's it to you? . . . You're not

jealous of him?"26
```

Original

From the boy's face one might suppose that sacred emblem to be, in his eyes, the crowning confusion of the great, confused city;—so golden, so high up, so far out of his reach.[27]

Cut version

```
"From the boy's face one might suppose that sacred emblem

to be, in his eyes, the crowning confusion of the great,

confused city; . . . so far out of his reach."27
```

Period followed by ellipsis

When another sentence follows either a complete or a cut sentence, place a period at the end of the sentence, without an intervening space, and add three ellipsis points. A complete sentence must precede the four dots, and a complete sentence must follow them.

Original

Great advances in the principles of research were made by the ancient Greeks. Building partly upon previous discoveries recorded by the Egyptians and Babylonians, the Greek thinkers delved particularly into astronomy, medicine, physics, and geography, and some of them explored literature and ethics. A few instances will illustrate the scope and the fundamental importance of their contributions to the sum of human learning. Among the earliest whose

---

[25] Ralph Waldo Emerson, "Self-Reliance," in *The American Tradition in Literature,* ed. George Perkins et al., vol. 1, 6th ed. (New York: Random House, 1985), 846.

[26] André Schwarz-Bart, *The Last of the Just,* trans. Stephen Becker (New York: Atheneum, 1981), 225.

[27] Charles Dickens, *Bleak House* (New York: Bantam, 1983), 253.

names we know were Thales and Anaximander (about 600 B.C.), whose principal work was done in astronomy.[28]

Cut version

In a chapter on "The Role of Research," Tyrus Hillway

points out that "great advances in the principles of

research were made by the ancient Greeks. . . . Greek

thinkers delved particularly into astronomy, medicine,

physics, and geography. . . . Among the earliest whose

names we know were Thales and Anaximander."[28]

(The first ellipsis follows a complete sentence in the original; the second ellipsis follows a cut
sentence.)

**Omission at
beginning of
paragraph**   In a set-off quotation, indicate the omission of words or sentences at the
beginning of a paragraph by starting at the indented margin, without the
additional three-space paragraph indention.

Original

The remarkable reduction in fertility that the American population has
achieved over the past two centuries is, perhaps, the most obvious cause for the
decline in mean household size. As the birthrate fell, the proportion of childless
households increased from about 20 percent in 1790 to 48.3 percent in 1950.
The effects of the postwar baby boom temporarily reversed this trend, so that
only 43.0 percent of all households were childless in 1960. But with the recent
decline in fertility, childless households have once again started to increase,
accounting for 46.0 percent of the total in 1975.

Increased life expectancy may also have helped to lower the average size of
the household. We have seen how the combination of lower fertility and longer
life meant that twentieth-century couples were among the first in history who
could expect to have a significant number of years together after their children
left home. Thus, an increase in childless households and households with one or
two children reflects not only lower levels of childbearing, but also more older
couples whose children have grown up and left home. For example, in 1970,
fully 82.2 percent of all married couples in which the husband's age was
between 55 and 64 had no children in their household, a remarkable contrast to
the 11.7 percent of couples without children when the husband was 35 to 44.

One other interesting change is the increasing tendency for women to head
the households. In part this is directly related to improved life expectancy,
although it seems likely that alterations in social attitudes are also involved.[29]

Cut version

Berkin and Norton attribute the decline in the size of the

American household to several factors.

An increase in childless households and
households with one or two children reflects not

---

[28] Tyrus Hillway, *Introduction to Research* (Boston: Houghton Mifflin, 1956), 15.
[29] Carol Ruth Berkin and Mary Beth Norton, *Women of America: A History* (Boston: Houghton
Mifflin, 1979), 29.

```
                    only lower levels of childbearing, but also more
                    older couples whose children have grown up and
                    left home.29
```
(The set-off sentence, which is in the second paragraph of the original, begins with *thus*.)

Omission of entire paragraph(s)

    Indicate the omission of one or more paragraphs in a prose quotation with an ellipsis at the end of the paragraph immediately preceding the omission. (Some writers prefer to use a full line of ellipsis points to indicate the omission of an entire paragraph.) The quoted passages in the following examples come from the excerpt from *Women of America*, cited in footnote 29.

Cut version

```
Berkin and Norton attribute the decline in the size of the

American household during the past two hundred years to a

variety of factors.

          The remarkable reduction in fertility that
          the American population has achieved over the
          past two centuries is, perhaps, the most
          obvious cause for the decline in mean household
          size. . . .
          Increased life expectancy may also have
          helped to lower the average size of the
          household.29
```
(The ellipsis points after *size* might indicate the omission of an entire paragraph; in this case, however, they signal only the omission of the rest of the sentences in the paragraph.)

Cut version (alternative)

```
Berkin and Norton point out that, in addition to an

increase in life expectancy, many other factors account

for the decline in size of the American household:

          The remarkable reduction in fertility that
          the American population has achieved over the
          past two centuries is, perhaps, the most obvious
          cause for the decline in mean household size.

          . . . . . . . . . . . . . . . . . . . . . . . .

          One other interesting change is the
          increasing tendency for women to head the
          households.29
```

Omission of line(s) of poetry

    Show the omission of one or more lines of poetry with a full line of ellipsis points equal in length to the longest line of the poem, as in this example from Alexander Pope's "An Essay on Criticism."

```
          'Tis with our judgments as our watches: none
          Go just alike, yet each believes his own.

          . . . . . . . . . . . . . . . . . . . . . . .

          Authors are partial to their wit, 'tis true,
          But are not critics to their judgment too?
```

Interpolation

Clarifying original source

Except for appropriate changes of beginning capitalization and end punctuation, direct quotations should not be altered. However, if you believe that a reader may find a quotation unclear or may miss the point you are trying to make by using the quotation, you may insert explanatory material within the quotation, enclosing it in brackets. Such an addition is called an *interpolation*.

```
"No society in which these liberties [liberty of

conscience, liberty of pursuits, and freedom to unite] are

not, on the whole, respected, is free, whatever may be its

form of government."30
```

Correcting errors

An error in a quotation should be designated in brackets immediately following the error. You may indicate your awareness of an error with the word *sic* (meaning "thus" in Latin) or with a correction.

When the correction would be obvious to your readers, as in most spelling or typographical errors, use *sic*.

Correction with sic

```
John Doe explained, "The results of the 1988 experiment

were quite surprizing [sic]."31
```

When the nature of the error might not be readily apparent, supply the correction in brackets.

Correction in brackets

```
Doe added, "The affects [effects] of radiation

exceeded our estimates."31

Doe advised that "Smith completed her experiments in

1987 [1986]."31
```

Unless you particularly want to call attention to the inaccuracy or carelessness of a source, you may want to try to avoid quoting sentences with errors.

Indicating source of italics

Indicate the source of italics with an explanatory phrase in brackets when the source might be misinterpreted. Note the following example:

```
          This is the story of an adolescent whose
       needs are not understood by his father, who
       thinks his son is stupid.  The son will not
```

---

30 John Stuart Mill, *On Liberty*, ed. David Spitz (New York: Norton, 1975), 14.
31 John Doe, letter to author, 19 May 1989.

develop himself as the father thinks he should,
but stubbornly insists on learning instead what
<u>he</u> [italics in original *or* original emphasis]
thinks is of real value. To achieve his
complete self—realization, the young man first
has to become acquainted with his inner being, a
process <u>no father can prescribe</u> [italics mine *or*
emphasis mine] even if he realizes the value of
it, as the youth's father does not.[32]

**Clarifying pronoun
reference**

If the referent of a pronoun in a quotation might be ambiguous, or if the
pronoun refers to a noun in a previous sentence that is not quoted, supply
the noun in brackets.

"The scientist refers to it [a datum] as an observation."[31]

"This ["The Three Languages"] is the story of an adolescent

whose needs are not understood by his father."[32]

---

[32] Bruno Bettelheim, *The Uses of Enchantment: The Meaning and Importance of Fairy Tales*
(New York: Vintage, 1977), 100. The bracketed material has been interpolated.

TYPING AND PRINTING INSTRUCTIONS

Superscripts

Within the text, a superscript should be placed without any intervening space after the end punctuation. In notes, the superscript should be indented five spaces and followed by one space. If you use a word-processing program that does not produce superscripts, check with an adviser about an acceptable alternative, such as placing the number in parentheses.

Run-in Prose Quotations

Run short prose quotations (fewer than five typed lines) into the text and enclose them in double quotation marks. If the original excerpt contains a direct quotation, change the double quotation marks around the internal quotation to single quotation marks.

Set-off Prose Quotations

Set off long quotations (five typed lines or more) in indented, block-style paragraphs. Unlike run-in quotations, quotations that are set off are not enclosed in quotation marks.

Set-off quotations may be single- or double-spaced. Single-spacing is often preferred for theses and dissertations to save space and to make the finished paper resemble a book. MLA format calls for the double-spacing of set-off quotations, particularly for materials to be set by a printer. Whichever spacing you select should be used consistently throughout the paper. Set-off quotations, whether single- or double-spaced, should be separated from the text by one double space both above and below, and they should be indented ten spaces from the left margin. Indent three spaces within set-off material to indicate indentions in the original. Indicate omissions, alterations, and corrections of quoted material as specified on pages 79 through 83.

Poetry

Short excerpts of poetry (two full lines or fewer) should be run into the text and enclosed in double quotation marks. Separate each line of poetry with a slanted line with a space on either side of it. Excerpts of three or more lines should be set off and may be single- or double-spaced. (See the discussion of spacing in the preceding section.) Double-space between stanzas. Indent poetry ten spaces from the left margin; indention may be five spaces when the line would otherwise have to be broken. Lines of poetry extending beyond one typescript line should be indented five spaces, broken, and indented ten spaces on the next line. Alignment and spacing within the set-off quotation should follow the original as closely as possible.

Epigraphs

Direct quotations that precede an entire text or a chapter should be aligned twenty spaces from the left margin and continue to the right margin. Double-space from the chapter title to the epigraph. Single-space the epigraph itself. Indention in the original is indicated with an additional three-space indention. The spacing suffices to indicate that the epigraph is a direct quotation; quotations marks are not needed. Single-space to the attribution of the quotation, which appears below the epigraph, flush with the right margin. Begin the attribution approximately at the middle of the page. Double-space to the first line of text.

Ellipsis

Indicate the omission of any portion of a quoted excerpt with three ellipsis points (three spaced dots). When an ellipsis is used within a sentence, leave a space before the first dot and after the third. Use four dots (a period plus three ellipsis points) to signify the omission of any of the following: (1) the end of a quoted sentence, (2) the beginning of the following sentence, (3) one or more sentences, (4) one or more paragraphs. Place the first of the four dots, with no intervening space, immediately after the last quoted word. The omission of the end of a sentence and the omission of one or more subsequent sentences are indicated in the same way. A complete sentence must precede the four dots, and another complete sentence must follow them. When you retain the original punctuation at the end of a cut or a complete sentence, that mark of punctuation (question mark, exclamation point, semicolon, colon, comma) takes the place of the period. A full line of ellipsis points running the length of the longest line indicates omission of one or more lines of poetry. When a line of ellipsis points is used to indicate the omission of a paragraph, the dots run from margin to margin.

Brackets

Enclose in square brackets ([ ]) corrections, clarifications, and editorial comments inserted in direct quotations. If your typewriter or printer does not have brackets, insert them neatly in black ink. Do not substitute parentheses or slanting brackets made with the slash and underline marks.

End Punctuation with Documentation

For end punctuation with superscripts or parenthetical documentation to identify original sources, see Chapter 4, pages 92 and 93, and pages 103 and 104.

Quotations in Notes

Run in all direct quotations in both footnotes and endnotes, regardless of the length of the quotation. Use single- or double-spacing consistent with other entries. If the quotation runs more than one paragraph, begin each paragraph at the left margin without indention. Place quotation marks at the beginning of each paragraph and at the beginning and end of the entire quotation. Provide any necessary bibliographical information for the quotation within parentheses directly after the quotation. Single- or double-space quotations according to your policy for notes.

[1] On other issues the Supreme Court handed down these decisions in 1989: "Ruling unanimously in a copyright case (Community for Creative Non-Violence v. Redi, No. 88-293), the Court held that freelance artists and writers retain the right to copyright what they create as long as they were not in a conventional employment relationship with the organization that commissioned their work.
"The court unanimously refused to narrow the scope of the Federal racketeering law. The decision, H.J. Inc. v. Northwestern Bell, No. 87-1252, left the law, originally aimed at organized crime, as a powerful weapon in private civil lawsuits." (Linda Greenhouse, "The Year the Court Turned Right," New York Times, 7 July 1989, A10)

4

NOTES AND PARENTHETICAL REFERENCES

Documentation, through either notes or parenthetical references, is the acknowledgment of the sources of ideas and information in your paper. The authority or source for both facts and opinions—whether quoted directly or indirectly or derived from primary or from secondary sources—must be cited to provide your reader with an accurate account of the materials on which you base your conclusions. Omission of full and precise documentation can result in inaccurate and invalid research or in plagiarism (see Chapter 3).

SYSTEMS OF DOCUMENTATION

The two basic systems for documenting materials from other sources are the note-bibliography system and the parenthetical-reference system. The note-bibliography format involves presentation of bibliographical information in footnotes or endnotes and in a bibliography. This system has been widely used for undergraduate and graduate research papers in the humanities and the social sciences and for papers in many of the professions. The parenthetical-reference system entails including documentation in parentheses within the text and in a list of works cited.

This book provides instructions for using both of these systems. The note-bibliography system here is based on *The Chicago Manual of Style*, 13th edition; the parenthetical reference system is the one recommended by the *MLA Handbook for Writers of Research Papers*, 3rd edition.

Choosing between *Chicago Manual* and MLA styles

Your choice between Chicago and MLA formats might be governed by the suggestions of your adviser, the requirements of your university, or your personal taste. If you wish to use the note-bibliography system and widely accepted traditional bibliographical forms, you will follow the basic format presented throughout *Form and Style* and use the note and bibliography forms presented on facing pages in Chapter 5 (pages 146–79). If you want to use more abbreviated bibliographical forms and the parenthetical-reference system favored by MLA, you can alter the basic format according to the instructions provided in parentheses and follow the instructions in the sections on parenthetical references and lists of works cited on pages 100 through 104, and 136 and 137. You should select a format in the beginning stages of research and follow it consistently throughout the process of preparing your paper.

Other formats

Parenthetical reference systems can take a number of forms. The Modern Language Association uses an author-page style, which is fully detailed in this chapter. The American Psychological Association uses an author-date style (see Appendix B). Some scientific disciplines use an author-number style (see Appendix C). A section on legal citation, which uses notes only, appears at the end of this chapter.

PURPOSES OF DOCUMENTATION

Documentation may serve one or more purposes: to acknowledge indebtedness, to establish the validity of evidence, to indicate cross-references within the paper, to amplify ideas in the text, and to provide additional bibliographical information.

Notes or parenthetical references may be used to accomplish the first three purposes; whether you use notes and bibliography or parenthetical references and a list of works cited, you may still use notes to amplify ideas and provide additional bibliography.

Acknowledging Indebtedness

All material gathered from sources, whether quoted directly or indirectly, requires documentation in a research paper. Information that qualifies as common knowledge (see page 65) does not need to be documented except when it is quoted directly. When the audience for a paper is very specialized, the amount of material that constitutes common knowledge may be greater than it is for a research paper directed to a general audience. The use of documentation to acknowledge indebtedness, then, sometimes requires making judgments about whether a piece of information is common knowledge and about the degree of your dependence on a source for the information. When you are in doubt about whether to document something, it is wise to do so, particularly in undergraduate papers.

Establishing the Validity of Evidence

Citation of sources of information gives readers a way to establish the accuracy of direct or indirect quotations and to verify the validity of your interpretation and use of sources.

Providing Cross-References within the Paper

References to materials in other parts of the paper or in the appendixes can help the reader establish the proper relationships among ideas and concepts. Cross-references may be made either in notes or in the text.

Amplifying Ideas

Informational notes can provide discussion or amplification of points in the text. They should be used only when such discussion cannot be included in the text without interrupting or complicating the development. Material such as technical discussions or definitions, incidental comments, corollary materials, additional information, and reconciliation of conflicting views might be presented in an informational note. These notes should be complete in themselves, and they should read as parenthetical statements that can be removed without changing the meaning of the text. The paper should read logically and coherently without the notes. Essential ideas and information should be presented in the text; unimportant and peripheral information should be omitted.

An example of an informational note follows:

Informational note

¹ Sophocles, <u>Antigone</u>, trans. Elizabeth Wyckoff, <u>The Complete Greek Tragedies: Sophocles I</u>, ed. David Grene and Richmond Lattimore (Chicago: Univ. of Chicago Press, 1954). The authorship of these lines has long been disputed, and difference of opinion remains though modern critics tend to accept them, as did Aristotle. Bernard Knox explains the scene as a solitary moment of self-discovery for Antigone: "She can at last identify the driving force behind her action, the private, irrational imperative. . . . It is her fanatical devotion to one particular family, her own, the doomed, incestuous, accursed house of Oedipus." Sophocles, <u>The Three Theban Plays</u>, trans. Robert Fagles and introd. Bernard Knox (New York: Viking, 1982), 33.

Providing Additional Bibliography

Bibliographical notes can allow you to mention sources indirectly relevant to your paper that you have not cited yourself but that another researcher might wish to pursue.

An example of a bibliographical note follows:

Bibliographical note

² For differing explanations of the causes of Mill's breakdown, see William Albert Levi, "The 'Mental Crisis' of John Stuart Mill," <u>Psychoanalytic Review</u> 23 (1945): 86–101; John Durham, "The Influence of John Stuart Mill's Mental Crisis on His Thoughts," <u>American Imago</u> 20 (1963): 369–84.

NOTES ACCOMPANIED BY A BIBLIOGRAPHY (*CHICAGO MANUAL*)

The citation of a source in the note-bibliography system is indicated in the text with a superscript (raised number), which refers to a note providing information about the source. The notes are called *footnotes* when they appear at the bottom of the page and *endnotes* when they are collected in a section at the end of each chapter or at the end of the entire paper. Dissertations to be microfilmed should have footnotes, because turning back to endnotes on a microfilm reader can be distracting. Most other papers can have endnotes.

Designation of Notes

A note is indicated in the text by a raised arabic numeral. The superscript should be raised one-half space (never a full space) above the line and should be placed directly after the material (without a space) for which the corresponding note provides the source. The best placement of the number is at the end of a sentence or, if that would cause confusion or inaccuracy, at the end of a clause. The number goes outside all punctuation except the dash, and it should not be underlined, circled, or followed by a period. The examples given below demonstrate correct and incorrect placement of the superscript.

Correct Mina P. Shaughnessy points out that "the beginning writer

does not know how writers behave."[1]

Incorrect Mina P. Shaughnessy[1] points out . . .

Incorrect Mina P. Shaughnessy points out that "the beginning writer

does not know how writers behave.[1]"

Correct Mina P. Shaughnessy speculated that the inexperienced

writer is handicapped by lack of knowledge about the

process of writing.[1]

Correct "The beginning writer does not know how writers

behave"[1]--all of the research points to this conclusion.

Numbering of notes Both endnotes and footnotes are usually numbered consecutively within a chapter, starting at number one in each new chapter. Some institutions recommend beginning the numbering afresh on each page when footnotes are used or numbering thoughout the entire thesis when endnotes are used.

See Chapter 6 for the placement and numbering of notes in figures and tables.

First References

The first time you cite a source in the notes, give a complete entry in the correct format for the bibliographical style you are using throughout the paper. For a book, a complete entry includes the following information (if applicable): complete name of the author; title of the book; editor, compiler, or translator; series and number; edition (other than first); number of volumes; city and state of publication; publisher; date of publication; volume number; page number(s). For an article in a periodical, a complete

---

[1] Mina P. Shaughnessy, *Errors and Expectations: A Guide for the Teacher of Basic Writing* (New York: Oxford Univ. Press, 1977), 79.

entry usually includes the following: complete name of the author; title of the article; name of the periodical; volume and/or number of the issue; date; page number(s). (See the first-reference forms on the "Notes" pages in Chapter 5, pages 146–79.)

Subsequent References

After the first complete reference note, you should use a shortened format for subsequent references to the same work. In most cases the last name of the author and the page number serve to identify the work. When you have more than one work by the same author, you will need to use the author's name, the title (abbreviated if it is lengthy) of the work, and the page number, as the examples below illustrate. Subsequent reference notes should provide enough information to allow the reader to locate the original note or the bibliography entry, but they should not be longer than necessary. Most style books now discourage the use of Latin abbreviations in subsequent references (see Appendix A for a discussion of their use).

Even when you use the note-bibliography system, you may wish to cite some works parenthetically, particularly when you have multiple references to the same work, as in papers on literature (see page 97).

LAST NAME OF THE AUTHOR   Subsequent references in the note-bibliography system usually consist of the last name of the author, the page number(s), and any other information required for identification of the source.

3 Martin Luther King, Jr., Why We Can't Wait (New York: New American Library, 1964), 78–80.

4 A. Powell Davies, The Meaning of the Dead Sea Scrolls (New York: New American Library, 1956), 50.

5 King, 45–47.

6 Davies, 81.
(MLA omits the comma before the page number.)

Subsequent references to work without author   When an article or book does not have a named author, the subsequent reference includes the title of the article or book (shortened when the title is long) and the page number(s). (See page 96 for rules concerning the shortening of titles.)

First reference   7 "Net-Weight Nonsense on Canned Food Labels," Consumer Reports, Oct. 1972, 665.
(MLA omits the comma before the date and uses a colon after the date.)

Intervening note   8 Morgan, 14.

Subsequent reference

9 "Net—Weight Nonsense," 666–67.
(MLA omits the comma before the page number.)

Subsequent references to more than one work by an author

When more than one work by an author is cited, each subsequent reference must include not only the name of the author, but also the title of the article or book (again, shortened when the title is long). The examples below show subsequent references for two works by the same corporate author:

First reference

10 Association for Supervision and Curriculum Development, Fostering Mental Health in Our Schools, 1950 Yearbook (Washington: National Education Association, 1950), 104–08 (hereafter referred to as ASCD).

Subsequent references

11 ASCD, Learning and Mental Health in the School, 1966 Yearbook (Washington: National Education Association, 1966), 127–29.

12 ASCD, Fostering Mental Health, 123–24.

13 ASCD, Learning and Mental Health, 130.
(MLA omits the comma before the page number.)

Subsequent references to work with more than one author

For a work with multiple authors, give the last names of up to three authors. When a work has four or more authors, give the name of the first author followed by *et al.* (the abbreviation for *et alii,* "and others").

First reference

14 Cleanth Brooks and Robert Penn Warren, Modern Rhetoric, 4th ed. (New York: Harcourt, 1979), 56.

Subsequent reference

15 Brooks and Warren, 89.

First reference

16 Janice M. Lauer et al., Four Worlds of Writing (New York: Harper and Row, 1981), 77.
(The book has four authors.)

Subsequent reference

17 Lauer et al., 80.
(MLA omits the comma before the page number.)

Authors with the same last name

When you have more than one author with the same last name, include first names or initials in subsequent references:

First references

18 Helen C. White, The Mysticism of William Blake (New York: Russell, 1964), 75.

19 E. B. White, Charlotte's Web (New York: Harper, 1952), 67.

Subsequent references

20 Helen C. White, 77.

21 E. B. White, 95.
(MLA omits the comma before the page numbers.)

Works with name of editor, compiler, or translator in place of name of author

Some works have the name of an editor, compiler, or translator in place of the name of an author. In subsequent references, you should list the name or names of an editor, compiler, or translator without the accompanying abbreviation (*ed.*, *comp.*, or *trans.*), which should appear in the bibliography:

Text

Many of the articles in Research on Composing advocate

further exploration of the motivation for writing.22

First reference

22 Charles R. Cooper and Lee Odell, eds. Research on Composing: Points of Departure. Urbana: NCTE, 1978, xi–xviii.

Subsequent reference

23 Cooper and Odell, xi–xviii.

(MLA omits the comma before the page numbers.)

Multivolume works

If a multivolume work has one general title, each subsequent citation must include the volume number:

First reference

24 Gerhard von Rad, Old Testament Theology, trans. D. M. G. Stalker, 2 vols. (New York: Harper and Row, 1962–65).

(This initial citation refers to the complete work rather than to any specific page within a volume.)

Subsequent reference

25 Rad, 1:76.

(This citation refers to material on page 76 of volume 1. MLA omits the comma before the volume and page numbers.)

When each volume in a multivolume work has a separate title, however, the title of the volume serves as identification:

26 James C. Crutchfield, ed., The Fisheries: Problems in Resource Management, vol. 1 of Studies on Public Policy Issues in Resource Management (Seattle: Univ. of Washington Press, 1965), 61.

27 Crutchfield, Fisheries, 62.

(MLA omits the comma before the page number.)

Shortening titles

Shortened titles should include significant identifying words. Abbreviations should not be used, and the original word order should not be changed. *Chicago Manual* does not advise shortening a title of fewer than five words except for the omission of an initial article; MLA recommends reducing titles to the shortest possible form, generally one word, which should be the first word other than an article. Subtitles should always be omitted in subsequent references. Decide on a principle for shortening titles, and use it consistently throughout your paper.

ORIGINAL TITLE	SHORTENED VERSION
The Modes of Modern Writing	Modes of Modern Writing *or* Modes
Teaching and Learning English as a Foreign Language	Teaching and Learning English *or* Teaching
The Drama of the Gifted Child	Gifted Child *or* Drama
Eagle against the Sun: The American War with Japan	Eagle against the Sun *or* Eagle

TITLE ONLY: WORKS OF LITERATURE   Although the first reference to a work of literature gives full details on the author, title, and facts of publication, subsequent references may be considerably abbreviated, sometimes leaving out the name of the author and shortening the title of the work when it is well known. Abbreviations should be used to designate the parts of a literary work: volume (vol.), part (pt.), number (no.), numbers (nos.) book (bk.), chapter (chap.). No abbreviation for lines should be used.

28 John Milton, Paradise Lost, ed. Merritt Y. Hughes (New York: Odyssey, 1962), bk. 9, lines 342–75.

Abbreviated references   After you have indicated the kinds of sections to which your numbers refer, as is done in note *28* with *bk.* and *lines,* you may omit the designations in following citations. Subsequent references to well-known works need not include the author's name:

29 Paradise Lost 3.1–55.

Citations for a play should include the numbers of acts, scenes, and lines in arabic numerals. These numerals should be separated by periods without spacing:

30 Othello 3.2.1–5.

You may wish to shorten the title even further. See the *MLA Handbook* for acceptable abbreviations of the works of Shakespeare and Chaucer.

31 Oth. 3.2.1–5.

Subsequent references for less well known works of literature may include the last name of the author (particularly for audiences outside the field of literature or in the case of obscure works). If the reader will understand the reference, subsequent citations may be reduced to a short-ened version of the title and designation of the sections:

32 Robert Browning, "Soliloquy of the Spanish Cloister," The Norton Anthology of English Literature, ed. M. H. Abrams et al., 3rd ed. (New York: Norton, 1975), stanza 4, lines 25–32.

33 Browning, "Soliloquy" 7.49–52.

or

34 "Soliloquy" 7.49–52.

When a work has other types of divisions or when the meaning of a sequence of numbers might not be clear, an explanatory note identifying each element of a citation allows you to abbreviate the note in subsequent references:

35 Jane Austen, Emma, ed. Stephen M. Parrish (New York: Norton, 1972). Subsequent references to this edition will appear as E. The first number of each citation refers to the volume, the second to the chapter, and the third to the page.

36 E 2.12.75.

Even when a page number would suffice to identify a passage, you should try to designate passages in works of literature by names and numbers of sections because readers often use many different editions of widely reprinted works.

Sacred writing   References to the Bible and other sacred writings begin with the particular chapter or book you wish to cite. The version or translation appears only in the bibliographic entry (see page 124). Books of the Bible should be abbreviated; chapters and verses are expressed in arabic numerals separated by a colon without spacing. See *The Chicago Manual of Style* or the *MLA Handbook* for accepted abbreviations of books of the Bible.

37 1 Sam. 14:6–9.

Classical works   Refer to classical works by title and main divisions—volume, book, chapter, pages, sections, or lines, as appropriate—in subsequent references. Numerals should be separated by periods without spacing. The initial citation must indicate the identity of the translator and editor. This is important information about any work, but it is essential for classical works, where the work of the translator can involve restoration of the text or theories about the meaning of particular words.

First reference   38 Aristotle, Poetics, trans. S. H. Butcher, ed. Francis Fergusson (New York: Hill and Wang, 1961), bk. 7, chap. 2.

Subsequent references to the classics omit the name of the author:

39 <u>Poetics</u> 8.1.

PARENTHETICAL REFERENCES IN THE TEXT   Even when you have chosen the note-bibliography format, you may wish to use some parenthetical references, particularly when, as in a paper on literature, you have multiple references to the same work. Parenthetical references should consist of short entries giving the last name of the author (or an abbreviated title) and the page number(s). Final punctuation follows the parentheses.

First reference

In 1680 the Pueblo Indians rebelled swiftly and ferociously. In just a few weeks they accomplished what no other Indians were able to do: they drove the invaders from their land, decisively and completely.40

---

40 Alvin M. Josephy, Jr., <u>The Patriot Chiefs</u> (1961; reprint, New York: Viking, 1969), 65–66.

Subsequent reference

The subsequent reference may appear in the text:

The guiding force and catalyst in the revolt was an Indian medicine doctor who had been denied the right to conduct his rituals (Josephy 87).

After the first reference, information such as act, scene, and line; part, verse, and line; and book, chapter, and page number may be included in parentheses after the quotation, whether it is run in or set off. When such a parenthetical reference follows a direct quotation, the punctuation for the sentence follows the parentheses. Particularly in a paper involving several works by one author, abbreviations may be substituted for the title:

Indeed, the truth about Jim's affair is so elusive that even after innumerable evenings spent spinning out the story on verandahs all over the Pacific, Marlow knows that "the last word is not said——probably shall never be said" (<u>LJ</u> 137).

(After the edition is cited in the first reference, the novel *Lord Jim* is indicated in subsequent parenthetical references with the abreviation *LJ*. The period follows the parenthesis rather than the last word in the sentence.)

PARENTHETICAL REFERENCES ACCOMPANIED BY A LIST OF WORKS CITED (MLA)

The use of parenthetical references and a list of works cited is an alternative to the note-bibliography system. The principles of documentation remain the same—that is, you document the source of any fact or opinion that you have taken from your reading (see page 65). The documentation that appears within the text is a brief parenthetical reference (rather than a note number) that directs your reader to a full bibliographical citation in a list of works cited. The system of parenthetical documentation described below is the one favored by the Modern Language Association (MLA).

You will be able to use parenthetical documentation most efficiently if you decide to use it before beginning to write because it requires a different kind of thinking about your bibliography and occasionally requires different stylistic choices. Parenthetical documentation depends on reference to a complete list of works cited, or bibliography (see Chapter 5). It is even more necessary with parenthetical documentation than with the note-bibliography format that you set up this list before you begin to write because the parenthetical references must correspond to it. For example, you need to know whether you have one or more than one work by the same author because your parenthetical reference for the same book will differ in each case.

Since your documentation actually appears within your text, you should keep it to a minimum to avoid distracting the reader. You should keep your parenthetical references as brief as possible, while giving the reader enough information to identify the source in the list of works cited. As you write, then, you should keep in mind the necessity for introducing both direct and indirect quotations in a way that will allow you to cite sources efficiently. At the same time, you should not let the need for documentation govern or alter your meaning. Each time you need a reference, you should evaluate your choices for documentation along with the demands of the style and sense of your writing. The sample sentences below illustrate some of the options available for parenthetical documentation.

Content of Parenthetical Citations

When you cite a source either directly or indirectly, indicate the name of the author either in the text or in parentheses and the page number in parentheses, as the following examples indicate:

```
Moffett has identified public narrative as one kind of

discourse (42–44).
```

```
At least one other educator has recently quarreled with

the traditional division of the curriculum into discrete

subjects (Moffett 5–10).
```

Entry in list of works cited
```
Moffett, James.   Teaching the Universe of Discourse.
     Boston: Houghton, 1968.
```

Work with more than one author
When a work has two or three authors, include all the names within parentheses:

```
One textbook defines rhetoric as "the art of using

language effectively" (Brooks and Warren 5).

Brooks and Warren define rhetoric as "the art of using

language effectively" (5).
```

Entry in list of works cited
```
Brooks, Cleanth, and Robert Penn Warren.   Modern Rhetoric.
     4th ed.   New York: Harcourt, 1979.
```

Work with four or more authors
When a work has four or more authors, give only the last name of the first author followed by *et al.* (the abbreviation for *et alii,* "and others"):

```
The authors of Four Worlds of Writing begin with the

premise that "writing represents a way of making meaning

of our experience" (Lauer et al. 2).
```

Entry in list of works cited
```
Lauer, Janice M., et al.   Four Worlds of Writing.   New
     York: Harper, 1981.
```

More than one author with same last name
When you have more than one author with the same last name, include first names in subsequent references. Subsequent references in a paper including references to Helen C. White's *The Mysticism of William Blake* and E. B. White's *Charlotte's Web* would read as follows: (Helen C. White 75) and (E. B. White 67).
List the names of an editor, compiler, or translator without the accompanying abbreviation that appears in the list of works cited:

```
Many of the articles in Research on Composing

advocate further exploration of the motivation for writing

(Cooper and Odell).
```

Entry in list of works cited
```
Cooper, Charles R., and Lee Odell, eds.   Research on
     Composing: Points of Departure.   Urbana: NCTE, 1978.
```

Work listed by title only
When you have a work listed only by title in your works cited section, use a shortened version of the title in parentheses.

The prime ministers of four Caribbean nations attended the

installation of the new Parliament in Grenada ("New

Parliament" 5).

Entry in list of works cited

"New Parliament Installed in Grenada." New York Times
    30 Dec. 1984, sec. 1: 5+.

(See page 122 for an explanation of MLA's use of + for articles on discontinuous pages.)

Corporate author

When you have a corporate author, use the name of the organization, abbreviated if it is lengthy, in place of the name of the author:

The 1950 yearbook emphasized this point (ASCD 123–24).

Works cited by author or by author and title

When you cite an entire work by the name of the author alone or by author and title, you do not need a parenthetical reference. A reader will be able to find bibliographical information by looking up the author's name in your list of works cited.

Murray's book allows a beginner to share the experience of

a professional writer.

Shaughnessy's study of her students' papers has inspired a

generation of teachers.

Multivolume works

To cite an entire volume of a multivolume work, use the author's name and the abbreviation *vol.*

This valuable reference work surveys the major operas of

Mozart and Puccini (Newman, vol. 2).

To cite a portion of a volume of a multivolume work, use an arabic numeral to indicate the volume followed by a colon and the page number(s).

Newman discusses the controversy surrounding the quality

of Mozart's The Magic Flute (2: 104–05).

Entry in list of works cited

Newman, Ernest. Great Operas: The Definitive Treatment of
    Their History, Stories, and Music. 2 vols. New
    York: Vintage, 1958.

Two or more works by same author When you have two works or more by the same author, use a shortened version of the title in each reference:

Shaughnessy points out that "the beginning writer does not know how writers behave" (Errors 79).

Teachers applauded Shaughnessy's assertion that "teaching them [basic writers] to write well is not only suitable but challenging work for those who would be teachers and scholars in a democracy" ("Diving In" 68).

Material cited in another source When you refer to material cited in a source other than the original, use the abbreviation *qtd. in* to indicate where you actually found the quotation:

Goethe wrote that "it takes more culture to perceive the virtues of The Magic Flute than to point out its defects" (qtd. in Newman 2: 104).

Multiple citations When you wish to include more than one work in a parenthetical citation, separate entries with a semicolon:

(Errors 79; "Diving In" 68; Brooks and Warren 5)

Placement and Punctuation of Parenthetical Documentation

Parenthetical references should generally be placed at the end of a sentence. Quotation marks, if any, precede the reference; end punctuation, as well as commas, colons, and semicolons, follows it:

Shaughnessy points out that "the beginning writer does not know how writers behave" (79).

Was it Shaughnessy who pointed out that "the beginning writer does not know how writers behave" (79)?

"The beginning writer does not know how writers behave," according to Shaughnessy (79).

If confusion might result about the distinction between your own conclusions and an idea from a source, place the parenthetical reference within a sentence, generally at the end of a clause or phrase:

```
"The beginning writer does not know how writers behave"

(Shaughnessy 79): all of the research confirms this

conclusion.
```
(The second half of the sentence represents the writer's conclusion from reading in works other than Shaughnessy's.)

Entry in list of works cited
```
Shaughnessy, Mina P.  Errors and Expectations: A Guide for
     the Teacher of Basic Writing.  New York: Oxford UP,
     1977.
```

For an ellipsis at the end of a sentence, the parenthetical reference follows three points indicating the omission and precedes the period:

```
Berkin and Norton report that "childless households have

once again started to increase . . ." (29).
```

A parenthetical reference at the end of a set-off quotation follows the period. Two spaces separate the period from the reference, which is not followed by a period.

```
Berkin and Norton attribute the decline in the size of the

American household to several factors.

        An increase in childless households and
        households with one or two children reflects not
        only lower levels of childbearing, but also more
        older couples whose children have grown up and
        left home.  (29)
```

Entry in list of works cited
```
Berkin, Carol Ruth, and Mary Beth Norton.  Women of
     America: A History.  Boston: Houghton, 1979.
```
(The original passage appears on page 82 of this book.)

LEGAL CITATION

Most legal writing, particularly briefs and other documents filed with courts, employs only notes. Citations are made either parenthetically in the text or in footnotes. There is only one format for legal references, whether they are placed within the text or at the bottom of the page. If you wish to include legal documents in a bibliography, the entries should take the same form as the notes.

The Harvard Law Review Association booklet *A Uniform System of Citation* (revised periodically) is the standard guide in matters of format and interpretation of entries. For meanings of abbreviations not contained there, consult *Black's Law Dictionary*.

In the United States, primary sources are judicial, statutory, and quasi-statutory material.

Judicial Material

The most common category of judicial material includes the reported decisions of court cases and the materials related to these decisions, such as briefs submitted by the parties or the transcript of a trial. The order of the elements in the citation of a reported decision is as follows: (1) names of the parties (only the first party on each side); (2) volume number; (3) name of the report or service in which the decision appears; (4) page on which the decision begins, or paragraph number of the decision, followed by the page on which the cited material appears; (5) in parentheses, the court of decision (if not apparent from the name of the report) followed by the year of decision; and (6) the subsequent history of the case.

U.S. Supreme Court
> 41 Traux v. Corrigan, 257 U.S. 312, 327 (1921).

The decision in the *Traux* case, cited in note 41, is contained in volume 257 of the official reports of decisions of the United States Supreme Court (*United States Reports*). It begins on page 312; the cited material appears at page 327. The decision was handed down in 1921; the court of decision is apparent from the name of the report.

State court, parallel citations
> 42 3 N.Y. 2d 155, 143 N.E.2d 906, 164 N.Y.S.2d 714 (1957).

Note 42 gives the citation to *Sabo* v. *Delman*. The name of the case appears in the text, where it is italicized; only the citation is given in the note. The fact that the abbreviation of the official report—*N.Y.* for *New York Reports*—is also the abbreviation of the name of the state indicates that the decision was handed down by the state's highest court (in this case, New York's Court of Appeals). The designation *2d* indicates that the decision is found in the second series of *New York Reports*. A parallel citation is also given to two unofficial reports, the *North Eastern Reporter, Second Series,* which gathers cases from several states into a single volume, and the *New York Supplement, Second Series,* which reports New York cases from several different levels.

Many decisions are reported only in unofficial reporters, particularly loose-leaf services, which attempt to compile the decisions relevant to a particular subject matter:

Decisions in unofficial reporters
> 43 Omega-Alpha, Inc. v. Touche Ross & Co., [1976–1977 Transfer Binder] Fed. Sec. L. Rep. (CCH) 95,663, at 90,268 (S.D.N.Y. 1976).

The decision cited in note 43 is reported at Paragraph 95,663 of the *Federal Securities Law Reporter,* compiled by the Commerce Clearing House, Inc. Although the decision first appeared in the "Current" binder of that service (updated weekly), it has now been transferred to the permanent binder of decisions handed down in 1976 and 1977. The particular material cited within the case is found at page 90,268 of the volume.

When the citation is to an unreported decision, the docket number of the case, the court in which it is pending, and the actual date of the decision are given:

Unreported decision

44 Lannen v. Simpson, No. 79-1527-J (162nd Jud. Dist. Ct. Tex., Feb. 3, 1980).

Materials submitted to a court or generated during court proceedings are cited by reference to a reported decision, if one exists, or to the case name, docket number, and court, if one does not.

Brief, U.S. District Court

45 Brief for Plaintiff at 10, Jones v. Smith, 139 F. Supp. 730 (W.D. La. 1956).

The reference in note 45 is to material appearing at page 10 of Jones's brief submitted to the United States District Court for the Western District of Louisiana in connection with a case with a decision reported in volume 139 of the *Federal Supplement.*

Statutory Material

The second kind of primary source material includes constitutions, statutes, bills and resolutions, and international agreements. Some of the elements found in judicial material are obviously not a part of statutory citations. The order of those elements that are relevant is the same, at least by analogy. The following examples indicate how this kind of citation can be read by someone who is familiar with legal abbreviations.

U.S. Constitution

46 U.S. Const. amend. XXI, § 2.

47 U.S. Const. art. III, §§ 1-2.

Notes 46 and 47 refer to the United States Constitution, section 2 of the twenty-first amendment and sections 1 and 2 of article III, respectively.

State constitution, with date

48 N.Y. Const. art. II, § 6 (1894, amended).

In note 48, citation of section 6, article II of the New York Constitution includes a date because the portion referred to has since been substantially amended or is no longer in force.

Statute, official and common names
[49] Labor Management Relations (Taft—Hartley) Act § 301 (a), 29 U.S.C. § 185 (a) (1986).

In note 49, the citation is to a federal enactment by both its official and common names, section 301, subsection (a); the law is codified in title 29 of the *United States Code*, section 185, subsection (a), 1986 edition. The citation should be to the latest edition of the code.

Bill not enacted into law
[50] S. 1975, 89th Cong. 1st sess., 111 Cong. Rec. 10502 (1965).

Note 50 refers to Senate Bill 1975, introduced in the first session of the Eighty-ninth Congress and cited in volume 111 of the *Congressional Record*, beginning on page 10502; the bill had not been enacted into law at the time of citation, 1965.

Senate resolution
[51] S. Res. 218, 83d Cong., 2d sess., 100 Cong. Rec. 2972 (1954).

Note 51 refers to Senate Resolution number 218, adopted at the second session of the Eighty-third Congress, 1954, and recorded in volume 100 of the *Congressional Record*, beginning on page 2972.

International agreement
[52] Agreement on Rural Health Services, Sept. 30, 1976, United States—Egypt, 28 U.S.T. 8877, T.I.A.S. No. 8775.

The agreement cited in note 52 was signed on 30 September 1976 and can be found in volume 28 of *U.S. Treaties and Other International Agreements*, the official source for such treaties, beginning on page 8877. Parallel citation is made to the Department of State publication *Treaties and Other International Acts Series*, number 8775; the latter is an unofficial source.

Quasi-statutory Material

Rules, regulations, and the like that are promulgated by nonlegislative organs of government are classified as quasi-statutory material. By analogy, citations to them are read in the same way as are citations to judicial and statutory sources.

Presidential Executive Order
[53] Exec. Order No. 10540, 19 Fed. Reg. 3983 (1954).

Note 53 refers to Presidential Executive Order number 10540, which is to be found in volume 19 of the *Federal Register* (an official report), 1954, beginning on page 3983.

Internal Revenue ruling

[54] Rev. Rul. 131, 1953–2 Cum. Bull. 112.

Note 54 refers to Revenue Ruling 131, which appears in part 2 of the 1953 volume of the *Cumulative Bulletin*, beginning on page 112. This is an Internal Revenue ruling of the Treasury Department.

Federal regulation

[55] SEC Reg. A, 17 C.F.R. §§ 230.251–230.264 (1980).

In note 55, the citation of Securities and Exchange Commission Regulation A to the Code of Federal Regulations shows that the regulation is currently in force. It is found in title 17, sections 230.251 through 230.264 in the 1980 edition.

TYPING AND PRINTING INSTRUCTIONS

Placement of the Superscript in the Text

Leave no space between the superscript (note number) in the text and the word or mark of punctuation that it follows. Place the superscript before a dash, but after all other marks of punctuation.

Internal Punctuation of Notes

When punctuating notes, place two spaces following each period; place one space following commas and colons. Be particularly careful to insert only one space after a colon (old styles called for two spaces).

Sequence of Note Numbers

The numbering of endnotes or footnotes should run consecutively through each chapter. Some institutions may want notes to run consecutively throughout the entire paper. You should check with your graduate office or adviser about the numbering of notes.

Location of Footnotes

Place every footnote at the bottom of the page on which the citation appears. Type a one-and-one-half-inch line with the underline key, starting from the left margin, one double space below the last line of the text. Place the first footnote one double space below the line.

Spacing of Footnotes

Indent the first line of each note five spaces. Subsequent lines start at the left margin. Place the superscript one-half space above the line and leave one space between the superscript and the first letter in the note. Single-space within footnotes, and double-space between them.

Continued Footnotes

When a footnote cannot be included without running into the bottom margin (one inch) and cannot be omitted without making the page noticeably short, the footnote may be split and carried over to the next page.

Conclude the footnote without indention, ahead of the next footnote in the series.

Location of Endnotes

Endnotes should be placed in a separate section entitled Notes (not Endnotes) either at the end of the entire paper immediately preceding the bibliography or at the end of each chapter. Endnotes should be numbered consecutively throughout each chapter or throughout the entire paper, as local regulations specify.

Spacing of Endnotes

Indent the first line of each note five spaces. Subsequent lines start at the left margin. Place the superscript one-half space above the line, and leave one space between the superscript and the first word of the note. Double-space throughout, both within and between entries.

Quotations in Notes

Run in all quotations in both footnotes and endnotes, regardless of the length of the quotation. If the quotation runs more than one paragraph, begin each paragraph at the left margin without indention. Place quotation marks at the beginning of each paragraph and at the beginning and end of the entire selection. Use single- or double-spacing consistent with other entries. Provide bibliographical information for the quotation within parentheses following the end of the quotation.

Punctuation with Parenthetical Documentation

Parenthetical references should be considered a part of the sentences in which they appear. All punctuation, either within a sentence or at the end of a sentence, comes after the parenthetical reference. When a parenthetical reference follows an ellipsis, three spaced dots precede the reference, and the fourth dot follows it to indicate the end of the sentence. After a set-off quotation, the parenthetical reference is placed two spaces after the period marking the end of the quotation and is not followed by a period (see sample sentences on pages 103 and 104).

5 BIBLIOGRAPHIES AND LISTS OF WORKS CITED

The concluding section of a research paper, thesis, or dissertation is usually an alphabetical listing of source materials. This list is generally entitled "Bibliography" with note-bibliography format and "Works Cited" with parenthetical documentation. This listing serves several functions. It allows the reader to observe the scope of the research behind the paper or to see if a particular work has been used. When parenthetical documentation is used, the list of works cited permits a reader to locate full bibliographic information for materials referred to in parenthetical notes. The bibliography may also provide the reader with a foundation for further research.

Types of bibliographies A bibliography may be one of several types, depending on the requirements of the assignment or the logic of the subject. The type most frequently required for both undergraduate and graduate research papers is a list of the works cited in notes or within the text. Another type of bibliography goes beyond works actually cited in a paper and includes all the works used in preparation for writing the paper. (Such a list is titled "Works Consulted" or "Bibliography.") A third type, a comprehensive compilation of works on a subject (entitled "Bibliography"), may be desirable for some subjects. Finally, there is the annotated bibliography—each entry is accompanied by a short descriptive or evaluative statement—which assesses the nature or value of the material.

A list of works cited should include only the sources you actually cite in the text of your paper. This list may be supplemented by additional bibliography references, generally in a separate section.

FORM OF THE BIBLIOGRAPHY ENTRY

The principles for constructing bibliography entries are the same for both formats presented in the text of *Form and Style*: notes accompanied by a bibliography and MLA-style parenthetical documentation accompanied by a list of works cited (see page 100 for a listing of some additional factors you need to consider when you use the latter format). Whichever format you use, it is wise to prepare a draft of the bibliography or list of works cited before you begin to write. If you have working bibliography cards written out in the correct form and arranged in alphabetical order, you can easily create a bibliography or list of works cited from them. Having a draft of a bibliography will allow you to make notes or parenthetical references quickly and accurately. For note-bibliography format, you will have all the information you need for first references. For parenthetical documentation, you will be able to make sound judgments about ways of introducing direct and indirect quotations to minimize parenthetical documentation in the text. If, after writing the paper, you find that you have not referred to one or more works, you can eliminate them from your list of works cited before typing the final copy.

This chapter presents entries based on the note-bibliography format described in the *Chicago Manual* and on the parenthetical-reference format favored by MLA. For many types of entries, the formats are identical. The places where MLA differs are noted in parentheses below each entry. Any system of documentation is a set of conventions. No system is more correct than another; systems are just different and acceptable to different audiences. It is important, however, to follow consistently whichever system you choose.

Three categories of information are needed for each bibliography entry: author, title, and facts of publication. Each of these categories may contain more than one piece of information. A book may have more than one author, and the facts of publication for some materials may be complicated. A period follows each category of information in a bibliography entry—that is, a period follows the author, the title, and the facts of publication. Because an entry in a bibliography (unlike an entry in a note) refers to the complete work rather than to a specific passage, a bibliography entry does not include page numbers. A bibliography entry for an article lists the inclusive pages of the entire article rather than specific pages from which material was selected for citation.

Books

The author category for a book may include one or more authors, editors, compilers, and translators, or a corporate author or institution. The title category includes the title and subtitle. The facts of publication category identifies the series in which the work appears, the number of volumes in a multivolume work or the particular number of a volume, the edition if it is other than the first, the city of publication (the state is generally omitted), the name of the publisher, and the year of publication.

The basic form for a bibliography entry for a book reads as follows:

Basic bibliography form

```
Bronowski, Jacob.  The Ascent of Man.  Boston: Little,
     Brown, 1973.
```

Notice that periods mark the end of the author, title, and facts of publication sections. Two spaces follow each period; one space follows commas and colons. Be careful to insert only one space after each colon (old styles required two spaces).

NAME OF AUTHOR   In a bibliography entry, the name of the author appears last name first for purposes of alphabetization. When there are two or three authors, the names are listed in the order in which they appear on the title page, whether or not that order is alphabetical. Only the name of the first author appears in inverted order. A comma separates the first name of the first author from succeeding names:

Two (or three) authors

```
March, James G., and Herbert A. Simon.  Organizations.
     New York: Wiley, 1958.
```

Note: See Appendix E for MLA policy on publishers' names.

More than three authors

If a book has more than three authors, list each of their names in the bibliography:

McPherson, William, Stephen Lehmann, Craig Likness, and
    Marcia Pankake. <u>English and American Literature:
    Sources and Strategies for Collection Development</u>.
    Chicago: American Library Association, 1987.

In the note form, use only the name of the author listed first on the title page, followed by *et al.* (an abbreviation of *et alii*, which means "and others").

Two authors with same last name

When two authors have the same last name, the name should be repeated:

Ebbitt, Wilma R., and David Ebbitt. <u>Writer's Guide and
    Index to English</u>. 6th ed. Glenview: Scott,
    Foresman, 1978.

Pseudonyms

When an author's name as given on the title page is a pseudonym (pen name), the bibliography entry begins with the pseudonym and continues with the author's real name in brackets. If the author's real name is unknown, the abbreviation *pseud.* within brackets follows the name.

Green, Hannah [Joanne Greenberg]. <u>I Never Promised You a
    Rose Garden</u>. New York: Holt, Rinehart and Winston,
    1964.

Well-known pseudonyms, such as George Eliot and Mark Twain, do not require the insertion of the writer's real name.

Anonymous works

When no author's name appears on a work or when the title page lists *Anonymous* as the author, the work is listed in the bibliography by title alone. If the author's name is known, it may be put in brackets and the work may be listed in the bibliography under the author's name. *Anonymous* is not used as an author entry.

[Scarborough, Dorothy]. <u>The Wind</u>. New York: Harper, 1925.

or

<u>The Wind</u>. New York: Harper, 1925.

Group or corporation as author

When the author is a group or corporation, the publication is listed under the name of the organization:

Holiday Magazine. <u>Spain</u>. New York: Random House, 1964.

Note: See Appendix E for MLA policy on publishers' names.

When the corporate author is also the publisher, the name does not need to be repeated with the other facts of publication:

Columbia University. The Faculty Handbook. New York,
      1987.

Compilations

Emphasis on author

When a work has been edited, compiled, or translated by a person other than the author, you have to decide under which name you should alphabetize the work. If the emphasis of your investigation or analysis is on the author, the author's name precedes the title and a period follows the title. The appropriate abbreviation and one or more names to indicate compiler, editor, or translator follow. (Use *comp., ed., trans.,* or the plural forms, *comps., eds., trans.*)

Hayes, William C. Most Ancient Egypt. Ed. Keith C.
      Seele. Chicago: Univ. of Chicago Press, 1965.

Emphasis on editor

If the emphasis in your research is on the work of the compiler, editor, or translator, the name of the compiler, editor, or translator, followed by a comma, the appropriate abbreviation, and a period, precedes the title. The names of the author and the title form a unit: the author's name follows the title in the first name–last name order preceded by a comma, one space, and the word *by.*

Seele, Keith C., ed. Most Ancient Egypt, by William C.
      Hayes. Chicago: Univ. of Chicago Press, 1965.

Macedo, Suzette, trans. Diagnosis of the Brazilian
      Crisis, by Celso Furtado. Berkeley: Univ. of
      California Press, 1965.
(MLA puts a period after the title and capitalizes *by.*)

When a bibliography entry begins with three or more editors, compilers, or translators, follow the rules for works with three or more authors. The plural form of the appropriate abbreviation (*eds., comps., trans.*) follows the names.

Compilations, or books consisting of discrete selections by one or more authors, may include either new materials or writing that originally appeared elsewhere. When the collection contains new materials, references to the book place the name of the compiler or editor first, with the abbreviation *comp.* or *ed.,* as appropriate.

Corrigan, Robert W., ed. Theatre in the Twentieth
      Century. New York: Grove, 1963.

Emphasis on author of one article

When you want to emphasize an article or chapter in the collection, place the name of the author of the article or chapter first.

Note: See Appendix E for MLA policy on publishers' names.

```
Miller, Arthur.  "The Playwright and the Atomic World."
    In Theatre in the Twentieth Century.  Ed. Robert W.
    Corrigan.  New York: Grove, 1963.
```
(MLA omits the word *In*.)

Emphasis on writer of introduction

When you want to cite the introduction or foreword to a book in your bibliography, place the name of the author of this section first.

```
Fiedler, Leslie A.  Introduction to Waiting for God, by
    Simone Weil.  1951.  Reprint.  New York: Harper and
    Row, Colophon, 1973.
```
(MLA puts a period after *Introduction*, omitting *to;* puts a period after the title; capitalizes *by;* and omits the word *Reprint*.)

Compilation of material previously published elsewhere

When a compilation consists of material previously published elsewhere, a complete entry gives the original facts of publication as well as the information concerning the compilation.

```
Ten, C. L.  "Mill on Self-Regarding Actions."  Philosophy
    43 (1968): 29—37; reprinted in John Stuart Mill, On
    Liberty, ed. David Spitz, 238—46.  Norton Critical
    Edition.  New York: Norton, 1972.
```
(MLA uses the abbreviation *rpt.* for *reprinted*, omits the word *in*, and puts the inclusive page numbers, followed by a period, after the date of publication).

When a compilation reprints an article under a title different from the original title, indicate that the title has been changed or another title added in the later collection.

```
Langer, Suzanne.  Feeling and Form.  New York: Scribner's,
    1953.  Reprinted as "The Great Dramatic Forms: The
    Comic Rhythm."  In Comedy: Plays, Theory, and
    Criticism.  Ed. Marvin Feldheim, 241—53.  New York:
    Harcourt, 1962.
```
(MLA uses the abbreviation *Rpt.* for *Reprinted*, omits the word *In*, and puts the inclusive page numbers, followed by a period, after the date of publication.)

TITLE   The title of a book should appear in the bibliography exactly as it is on the title page. Capitalization, however, may be changed to conform to principles outlined in Chapter 7. Any subtitle should be separated from the main title with a colon followed by one space. In notes the subtitle is optional, but it must appear in the bibliography entry. The full title should be underlined.

```
Walker, Ronald G.  Infernal Paradise: Mexico and the
    Modern English Novel.  Berkeley: Univ. of California
    Press, 1978.
```

Note: See Appendix E for MLA policy on publishers' names.

Titles of articles or chapters within a book should be placed within double quotation marks. Names of series and manuscript collections are not underlined. (See the section on multivolume works on page 119.)

Edition other than the first When the edition you use is not the first, the number of the edition as well as its date of publication should be provided. Unless you have a particular reason for using an earlier edition, refer to the latest edition of a work. Additional editions may have a variety of designations, such as *2nd rev. ed.* (second revised edition), *3rd enl. and rev. ed.* (third enlarged and revised edition), and these should be recorded as they appear on the title page.

```
Cochran, John A.  Money, Banking, and the Economy.  3rd
     ed.  New York: Macmillan, 1975.
```

Previously published with another title If a book was previously published with another title, whether a different title in English or a title in a foreign language, you may give the original title within parentheses. In the following example, the French title is included because it differs considerably from the title chosen for the English translation:

```
Foucault, Michel.  The Order of Things: An Archaeology of
     the Human Sciences [Les Mots et les choses].  New
     York: Vintage, 1973.
```
(Words in the original title are capitalized according to rules for titles in French.)

FACTS OF PUBLICATION The facts of publication are the place of publication, the name of the publishing house, and the date of publication. The city name alone (without the state name) may serve as the place of publication except when it might be confused with another city of the same name. When a publisher lists several cities, select the first as the place of publication. When a book is published simultaneously by two companies, name either the first publisher mentioned on the title page or both publishers, separating the names with a semicolon.

Shortening the name of the publisher The name of the publisher may be shortened as long as its identity remains clear. Abbreviations such as *Inc., Co.,* and *Ltd.* and an initial *The* should be omitted. *Chicago Manual* preserves the rest of the name, as in *Holt, Rinehart and Winston* and *University* (or *Univ.*) *of Chicago Press.* In MLA style, the names of publishers are shortened to one word whenever possible, as in *Holt. University* and *press* are abbreviated, as in *U of Chicago P.* MLA puts the name of the imprint, or division, of a publisher before the name of the publisher, citing a book published in the Colophon series as Colophon-Harper, while *Chicago Manual* style cites the same publisher as Harper and Row, Colophon. See Appendix E for MLA policy on the names of publishers and imprints.

You should decide on a policy for shortening names of publishers and use it consistently throughout your paper. When you cannot find an unambiguous or widely accepted way to shorten a name, it is best to write out the full name.

Note: See Appendix E for MLA policy on publishers' names.

Date of publication

    The date of publication for any work other than an article in a periodical is the year alone, without the month or day. This date generally appears on the title page or on the copyright page. When various printings are listed, the date of the first printing is used in the bibliography or list of works cited. A printing is a press run of a book. An edition is a new version of a text. The most recent edition of a book should be cited unless there is some reason to cite a previous edition. Ordinal numbers are used to designate editions: *2nd, 3rd, 4th,* and so on.

Work out of print

    An entry for a work that was out of print but has been republished should indicate the original date of publication and the fact that the work is a reprint.

Markham, Beryl. West with the Night. 1942. Reprint.
        Berkeley: North Point Press, 1983.

(MLA omits the word *Reprint.*)

Paperbound editions

    When a paperbound book is an original edition, it is listed just as any other book would be.

Mumford, Lewis. The City in History. Harmondsworth:
        Penguin, 1961.

    When a paperbound book is a reprint of the original hardcover edition, the entry indicates the date of publication of the hardcover edition. This information generally appears on the copyright page.

Bowra, C. M. The Romantic Imagination. 1949. Reprint.
        New York: Oxford Univ. Press, Galaxy, 1961.

(MLA omits the word *Reprint.*)

    When the publisher of the paperbound edition is a division of a publishing company, that information should appear in the entry. In the following entry, Harvest is a division of Harcourt, Brace and World:

Jung, C. G. Modern Man in Search of a Soul. Trans. W. S.
        Dell and Cary F. Baynes. New York: Harcourt, Brace
        and World, Harvest, 1933.

Missing information

    When you cannot locate one or more pieces of information concerning publication, you should use one of the following abbreviations in the appropriate place in the entry:

    No place: n.p.
    No publisher: n.p.
    No date: n.d.
    No page: n.pag. *or* unpaginated

Note: See Appendix E for MLA policy on publishers' names.

Capitalize the abbreviation only when it begins a section of the entry.

```
Eliot, George.   Felix Holt.   Edinburgh: William
     Blackwood, n.d.
```

```
Eliot, George.   Felix Holt.   N.p.: William Blackwood, n.d.
```

Multivolume Works and Series

A multivolume work consists of two or more volumes under one general title. Each separate volume may either have its own title or be identified by volume number only.

Reference to complete multivolume work

When you wish to refer to a complete multivolume work rather than to any specific volume, the bibliography entry should include the total number of volumes and the inclusive dates of publication, if applicable.

```
Bowsky, William M., ed.   Studies in Medieval and
     Renaissance History.   4 vols.   Lincoln: Univ. of
     Nebraska Press, 1963-67.
```

The entry for the date indicates that the first volume was published in 1963 and the fourth volume in 1967. It is not necessary to specify intermediate dates. Your note or parenthetical reference will specify the particular volume cited in each instance.

Reference to volume with individual title

When each volume in a multivolume work has an individual title, the entry takes the following form:

```
Crutchfield, James C., ed.   The Fisheries: Problems in
     Resource Management.   Vol. 1 of Studies on Public
     Issues in Resource Management.   Seattle: Univ. of
     Washington Press, 1965.
```
(MLA gives the total number of volumes and the inclusive dates of publication.)
```
Crutchfield, James C., ed.   The Fisheries: Problems in Resource
     Management.   Seattle: U of Washington P, 1965.   Vol. 1 of
     Studies on Public Policy Issues in Resource Management.
     12 vols.   1965-75.
```

Independent works in a series

A series consists of works independent of each other but numbered as belonging to a particular series. The name of the series follows the title and is not underlined.

```
Presseisen, Ernest L.   Before Aggression: Europeans
     Prepare the Japanese Army.   Monographs and Papers of
     the Association for Asian Studies, no. 21.   Tucson:
     Univ. of Arizona Press, 1965.
```
(MLA omits the abbreviation *no.* and the preceding comma.)

Note: See Appendix E for MLA policy on publishers' names.

When works in a series have editors or translators, identify and place their names according to the principles described above for works with editors, compilers, and translators. (See facing pages, beginning on page 146, for note and bibliography forms for such variations on the basic entry for a work in a series.)

Periodicals

Any publication that comes out at regular intervals is a periodical. Periodicals for an academic or professional audience are usually called *journals;* periodicals intended for the general public are often called *magazines.* The bibliography entry for periodicals includes the author's complete name, the title of the article, and the facts of publication, which include the name of the periodical, the number of the volume, the date of the volume or the issue number, and the inclusive page numbers for the entire article. (See Chapter 7 for rules regarding inclusive page numbers.) A period follows both the author and title segments, a colon introduces the page numbers, and a period closes the entry.

JOURNALS Most journals paginate continuously through each volume; that is, each issue continues the numbering of the previous issue rather than beginning anew with page 1. Two spaces follow the author and title entries; one space separates the elements of the facts of publication section. The basic format for an entry referring to such a continuously paginated journal is the following:

Basic form for periodicals

```
Aron, Raymond.  "The Education of the Citizen in
     Industrial Society."  Daedalus 91 (1962): 249-63.
```

When the season or month of the issue is necessary for identification, as in a journal that does not use issue numbers and begins new pagination with each issue, or when you wish to indicate the month or season for any reason, that information should precede the date within the parentheses.

```
Harding, D. W.  "Regulated Hatred: An Aspect of the Work
     of Jane Austen."  Scrutiny 8 (Mar. 1940): 346-62.
```

When a journal begins each issue in a volume with page 1, you need to include the number of the issue, as follows:

```
Bird, Harry.  "Some Aspects of Prejudice in the Roman
     World."  University of Windsor Review 10, no. 1
     (1975): 64.
```

(In MLA style, a period and the issue number follow the volume number with no intervening space: 10.1 (1975): 64.)

Abbreviations

Avoid including any information that is repetitive or unnecessary. If the volume serves to identify the source, the season or month should be omitted.

Months should be abbreviated as follows: *Jan., Feb., Mar., Apr., Aug., Sept., Oct., Nov.,* and *Dec.* The months May, June, and July are not abbreviated. Some journals use seasons to identify the volume. Seasons (fall or autumn, winter, spring, summer) should not be abbreviated, but they should be capitalized in note and bibliography forms.

```
Hall, David D.  "On Common Ground: The Coherence of
     American Puritan Studies."  William and Mary
     Quarterly 44 (Apr. 1987): 310-32.

Heaney, Howell J.  "A Century of Early American Children's
     Books in German."  Phaedrus 6 (Spring 1979): 22-26.
```

In some fields, abbreviations for titles of periodicals are used. If you want to use such abbreviations, follow an authoritative source as a guide to acceptable forms. Many indexes, such as the *Applied Science and Technology Index,* the *Cumulated Index Medicus,* the *Education Index,* the *MLA International Bibliography,* and the *Music Index,* contain glossaries of journal abbreviations used in their compilations.

For a journal that numbers only issues rather than volumes and issues, the entry appears as follows:

```
Nwezeh, C. E.  "The Comparative Approach to Modern African
     Literature."  Yearbook of General and Comparative
     Literature, no. 28 (1979): 22.
```
(MLA omits *no.* and the preceding comma. In subsequent references, *Yearbook of General and Comparative Literature* may be abbreviated *YGCL* if you provide the full title the first time or if you provide a key to abbreviations.)

Designation of series

Include a series number or designation in citing periodicals that have been published in more than one series. *Old series* or *original series* is indicated by o.s. (os in MLA style); *new series* is identified by n.s. (ns). Numbered series are indicated by ordinal numbers, for example, 3rd ser., preceding the volume number.

```
Dwork, Bernard M.  "On the Zeta Function of a
     Hypersurface."  Annals of Mathematics, 2nd ser., 83
     (1966): 518-19.
```
(MLA omits the comma after the name of the journal and before the volume number.)

Quotation within titles

When double quotation marks appear within the title of an article, they should be changed to single quotation marks.

```
Sanders, Charles.  "'The Waste Land': The Last Minstrel
     Show?"  Journal of Modern Literature 8 (1980): 23-28.
```

When another mark of punctuation, such as the question mark in the example above, comes at the end of the title, it takes the place of the period.

MAGAZINES   Issues of magazines are most often identified by date only, even when they have volume numbers. Page numbers are separated from the date by a comma (rather than a colon, as in journal entries). When magazine articles run on discontinuous pages, enter the page numbers on which the article actually appears, as in the Tuchman entry below: 38–45, 50, 53–57, for an article that begins on page 38 and ends on page 57 but is interrupted by other material. A comma between page numbers indicates discontinuous pagination. An alternative for indicating discontinuous pages is to cite the first and final pages only.

Tuchman, Barbara W. "The Decline of Quality." <u>New York
     Times Magazine</u>, 2 Nov. 1980, 38–45, 50, 53–57. (*or*
     38–57.)

(MLA omits the comma after the name of the magazine and puts a colon rather than a comma after the date. To indicate that an article continues over several discontinuous pages, MLA enters a plus sign (+) after the number of the first page of the article: Tuchman, Barbara W. "The Decline of Quality." <u>New York Times Magazine</u> 2 Nov. 1980: 38+.)

Brown, Norman O. "Apocalypse: The Place of Mystery in the
     Life of the Mind." <u>Harper's</u>, May 1961, 27–35.

(MLA omits the comma after the name of the magazine and puts a colon rather than a comma after the date.)

"Report on Hepatitis in Blood." <u>U.S. News and World
     Report</u>, 7 June 1976, 78.

(MLA omits the comma after the name of the magazine and puts a colon rather than a comma after the date.)

NEWSPAPERS   Newspapers may be published daily, weekly, or according to some other schedule, but if they appear at intervals, they are considered periodicals.

The bibliography entry for a newspaper should include the name of the author (if available), the title of the article (headline) in quotation marks, and the name of the newspaper underlined. If the name of the newspaper does not indicate its place of publication, the name of the city, state, or nation must be interpolated in brackets before or after the title; such interpolations are not underlined. Nationally circulated newspapers, such as the *Christian Science Monitor*, do not require the addition of the place of publication. When a newspaper has more than one section, enter the number or the letter of the section along with the page number. When the section carries a number, use the abbreviation *sec*. When a page number follows a section number, insert the abbreviation *p*. or *pp*. for *page* or *pages* to avoid confusion.

Interpolation of city and state

Section numbers

Basic entry

Rasky, Susan F. "Senate Calls for Revisions in New Tax
     for Health Care." <u>New York Times</u>, 8 June 1989, A20.

(MLA omits the comma after the name of the newspaper and puts a colon rather than a comma after the date.)

State interpolated

"Unknown Author of <u>Wind</u> Answers Crane Criticism."
     <u>Sweetwater [Texas] Daily Reporter</u>, 15 Dec. 1925, 6.

(MLA omits the comma after the name of the newspaper and puts a colon rather than a comma after the date.)

City interpolated, with section number

Times [London], 19 May 1943, sec. 2, pp. 5, 8.
(MLA omits the comma after [*London*], puts a colon rather than a comma after *sec. 2*, omits *pp.*, and enters a plus sign (+) after the opening page number to indicate that the article continues on discontinuous pages: Times [London] 19 May 1943, sec. 2: 5+.)

If a newspaper prints more than one edition (for example, the late city edition, the Long Island edition), the edition cited is designated after the date.

Green, Wayne E. "Cold—Fusion Development Spurs Hot Race
        for Patents." Wall Street Journal, 9 June 1989,
        eastern ed., B1.
(MLA omits the comma after the name of the newspaper and puts a colon rather than a comma after *eastern ed.*)

Special types of articles

Editorials and other special classes of articles should be designated.

"Credit for All at the World Bank." Editorial. New York
        Times, 1 Nov. 1980, A24.
(MLA omits the comma after the name of the newspaper and puts a colon rather than a comma after the date.)

Romero—Barcelò, Carlos. Letter. New York Times,
        1 Nov. 1980, A25.
(MLA omits the comma after the name of the newspaper and puts a colon rather than a comma after the date.)

BOOK REVIEWS An entry for a book review begins with the name of the reviewer, includes the title (if any) of the review, gives the name of the author and the work being reviewed, and ends with the name of the periodical in which the review appeared, together with the volume number (if applicable), date and page(s). If the review is unsigned and untitled, the entry begins with *Review* or *Rev.* Examples of several types of review entries follow.

Dershowitz, Alan M. "Inside the Sanctum Sanctorum."
        Review of Independent Journey: The Life of William O.
        Douglas, by James F. Simon. New York Times Book
        Review, 2 Nov. 1980, 9.
(MLA abbreviates *Review* as *Rev.*, omits the comma before the date, and puts a colon rather than a comma after the date.)

Lott, Robert E. Review of Emilia Pardo Bazán, by Walter
        T. Pattison. Symposium 28 (1974): 382.
(MLA abbreviates *Review* as *Rev.*)

Review of Married to Genius, by Jeffrey Meyers. Journal
        of Modern Literature 7 (1979): 579—80.
(MLA abbreviates *Review* as *Rev.*)

Works of Literature

The bibliography entry for a book-length work of literature should follow the principles of creating an entry for a book; for a short work included in a book or periodical, the entry follows the form for an article in a collection.

Basic form
When the entry refers to the work in an edition without editing or commentary, the basic form for a book is used.

```
Lowry, Malcolm.  Under the Volcano.  New York: Reynal and
     Hitchcock, 1947.
```

When the entry refers to a particular edition or translation of a work, the name of the editor or translator should be supplied. When the emphasis is on the work rather than the editor, the note begins with the name of the author.

```
Conrad, Joseph.  Lord Jim.  Ed. Thomas C. Moser.  New
     York: Norton, 1968.
```

Emphasis on translator
When the editor or translator has most importance, that name begins the entry.

```
Bergin, Thomas G., trans. and ed.  The Divine Comedy, by
     Dante Alighieri.  New York: Appleton-Century-Crofts,
     1955.
```
(MLA puts a period after the title and capitalizes *by*.)

Emphasis on writer of introduction
When the emphasis is on the author of the introduction to a particular edition, the entry may begin with that name.

```
Daiches, David.  Introduction to Pride and Prejudice, by
     Jane Austen.  New York: Modern Library, 1950.
```
(MLA puts a period after *Introduction* and omits *to*, puts a period after the title, and capitalizes *by*.)

Titles of full-length works, including novels, plays, and long poems, are underlined in bibliography and note entries. Titles of parts of books, such as chapters, short poems, short stories, and essays, are placed within quotation marks. (See Chapter 7 for further information on capitalization of titles.)

SACRED WORKS   The title of the version or translation that you use goes into the bibliography. The titles of sacred works should not be underlined. The name of the translation or version generally suffices without further facts of publication.

```
The Bible.  Revised Standard Version.
```

Note: See Appendix E for MLA policy on publishers' names.

```
The Book of Mormon.
```

See Chapter 4, page 98, for note and parenthetical-reference forms.

CLASSICAL WORKS   Give full information in the bibliography concerning the edition. If your subsequent reference notes or parenthetical reference will cite the name of the classical author, that name should appear first in the bibliography entry.

```
Aristotle.  Poetics.  Trans. S. H. Butcher.  Ed. Francis
     Fergusson.  New York: Hill and Wang, 1961.
```

```
Plato.  The Republic.  Trans. Desmond Lee.  Harmondsworth:
     Penguin, 1955.
```

See Chapter 4, page 98, for note and parenthetical-reference forms.

Reference Works

Entries for widely known reference works, such as dictionaries, encyclopedias, atlases, and yearbooks, need not include the facts of publication. The edition number or the year suffices for identification of the work. The article or entry appears within quotation marks, and the title of the reference work is underlined.

Encyclopedia entry
```
"Huygens, Christiaan."  Encyclopaedia Britannica.  13th ed.
```

Dictionary entry
```
"Advertisement."  Webster's Third International
     Dictionary.
```
(Because the number of the edition appears in the title, the date is not necessary.)

Atlas entry
```
"Hidden Face of the Moon."  Times Atlas of the World.
     1971 ed.
```

Signed entry
When an article or entry is signed, the name of the author may be included. When only the initials of the author are given, the full name, if you can locate it in a list of contributors for the work, should be supplied in brackets.

```
Markowitz, William.  "Time, Measurement and Determination
     of."  Encyclopedia Americana.  1965 ed.
```

```
W[heat], J[oe] B[en].  "Cliff Dwellings."  Encyclopaedia
     Britannica.  1964 ed.
```

Note: See Appendix E for MLA policy on publishers' names.

Specialized reference works　　Entries for little-known or specialized reference works should include the full facts of publication.

> English, Horace B., and Ava Champney English. A
> Comprehensive Dictionary of Psychological and
> Psychoanalytical Terms. New York: McKay, 1958.

When you cite a particular author in a specialized reference work, your bibliography entry should begin with the name of the author(s) of the article.

> Bloom, Benjamin S., and Ernest A. Rakow. "Higher Mental
> Processes." In Encyclopedia of Educational Research.
> Ed. Robert L. Ebel. 4th ed. New York: Macmillan,
> 1969.

(MLA omits the word *In.*)

Public Documents

A publication authorized or printed by a government entity, such as a nation, state, or city, is called a *public document*. Public documents take a wide variety of forms: records of meetings and proceedings, regulations, reports of research, guidelines for industries, statistics on current and future trends. The *Monthly Catalog of U.S. Government Publications*, 1930–, provides a full listing of the publications of various branches of government in the United States. Many states and cities also publish such listings. In addition, the federal government regularly publishes a *Checklist of United States Public Documents*.

Bibliographic entries for public documents, like those for other kinds of works, consist of three parts—author, title, and facts of publication—each of which may contain several elements. Each part ends with a period, followed by two spaces.

Because there are many types and sources of documents, it may be difficult to know where to place all the information. When you cannot follow the rules given below, use your judgment about presenting the information in a way that allows your reader to locate the document.

Author entry　　The author entry may include several elements, presented in this order:

1. The governing body—such as nation, state, county, or city—in order of size and importance
2. The identity of the division of government—such as Congress, Senate, or Department of State
3. The name of any particular committee and subcommittee within the division

The author entry for a document prepared by a subcommittee of the Senate Committee on Agriculture would read as follows:

Note: See Appendix E for MLA policy on publishers' names.

```
U.S.   Senate.   Committee on Agriculture.   Subcommittee on
      Loans.
```
(MLA spells out *United States*.)

Even when the name of an individual author appears on the title page, in most cases the author of a document is still considered to be the governing body that commissioned and published the work. The personal names of individual authors usually follow the title.

Title entry   The title entry for a public document includes the following:

1. The name of the publication, underlined
2. The name of any individual authors (or editors or compilers)
3. A designation of the document's identity—such as *Hearing, Proclamation, Executive Order, Report,* or *Document*—when applicable
4. Information about the date or origin, such as the session of Congress or the number of the document

Within the title entry, you may use abbreviations: *S.* for Senate, *H.* for House, *Cong.* for Congress, *res.* for resolution, *doc.* for document, *sess.* for session. The title entry for a document that has an individual author would read as follows:

```
Precedents, Decisions on Points of Order, with
      Phraseology, in the United States Senate.   Report
      prepared by Henry Gilfry.   62nd Cong., 2nd sess.
      1938.   S. Doc. 1123.
```

Alternatively, if the name of the author seems to be more important than the name of the government body, either for the purposes of your research or for accurate attribution of the work, you may begin the entry with the name of the individual author:

```
Hunt, G. Halsey, and Stanley R. Mohler.   Aging: A Review
      of Research and Training Grants Supported by the
      National Institutes of Health.   U.S. Public Health
      Service Publication, no. 652.   Bethesda: National
      Institutes of Health, 1958.
```
(MLA omits *no.* and the preceding comma.)

Facts of   The facts of publication include the following:
publication

1. The city of publication
2. The publisher
3. The date of publication, as distinct from the date of the session of Congress that produced the information

The publisher of most United States government documents is the Government Printing Office, abbreviated *GPO*, located in Washington, D.C. The usual facts of publication for a U.S. government document read as follows: Washington: GPO, 19XX. These facts of publication may be omitted in citations to congressional and other documents that already contain detailed identifying information. When a document has another publisher, follow the general rules for the facts of publication.

Enter the page number, following the rules for a book or article, as appropriate. When a page number follows the number for a part or section, introduce it with the abbreviation *p.* or *pp.* to avoid confusion.

A bibliography entry for a document with author, title, and facts of publication, then, reads as follows:

```
U.S.  Congress.  House.  Committee on Agriculture.
     Subcommittee on Dairy and Poultry.  Federal Loan for
     Poultry Processing Plant in New Castle, Pa.  Hearing.
     89th Cong., 1st sess., 19 Oct. 1965.  Washington:
     GPO, 1966.
```
(MLA spells out *United States*.)

Congressional Record

Because the *Congressional Record* is widely known and often cited, it may be entered without the author entry or the facts of publication:

```
Congressional Record.  89th Cong., 2nd sess., 1966.
     Vol. 72, pt. 5, pp. 12161-214.
```
(MLA shortens this type of entry: Cong. Rec. 17 Nov. 1980: 3852.)

Although you may encounter numerous kinds of documents, the most frequently used may be categorized as follows:

Constitution of the United States

A bibliography entry for the Constitution of the United States should contain only the name:

```
Constitution of the United States.
```

The note or parenthetical reference should include the article or amendment and section, as well as the clause, if appropriate.

Congressional documents

An entry for a hearing, a transcript of the testimony of witnesses before congressional committees, should include the name of the committee to which testimony was presented:

```
U.S.  Congress.  Senate.  Committee on Environment and
     Public Works.  Construction and Repair Programs to
     Alleviate Unemployment.  Hearing.  97th Cong., 2nd
     sess., 1 Dec. 1982.  Washington: GPO, 1983.
```
(MLA spells out *United States*.)

Individual acts of Congress are published separately after passage. These separate publications should be cited as documents:

```
U.S.  Congress.  Senate.  Committee on Commerce, Science,
     and Transportation.  Subcommittee on Surface
     Transportation.  Household Goods Transportation Act
     of 1980.  Washington: GPO, 1983.
```
(MLA spells out *United States*.)

After the laws have been compiled in the *Statutes at Large*, they should be cited as laws (see the discussion of legal citation in Chapter 4).

Entries for reports prepared by Congress should follow the basic form for a document:

```
U.S. Congress. House. Committee on Post Office and
     Civil Service. Background on the Civil Service
     Retirement System. Report prepared by the
     Congressional Research Service. Washington: GPO,
     1983.
```
(MLA spells out *United States*.)

Executive documents

The executive branch issues presidential proclamations, executive orders, and reports of executive departments and bureaus.

```
U.S. President. Proclamation. Martin Luther King Day.
     15 January 1988.
```
(MLA spells out *United States*.)

```
U.S. Department of Commerce. Bureau of the Census.
     Aircraft Propellers. Washington: Bureau, 1979.
```
(MLA spells out *United States*.)

Treaties made by the United States since 1950 have been published in *United States Treaties and Other International Agreements*. Entries for treaties, as well as for other kinds of documents published in books, include the title of the collection.

```
U.S. Department of State. "Nuclear Weapons Test Ban,"
     15 Aug. 1992, TIAS no. 1943. United States Treaties
     and Other International Agreements, vol. 34.
```
(MLA spells out *United States*.)

Entries for documents published by states and cities, as well as by other nations, follow the same principles for note and bibliography entries.

Unpublished documents

Unpublished documents, or those published for a small audience, often do not include all of the information necessary for a complete bibliography entry. When that is the case, you will fill in the entry with descriptions of the material sufficient to enable the reader to locate it. Titles of unpublished materials are placed within quotation marks rather than underlined, as in the following examples:

```
"Automobile, Aerospace and Agricultural Implement Workers
     of America: International Union, United, AFL-CIO, and
     the Ford Motor Company, Agreement between."
     20 Oct. 1961.
```

```
Stone Cutters Association of North America, Journeymen,
     "Constitution and By-Laws." 1926.
```

For further examples of note and bibliography forms for documents, see pages 166 through 171.

Unpublished Sources

In the citation of unpublished sources, improvisation is occasionally necessary. You may encounter sources that do not provide all of the usual information. When that is the case, include any other piece of information essential for locating the source according to the principles of the style you are using.

If the source has an individual or corporate author, list the name as in any author entry. Titles of unpublished works are not underlined but are enclosed in double quotation marks. If you have to supply a title for the source, that title is neither underlined nor quoted. The facts of publication include the origin or location of the source and the date.

Manuscript materials   A citation to manuscript materials—such as letters, scrapbooks, diaries, sermons, financial records, minutes of meetings, and legal transactions—includes the name of the author, the name of the collection and the library, the location of the library, the nature of the materials, and any other relevant information.

An entry for a letter gives the names of the sender and addressee, the date, and the location.

```
Cockburn, Robert.  Letter to Lord Melville.  17 May 1819.
     Group 125, Manuscript Collection, Rutgers University,
     New Brunswick, N.J.
```
(MLA puts a period after *125*, abbreviates *University*, and omits the name of the state.)

For a letter cited from a published volume, the entry follows the format for citation of a book or a collection, as appropriate.

The nature of the manuscript materials should be indicated in the entry.

```
Towne, Zaccheus.  Diary.  July 1776–Feb. 1777.  Group 615,
     Manuscript Collection, Rutgers University, New
     Brunswick, N.J.
```
(MLA puts a period after *615*, abbreviates *University*, and omits the name of the state.)

Supplied titles   When a manuscript does not have an author or a title, the writer supplies a description of the materials so they can be identified and located. Supplied titles and descriptions are neither underlined nor enclosed in quotation marks.

```
Papers on Industrial Espionage.  Report of Agent 106.
     17 July 1919.  University of Washington, Seattle.
```
(MLA uses the abbreviation *U* for *University*.)

Manuscript: MS   A manuscript—a handwritten copy—is indicated by the abbreviation *MS*.

```
Scarborough, Dorothy.  "The Wind."  MS.  Dorothy
     Scarborough Papers.  The Texas Collection, Baylor
     University, Waco, Tex.
```
(MLA puts a comma after the title, abbreviates *manuscript* as *ms.*, and omits the name of the state.)

Typescript: TS   A typescript—a typewritten copy of a work or a transcription of an oral source such as an interview—is designated with the abbreviation *TS*.

```
The Oral Memoirs of J. R. Smith.  TS.  Oral History
     Division.  Butler College, Butler, N.Y.
```
(MLA puts a comma after the title, abbreviates *typescript* as *ts.*, and omits the name of the state.)

Photocopied material   The form of a work duplicated by photocopying machine, mimeograph, or ditto should be indicated in the citation.

```
Yaffe, James.  "A Report on the [University of Nebraska]
     Summer Writing Institute: 1979."  Photocopy.  N.d.
```
(MLA uses the abbreviation *U* for *University*.)

Dissertations

When cited as unpublished sources, the titles of dissertations and theses appear within quotation marks.

```
Rosenthal, Marilyn.  "Poetry of the Spanish Civil War."
     Ph.D. diss., New York University, 1972.
```
(MLA gives the facts of publication as Diss. New York U., 1972. The abbreviation *Ph.D.* is omitted.)

A dissertation published by a microfilm service should be entered in a bibliography according to the guidelines for a book, with the title appearing in italics.

```
Casari, Laura Elizabeth Rhodes.  Malcolm Lowry's Drunken
     Divine Comedy: Under the Volcano and Shorter Fiction.
     Ph.D. diss., University of Nebraska, 1967.  Ann
     Arbor: UMI, 1967.  67-15812.
```
(Notice that a title within a title is not underlined. MLA identifies the work as Diss. U of Nebraska, 1967. The abbreviation *Ph.D.* is omitted.)

When you cite the abstract for a dissertation, refer to *Dissertation Abstracts International (DAI)*, published until 1969 as *Dissertation Abstracts (DA)*, for the facts of publication.

Blair, Catherine Pastore. "Mark Twain, Anatomist."
        <u>DAI</u> 41 (1981): 4387A—88A.
(MLA includes after the page reference the name of the university granting the degree, followed by a period.)

Nonprint Sources

With nonprint sources, as with unpublished sources, use your judgment about supplying the information a reader would need to locate the source.

Films   In an entry for a film, the writer, producer, or director may take the position of author, depending on the relative importance of each. The title of the film is underlined, and the entry should include the company and the year of release.

Robinson, Phil Alden, dir. <u>Field of Dreams</u>. With
        Kevin Costner, Amy Madigan, and James Earl Jones.
        Universal, 1989.

Performances   Performances of music, ballet, or drama should be identified by the author, director, conductor, choreographer, and/or the principal participants, depending on your emphasis. The entry should include the name of the theater, the city, and the date.

Robbins, Jerome, dir. and chor. <u>Jerome Robbins' Broadway</u>.
        Imperial Theatre, New York, 14 June 1989.
(MLA puts a period after *New York*.)

Mehta, Zubin, dir. New York Philharmonic, Avery Fisher
        Hall, Lincoln Center, New York, 25 Nov. 1980.
(MLA puts a period after *New York*.)

Kylian, Jiri. <u>Return to the Strange Land</u>. With Cynthia
        Anderson and Michael Bjerknes. Joffrey Ballet, City
        Center, New York, 19 Nov. 1980.
(MLA puts a period after *New York*.)

Hellman, Lillian. <u>The Little Foxes</u>. Dir. Austin
        Pendleton. With Elizabeth Taylor. Martin Beck
        Theatre, New York, 23 May 1981.
(MLA puts a period after *New York*.)

Musical compositions   When musical compositions are identified by the type or key of the work, they are not underlined. When another title is normally given the composition, that title is underlined.

Mozart, Wolfgang Amadeus. Piano Concerto in B—flat major,
        K. 595.

Schubert, Franz. Symphony No. 8 (<u>Unfinished</u>).

Recordings   References to recordings should give the name of the composer and/or the performer(s), the title of the piece or of the recording, the record label, the catalog number, and the year of release.

Monteverdi, Claudio. <u>L'Orfeo</u>. Dir. Nikolaus Harnoncourt.
 With Lajos Kozma. Concentus Musicus Wien.
 Telefunken, SKH 21/1-3, n.d.

Karajan, Herbert von, cond. Brahms' Symphony No. 1
 in C minor, op. 68. Vienna Philharmonic Orchestra.
 London Records, STS 15194, 1960.

The Beatles. "The Long and Winding Road." <u>Let It Be</u>.
 Apple Records, n.d.

Thomas, Dylan. "Fern Hill." <u>Dylan Thomas Reading</u>.
 Vol. 1. Caedmon, TC 1102, n.d.

Tapes and cassettes   Citations for tape recordings, audiocassettes, or videocassettes should follow the format for recordings. Specify the nature of the material.

Paolucci, Anne. Audiocassette. <u>Dante and Machiavelli</u>.
 Deland, Fla.: Everett/Edwards, n.d.

Works of art   Works of art are underlined and identified by their location, either in a museum or other collection or institution or in a book with reproductions.

Gainsborough, Thomas. <u>The Morning Walk</u>. National
 Gallery, London.

Vallayer-Coster, Anne. <u>The White Soup Bowl</u>. Private
 Collection, Paris. Plate 52 in <u>Women Artists:
 1550-1950</u>, by Ann Sutherland Harris and Linda
 Nochlin. New York: Knopf, 1977.
(MLA puts a period after the book title and capitalizes *by*.)

Television and radio programs   Citations for television and radio programs should include any of the following information: title of the segment in quotation marks; name of the series underlined; producer, director, and/or writer; actors or performers; the name of the broadcasting corporation; and the date of the broadcast.

Gorin, Norm, prod. "The Cop, the Kid, and the Knife."
 Narr. Morley Safer. <u>Sixty Minutes</u>. CBS, New York,
 16 Nov. 1980.
(MLA puts a period after *New York*.)

Personal contact with sources   Sources derived from personal contact between the writer and another scholar or expert in the field might include interviews, lectures, telephone conversations, and letters. All of these are treated in notes and bibliography as unpublished sources. When you cite such a source, you must obtain permission to use it, unless, as in the case of a speech or an address, general permission for recording has been granted.

```
Pearl, Arthur.  Letters to author.  7 Feb. to
     22 Mar. 1968.
```

```
Purcell, Thomas.  Telephone interview.  25 Oct. 1980.
```

```
Teller, Edward.  Personal interview.  12 July 1962.
```

Speeches

References to a speech or paper delivered at a meeting should include the name of the speaker, the title of the address, the name of the group, and the date and location of the meeting.

```
Nichols, J. R.  "Opiates as Reinforcing Agents: Some
     Variables Which Influence Drug-Seeking in Animals."
     Paper delivered at the American Psychological
     Association.  Washington, 7 Sept. 1967.
```
(MLA omits *Paper delivered at the.*)

Information services

Entries for materials available in microform—microfilm, microfiche, or any other type of film reproduction—should follow the format for the type of material reproduced in the author and title entries. Facts of publication may include the information service supplying the microfilm, such as Educational Resources Information Center (ERIC), Congressional Information Service (CIS), or National Technical Information Service (NTIS), along with identifying numbers or dates. Well-known information services such as those may be abbreviated.

```
Groark, James J.  Utilization of Library Resources by
     Students in Non-residential Degree Programs.  ERIC,
     1974.  ED 121 236.
```

When the nature of the reproduction may not be apparent, the type of microform may be specified in the entry.

```
Nicoll, Allardyce, and George Freeley, eds.  American
     Drama of the Nineteenth Century.  Micro-opaque.  New
     York: Readex Microprint, 1965-.
```

Computer Materials

A bibliography entry for computer software, such as programs, languages, and systems, should include the following information, if it is available: the title (underlined), identification of the version or date, the company owning the copyright and the city in which the company is located, numbers necessary for identification of the software, and the physical nature of the item. Because the information available for these relatively unstandardized materials differs greatly, in many cases it will be necessary to follow the principles for creating bibliography entries rather than to use any specific bibliography form. The entry below refers to the program for checking spelling that accompanies the word-processing program *Visiword*.

Computer programs

```
Visispell: Fut.heuristix.   Computer software.   Version
     1.00.   San Jose: Visicorp, 1983.   Disk.
```
(A manual for computer software should be treated like a book.)

Material from computer retrieval service

Material received from a computer retrieval service should be treated like other printed material of the same type, for example, articles or encyclopedia entries. At the end of the entry, however, you should give the name of the service and numbers identifying the document.

```
"Johnson, Susannah Carrie."   American Men and Women of
     Science.   15th ed.   New York: Bowker, 1983.   DIALOG
     file 257, item 0105622.
```

```
Million Dollar Directory.   CD-ROM.   New York: Dun's
     Marketing Service, 1988.
```

NOTE-BIBLIOGRAPHY FORMAT

The note-bibliography format uses either footnotes or endnotes, as described in Chapter 4, along with a bibliography. Prepare the bibliography entries by following the examples shown on pages 113 through 135. When you have a work that does not fit exactly into any of the categories, follow the principles for constructing bibliography entries discussed above. Follow the guidelines for alphabetization of entries and the typing instructions given below.

You may wish to classify the entries in a long bibliography by one of several principles: by form of publication, by section or chapters of the paper, or by primary and secondary sources. Lists of work cited should not be divided. Short research papers and reports usually do not require classified bibliographies.

Classification by form of publication

Grouping references according to their form of publication often facilitates the use of a bibliography; for example, books may be listed in one group, periodicals in a second group, and government publications in still another. A general guideline for this sort of classification is to divide bibliographies of more than thirty entries, to divide bibliographies of twenty to thirty items only if the nature or variety of entries warrants classification, and to use a single alphabetical listing for fewer than twenty entries.

Classification by primary and secondary sources

The distinction between primary sources and secondary sources is often used as a basis of classification, especially in the humanities and social sciences. The distinction is an important one in investigations that rely on documents because original documents and accounts, or exact copies of them, are generally superior to secondary sources in satisfying criteria of scholarship and because a writer reflects a standard of scholarship in making an accurate distinction between the two kinds of sources in the bibliographic listing. The writer of the history of a university, for example, might want to distinguish between primary sources (such as minutes of meetings, university catalogs, financial records, and students' diaries) and secondary sources (such as previous historical accounts).

Classification by subject or chapter

A bibliography may also be divided by subject or chapter. A study of the history of religious education in the United States might have bibliography entries grouped by denominations or by period, such as decades or centuries.

WORKS CITED FORMAT

With MLA-style parenthetical documentation, a works cited section at the end of your paper is the key to the references cited in your text. The entries for this section should be prepared as indicated in the examples on pages 146 through 179 and according to the principles explained above. When you have a work that does not fit exactly into any of the categories, follow the principles for constructing bibliography entries outlined above. Follow the guidelines for alphabetization of entries and the typing instructions given below.

A works cited list should not be divided into categories. Your reader needs to be able to locate bibliographic information by looking up the reference in one alphabetized list.

The first word of each entry in a works cited list is of particular importance, since that word, whether the last name of an author or the first word of a title, identifies the entry in the text. In deciding whether to place a translator's or editor's name first rather than the author's name, for example, you need to know the purpose for which you will cite the work in your paper. If your text will refer primarily to the decisions made by a translator, the translator's name should appear first in the entry, as in example 11 on page 148. If, on the other hand, you plan to discuss only the original work, the author's name should appear first and the name of the translator should follow the title, as was done with the editor's name in example 10 on page 148.

When you use a compilation and refer to more than one of the articles in it, you must list each article by author in the works cited section. The works cited entries should be constructed as follows:

Compilation

```
Tate, Gary, ed.  Teaching Composition: Ten Bibliographical
     Essays.  Fort Worth: Texas Christian UP, 1976.
```

Article in compilation

```
Winterowd, W. Ross.  "Linguistics and Composition."  Tate
     197—222.
```

(In a bibliography you could list only the one edited work, since your notes would mention specific articles from the compilation.)

When you cite more than one work by the same editor(s) or compiler(s), use a shortened form of the title to identify the compilation in the works cited list.

Compilation	Cooper, Charles R., and Lee Odell, eds. <u>Evaluating Writing: Describing, Measuring, Judging</u>. Urbana: NCTE, 1977.
Compilation, same editors	———. <u>Research on Composing: Points of Departure</u>. Urbana: NCTE, 1978.
Article in first compilation	Lloyd-Jones, Richard. "Primary Trait Scoring." Cooper and Odell, <u>Evaluating</u> 77–99.
Article in second compilation	Petty, Walter T. "The Writing of Young Children." Cooper and Odell, <u>Research</u> 73–84.
	Young, Richard E. "Paradigms and Problems: Needed Research in Rhetorical Invention." Cooper and Odell, <u>Research</u> 29–48.

See Chapter 4 for the parenthetical-reference forms that would accompany these entries in a works cited listing.

ALPHABETIZATION OF ENTRIES

Entries in a bibliography and works cited list are alphabetized by the last name of the author or the first word, excluding articles, of a group or corporate author. An entry for which the author is unknown, such as a newspaper article or unsigned review, is alphabetized by the first word of the title, excluding *A*, *An*, and *The*. The entry for an anonymous work begins with the name of the author in brackets; if the name of the author is not known, the entry is alphabetized by the first word of the title, excluding articles. *Anonymous* is never used as an author entry. Letter-by-letter alphabetization is generally preferred to word-by-word alphabetization for research papers and dissertations. (See page 10 for an explanation of the difference between word-by-word and letter-by-letter systems of alphabetization.) The following list shows letter-by-letter alphabetizing:

Barzun, Jacques. <u>The Modern Researcher</u> . . .

Bazerman, Charles. <u>The Informed Writer</u> . . .

"Breakdown in Communication" . . .

<u>Break of Day</u>

<u>Business Books in Print</u> . . .

```
"Businesses Tighten Accounting Procedures" . . .

"The Businesswoman and the Corporation" . . .
```

The entry for a work by two or more authors is alphabetized by the surname of the author who is listed first on the title page, regardless of whether the names on the title page are in alphabetical order.

```
Smith, B. Othanel, William O. Stanley, and J. Harlan
    Shores. Fundamentals of Curriculum Development.
    2nd ed. . . .
```

When you have two or more works by the same author, entries after the first begin with three hyphens positioned flush with the left margin and followed by a period and two spaces.

```
Burke, Kenneth.  A Grammar of Motives.  Englewood Cliffs:
    Prentice-Hall, 1954.


---.  A Rhetoric of Motives.  Englewood Cliffs: Prentice-
    Hall, 1950.
```

The hyphens stand for the same author or authors named in the preceding entry. If the person named served as editor, translator, or compiler, place a comma and the appropriate abbreviation after the hyphens. When an author listed alone is listed later as a co-author, you must spell out the full author entry. An author entry precedes an entry for the same person as an editor, which precedes an entry for the same person as a co-editor or co-author.

```
Good, Carter V.  The Basics of Research in Education.
    N.p.: Hill, 1960.


---.  Essentials of Educational Research.  New York:
    Appleton-Century-Crofts, 1966.


---, ed.  Dictionary of Education.  3rd ed.  New York:
    McGraw-Hill, 1973.


Good, Carter V., and Douglas E. Scates.  Methods of
    Research.  New York: Appleton-Century-Crofts, 1954.
```

All listings for one author appear in alphabetical order by the first word of the title (excluding the articles *a, an,* and *the*).

Note: See Appendix E for MLA policy on publishers' names.

STYLE MANUALS FOR VARIOUS PROFESSIONS AND DISCIPLINES

American Chemical Society. *Handbook for Authors of Papers in American Chemical Society Publications.* Washington: American Chemical Society, 1978.

American Institute of Physics. Publications Board. *Style Manual for Guidance in the Preparation of Papers.* 3rd ed. New York: American Institute of Physics, 1978.

American Mathematical Society. *A Manual for Authors of Mathematical Papers.* 7th ed. Providence: American Mathematical Society, 1980.

American Psychological Association. *Publication Manual of the American Psychological Association.* 3rd ed. Washington: American Psychological Association, 1983.

Council of Biology Editors. Style Manual Committee. *CBE Style Manual: A Guide for Authors, Editors, and Publishers in the Biological Sciences.* 5th ed. Bethesda: Council of Biology Editors, 1983.

Fleischer, Eugene B. *Style Manual for Citing Microform and Nonprint Media.* Chicago: American Library Association, 1978.

Garner, Diane L., and Diane H. Smith. *The Complete Guide to Citing Government Documents: A Manual for Writers and Librarians.* Bethesda: Congressional Information Service, 1984.

The Geological Society of America. *Information for Contributors to Publications of the Geological Society of America.* Boulder: Geological Society of America, 1979.

International Steering Committee of Medical Editors. "Uniform Requirements for Manuscripts Submitted to Biomedical Journals." *Annals of Internal Medicine* 90 (Jan. 1979): 95–99.

Irvine, Demar, ed. *Writing about Music: A Style Book for Reports and Theses.* 2nd ed. Seattle: Univ. of Washington Press, 1968.

Modern Language Association of America. *MLA Handbook for Writers of Research Papers,* by Joseph Gibaldi and Walter S. Achtert. 3rd ed. New York: Modern Language Association, 1988.

Skillin, Marjorie E., and Robert M. Gay, eds. *Words into Type.* 3rd ed. Englewood Cliffs: Prentice-Hall, 1974.

A Uniform System of Citation. 13th ed. Cambridge: Harvard Law Review Association, 1981.

U.S. Geological Survey. *Suggestions to Authors of Reports of the United States Geological Survey.* 6th ed. Washington: GPO, 1978.

U.S. Government Printing Office. *Style Manual.* Washington: GPO, 1984.

University of Chicago. *The Chicago Manual of Style.* 13th ed. Chicago: Univ. of Chicago Press, 1982.

TYPING AND PRINTING INSTRUCTIONS

Title

Type `Bibliography, Works Cited` (*or* `BIBLIOGRAPHY, WORKS CITED`), or another appropriate heading a double space from your name and the page number, centered between margins and without end punctuation. Double-space to the first entry or heading. Any subheadings should be placed as in the text: first level, centered and underlined; second level, flush with the left margin and underlined; third level, indented five spaces, underlined, and followed by a period.

Spacing

Bibliographies and works cited lists may be double-spaced or single-spaced. Double spacing is generally preferred; single spacing may be required for dissertations to save space. Double-spaced entries should be double-spaced both within and between entries. Single-spaced bibliographies and works cited lists should be single-spaced within entries and double-spaced between entries. (See the sample bibliography and works cited pages at the end of Chapter 1.)

Punctuation

Periods mark the end of the author, title, and facts of publication sections. Two spaces follow each period; one space follows commas and colons. Be careful to insert only one space after the colon (old styles required two spaces).

Placement

Use a hanging indention. Begin each entry at the left margin, and indent succeeding lines in the entry five spaces. If there are two or more entries by one author, type three hyphens (followed by a period or a comma, as appropriate) in place of the name for the second and following listings.

Annotations

Begin annotations either immediately following the end of an entry or on the next line, indented ten spaces. In either case, indent succeeding lines five spaces from the left margin.

BIBLIOGRAPHIES AND LISTS OF WORKS CITED

Sample Pages

The following sample pages illustrate principles of layout and format for bibliographies and lists of works cited.

Bibliography

Primary Sources

Collected Documents

Commager, Henry Steele, ed. Documents of American History. 2 vols. in 1. 5th ed. New York: Appleton-Century-Crofts, 1949.

MacDonald, William H., ed. Select Charters and Other Documents Illustrative of American History, 1606-1775. New York: Macmillan, 1899.

Whitmore, William H., ed. The Andros Tracts: Being a Collection of Pamphlets and Official Papers. 3 vols. Boston: n.p., 1868-74.

Diaries, Letters, and Narratives

Andrews, Charles McL., ed. Narratives of the Insurrections, 1675-1690. Original Narratives of Early American History. New York: Scribner's, 1915.

Bradford, William. Of Plymouth Plantation, 1620-1647. Ed. Samuel E. Morison. New York: Knopf, 1952.

Dreuilletes, Father Gabriel. "Narrative of a Journey to New England, 1650." The Jesuit Relations and Allied Documents . . . 1610-1791. Ed. Reuben G. Thwaites. Cleveland: n.p., 1898.

Dudley, Thomas. "Letter to the Countess of Lincoln." Collections of the New Hampshire Historical Society. Concord: New Hampshire Historical Society, 1834.

Homes, William. "Diary of Rev. William Homes of Chilmark, Martha's Vineyard, 1689-1746." New England Historical and Genealogical Register 48 (1894): 446-53; 49 (1895): 413-16; 50 (1896): 155-66.

Usher, John. "Report on Northern Colonies, 1698." William and Mary Quarterly, 3rd ser., 7 (1950): 95.

Bibliography page divided by type of source

Smith 79

Annotated Bibliography

Daiute, Colette A. "The Computer as Stylus and Audience." <u>College</u>
<u>Composition and Communication</u> 34 (May 1983): 134—45.
   Daiute argues that computers can help writers overcome
what she calls "psychological difficulties" in writing, such as
the limits of short—term memory and the necessity of considering
the reader's point of view.

Dobrin, David N. "Some Ideas about Idea Processors." In <u>Writing at</u>
<u>Century's End: Essays on Computer—Assisted Instruction</u>. Ed.
Lisa Gerrard (New York: Random House, 1987).
   Dobrin argues that idea processors, programs such as
ThinkTank that produce outlines, can help some writers to order
their thoughts, but for most writers they limit creativity.

Gottesman, Polly. "Writing Papers on the Word Processor: A Winter
Study Experiment, 1984." Photocopy, n.d.
   In an independent study project in science writing,
Gottesman experimented with teaching students to write and
revise on computers. Although the computer ultimately promoted
revision, students had to overcome the tendency to see a
beautifully typed draft as correct, and they had to learn to
shift and alter large sections of the text.

Schwartz, Helen J. "Teaching Writing with Computer Aids." <u>College</u>
<u>English</u> 46 (Mar. 1984): 239—47.
   Schwartz analyzes programs useful for teaching invention,
organization, and revision in the composition classroom.

Teichman, Milton. "What College Freshmen Say about Word
Processing." <u>Perspectives in Computing</u> 5 (1985): 43—48.
   In response to a questionnaire prepared by Teichman,
students listed the benefits and drawbacks of word processing.
The most important advantages they cited were saved time, ease
of revision, and a professional—looking copy. Among the
disadvantages mentioned were the inconvenience of working in
one place, preoccupation with the machine itself, and technical
difficulties.

Annotated bibliography

Works Cited

Brodman, John, and Jack Moore. "The Outlook for the World's Oil
    Supply and Demand Through 1983." Journal of Energy and
    Development 7 (Autumn 1981): 1–12.

Brown, William M. "Can OPEC Survive the Glut?" Fortune
    30 Nov. 1982: 89–90.

Croll, Donald O. "World Oil Production: Five-Year Low in First
    Half." Petroleum Economist 48 (Sept. 1981): 373–74.

---. "World Survey: 1981 Oil Production." Petroleum Economist 49
    (Jan. 1982): 5–7.

House, Karen Elliott. "Petroleum Politics." Wall Street Journal
    29 Apr. 1982: 21+.

"How the World Oil Glut Pinches Mexico." Business Week 9 Nov. 1981:
    62–65.

Katz, James E. "The International Energy Agency: Energy Cooperation
    or Illusion?" World Affairs 144 (Summer 1981): 55–82.

Nakame, Tadashi. "Thrifty Oil Users May End the OPEC Surplus."
    Euromoney [London] Dec. 1981: 63–67.

Rahmer, B. A. "West Germany: Oil Consumption in Decline."
    Petroleum Economist 48 (Dec. 1981): 529–31.

United States. Senate. Committee on Energy and Natural Resources.
    Government Responses to Oil Supply Disruptions. Hearings on
    S. 409. 97th Cong., 1st sess., 28 and 30 July 1981.
    Washington: GPO, 1982.

MLA-style works cited page

NOTE FORMS AND BIBLIOGRAPHY (OR LIST OF WORKS CITED) FORMS

Examples

The following pages show examples of note forms and bibliography (or list of works cited) forms. The form for notes is on the left-hand page; the corresponding form for the bibliography (or the list of works cited) is on the right. Except where differences are noted in parentheses, the forms reflect both *Chicago Manual* and MLA styles. (MLA prefers parenthetical references with a list of works cited but permits a note-bibliography style.) Chapters 4 and 5 provide explanations of the principles governing the entries shown here.

NOTES

Books

Basic form

1 Jacob Bronowski, <u>The Ascent of Man</u> (Boston: Little, Brown, 1973), 57–67.
(MLA omits the comma before the page numbers.)

Two authors

2 James G. March and Herbert A. Simon, <u>Organizations</u> (New York: Wiley, 1958), 79.
(MLA omits the comma before the page number.)

More than three authors

3 William McPherson et al., <u>English and American Literature: Sources and Strategies for Collection Development</u> (Chicago: American Library Association, 1987), 67.
(The note form uses only the first author listed on the title page and *et al.*, an abbreviation of *et alii*, which means "and others." MLA omits the comma before the page number.)

Two authors with same last name

4 Wilma R. Ebbitt and David Ebbitt, <u>Writer's Guide and Index to English</u>, 6th ed. (Glenview: Scott, Foresman, 1978), 67.
(MLA omits the comma before the page number.)

Pseudonym (real name supplied)

5 Hannah Green [Joanne Greenberg], <u>I Never Promised You a Rose Garden</u> (New York: Holt, Rinehart and Winston, 1964), 15.
(MLA omits the comma before the page number.)

Author's name missing

6 [Dorothy Scarborough], <u>The Wind</u> (New York: Harper, 1925), 27.

or

7 <u>The Wind</u> (New York: Harper, 1925), 27.
(MLA omits the comma before the page number.)

Group or corporation as author

8 Holiday Magazine, <u>Spain</u> (New York: Random House, 1964), 52.
(MLA omits the comma before the page number.)

Group or corporation as author and publisher

9 Columbia University, <u>The Faculty Handbook</u> (New York, 1987), 55.
(MLA omits the comma before the page number.)

Note: See Appendix E for MLA policy on publishers' names.

BIBLIOGRAPHY (OR LIST OF WORKS CITED)

Books

Bronowski, Jacob. The Ascent of Man. Boston: Little, Brown, 1973.

March, James G., and Herbert A. Simon. Organizations. New York: Wiley, 1958.

McPherson, William, Stephen Lehmann, Craig Likness, and Marcia Pankake. English and American Literature: Sources and Strategies for Collection Development. Chicago: American Library Association, 1987.

Ebbitt, Wilma R., and David Ebbitt. Writer's Guide and Index to English. 6th ed. Glenview: Scott, Foresman, 1978.

Green, Hannah [Joanne Greenberg]. I Never Promised You a Rose Garden. New York: Holt, Rinehart and Winston, 1964.

[Scarborough, Dorothy]. The Wind. New York: Harper, 1925.

or

The Wind. New York: Harper, 1925.

Holiday Magazine. Spain. New York: Random House, 1964.

Columbia University. The Faculty Handbook. New York, 1987.

Note: See Appendix E for MLA policy on publishers' names.

NOTES

Books continued

Editor and author, emphasis on author

> 10 William C. Hayes, <u>Most Ancient Egypt</u>, ed. Keith C. Seele (Chicago: Univ. of Chicago Press, 1965), 5.
> (MLA omits the comma before the page number.)

Translator and author, emphasis on translator

> 11 Suzette Macedo, trans., <u>Diagnosis of the Brazilian Crisis</u>, by Celso Furtado (Berkeley, Univ. of California Press, 165), 147–53.
> (MLA omits the comma before the page numbers.)

Two editors

> 12 Arthur S. Link and Rembert W. Patrick, eds., <u>Writing Southern History: Essays in Historiography in Honor of Fletcher M. Green</u> (Baton Rouge: Louisiana State Univ. Press, 1966), 384.
> (MLA omits the comma before the page number.)

Compilation, emphasis on editor

> 13 Robert W. Corrigan, ed., <u>Theatre in the Twentieth Century</u> (New York: Grove, 1963), 15.
> (MLA omits the comma before the page number.)

Compilation, emphasis on author of one article

> 14 Arthur Miller, "The Playwright and the Atomic World," in <u>Theatre in the Twentieth Century</u>, ed. Robert W. Corrigan (New York: Grove, 1963), 29.
> (MLA omits the word *in* and the comma before the page number.)

Emphasis on author of introduction, afterword, or preface

> 15 Leslie A. Fiedler, introduction to <u>Waiting for God</u>, by Simone Weil (1951; reprint, New York: Harper and Row, Colophon, 1973), 3–5.
> (MLA omits the word *reprint* and the comma before the page numbers.)

Reprint of article in a compilation

> 16 C. L. Ten, "Mill on Self-Regarding Actions," <u>Philosophy</u> 43 (1968): 29–37; reprinted in John Stuart Mill, <u>On Liberty</u>, ed. David Spitz, Norton Critical Edition (New York: Norton, 1972), 239.
> (MLA uses the abbreviation *rpt.* for *reprinted*, omits the word *in*, and omits the comma before the page number.)

Note: See Appendix E for MLA policy on publishers' names.

BIBLIOGRAPHY (OR LIST OF WORKS CITED)

Books *continued*

Hayes, William C. Most Ancient Egypt. Ed. Keith C. Seele.
     Chicago: Univ. of Chicago Press, 1965.

Macedo, Suzette, trans. Diagnosis of the Brazilian Crisis, by
     Celso Furtado. Berkeley: Univ. of California Press, 1965.
(MLA puts a period after the title and capitalizes *by*.)

Link, Arthur S., and Rembert W. Patrick, eds. Writing Southern
     History: Essays in Historiography in Honor of Fletcher M.
     Green. Baton Rouge: Louisiana State Univ. Press, 1966.

Corrigan, Robert W., ed. Theatre in the Twentieth Century. New
     York: Grove, 1963.

Miller, Arthur. "The Playwright and the Atomic World." In Theatre
     in the Twentieth Century. Ed. Robert W. Corrigan. New York:
     Grove, 1963.
(MLA omits the word *In.*)

Fiedler, Leslie A. Introduction to Waiting for God, by Simone
     Weil. 1951. Reprint. New York: Harper and Row, Colophon,
     1973.
(MLA puts a period after *Introduction*, omitting *to*; puts a period after the title and capitalizes *by*;
and omits the word *Reprint*.)

Ten, C. L. "Mill on Self-Regarding Actions." Philosophy 43
     (1968): 29–37; reprinted in John Stuart Mill, On Liberty, ed.
     David Spitz, 238–46. Norton Critical Edition. New York:
     Norton, 1972.
(MLA uses the abbreviation *rpt.* for *reprinted*, omits the word *in*, and puts the inclusive page
numbers, followed by a period, after the date of publication.)

Note: See Appendix E for MLA policy on publishers' names.

NOTES

Books *continued*

Reprint with change of title

17 Suzanne Langer, Feeling and Form (New York: Scribner's, 1953); reprinted as "The Great Dramatic Forms: The Comic Rhythm" in Comedy: Plays, Theory, and Criticism, ed. Marvin Feldheim (New York: Harcourt, 1962), 241.

(MLA uses the abbreviation *rpt.* for *reprinted*, omits the word *in*, and omits the comma before the page number.)

Subtitle, optional in note

18 Ronald G. Walker, Infernal Paradise: Mexico and the Modern English Novel (Berkeley: Univ. of California Press, 1978), 17.

or

19 Ronald G. Walker, Infernal Paradise (Berkeley: Univ. of California Press, 1978), 17.

(MLA omits the comma before the page number.)

Book, edition other than the first

20 John A. Cochran, Money, Banking, and the Economy 3rd ed. (New York: Macmillan, 1975), 77.

(MLA omits the comma before the page number.)

Work originally published with a different title

21 Michel Foucault, The Order of Things: An Archaeology of the Human Sciences [Les Mots et les choses] (New York: Vintage, 1973), 100.

(MLA omits the comma before the page number. When the original title is in a foreign language, follow the rules for capitalization of titles in that language.)

Republished work

22 Beryl Markham, West with the Night (1942; reprint, Berkeley: North Point Press, 1983), 17.

(MLA omits the word *reprint* and the comma before the page number.)

Original edition paperbound

23 Lewis Mumford, The City in History (Harmondsworth: Penguin, 1961), 251–55.

(MLA omits the comma before the page numbers.)

Paperbound reprint

24 C. M. Bowra, The Romantic Imagination (1949; reprint New York: Oxford Univ. Press, Galaxy, 1961), 10.

(MLA omits the word *reprint* and the comma before the page number.)

Note: See Appendix E for MLA policy on publishers' names.

BIBLIOGRAPHY (OR LIST OF WORKS CITED)

Books *continued*

Langer, Suzanne. <u>Feeling and Form</u>. New York: Scribner's, 1953.
Reprinted as "The Great Dramatic Forms: The Comic Rhythm." In
<u>Comedy: Plays, Theory, and Criticism</u>. Ed. Marvin Feldheim,
241-53. New York: Harcourt, 1962.

(MLA uses the abbreviation *Rpt.* for *Reprinted*, omits the word *In*, and puts the inclusive page
numbers, followed by a period, after the date of publication.)

Walker, Ronald G. <u>Infernal Paradise: Mexico and the Modern English
Novel</u>. Berkeley: Univ. of California Press, 1978.

Cochran, John A. <u>Money, Banking, and the Economy</u>. 3rd ed. New
York: Macmillan, 1975.

Foucault, Michel. <u>The Order of Things: An Archaeology of the Human
Sciences [Les Mots et les choses]</u>. New York: Vintage, 1973.

(When the original title is in a foreign language, follow the rules for capitalization of titles in that
language.)

Markham, Beryl. <u>West with the Night</u>. 1942. Reprint. Berkeley:
North Point Press, 1983.

(MLA omits the word *Reprint.*)

Mumford, Lewis. <u>The City in History</u>. Harmondsworth: Penguin,
1961.

Bowra, C. M. <u>The Romantic Imagination</u>. 1949. Reprint. New York:
Oxford Univ. Press, Galaxy, 1961.

(MLA omits the word *Reprint.*)

Note: See Appendix E for MLA policy on publishers' names.

NOTES

Books *continued*

Paperback publication by a division of publisher

25 C. G. Jung, <u>Modern Man in Search of a Soul</u>, trans. W. S. Dell and Cary F. Baynes (New York: Harcourt, Brace and World, Harvest, 1933), 156.
(MLA omits the comma before the page number.)

Facts of publication missing

26 George Eliot, <u>Felix Holt</u> (Edinburgh: William Blackwood, n.d.), 17.
(In the position of the date, *n.d.* means "no date." MLA omits the comma before the page number.)

27 George Eliot, <u>Felix Holt</u> (N.p.: William Blackwood, n.d.), 17.
(In the position of the place of publication, *n.p.* means "no place." MLA omits the comma before the page number.)

28 George Eliot, <u>Felix Holt</u> (Edinburgh: n.p., n.d.), 17.
(In the position of the publisher, *n.p.* means "no publisher." MLA omits the comma before the page number.)

29 George Eliot, <u>Felix Holt</u> (Edinburgh: William Blackwood, n.d.), n. pag. (*or* unpaginated).
(MLA omits the comma before the abbreviation *n. pag.*)

NOTES

Multivolume Works and Series

Multivolume work, general title, reference to a particular volume

30 William M. Bowsky, ed., <u>Studies in Medieval and Renaissance History</u>, 4 vols. (Lincoln: Univ. of Nebraska Press, 1963–67), 2:273–96.

or

31 William M. Bowsky, ed., <u>Studies in Medieval and Renaissance History</u>, vol. 2 (Lincoln: Univ. of Nebraska Press, 1963–67), 273–96.
(MLA uses the second form, omitting the comma before the page numbers.)

Note: See Appendix E for MLA policy on publishers' names.

BIBLIOGRAPHY (OR LIST OF WORKS CITED)

Books continued

Jung, C. G. Modern Man in Search of a Soul. Trans. W. S. Dell and
　　　Cary F. Baynes. New York: Harcourt, Brace and World, Harvest,
　　　1933.

Eliot, George. Felix Holt. Edinburgh: William Blackwood, n.d.

Eliot, George. Felix Holt. N.p.: William Blackwood, n.d.

Eliot, George. Felix Holt. Edinburgh: n.p., n.d.

Eliot, George. Felix Holt. Edinburgh: William Blackwood, n.d.
(Indication that a work is unpaginated is not necessary in a bibliography. An entry in a list of works
cited would add *n.pag.* or *Unpaginated* at the end, followed by a period.)

BIBLIOGRAPHY (OR LIST OF WORKS CITED)

Multivolume Works and Series

Bowsky, William M., ed. Studies in Medieval and Renaissance
　　　History. 4 vols. Lincoln: Univ. of Nebraska Press, 1963–67.

Note: See Appendix E for MLA policy on publishers' names.

NOTES

Multivolume Works and Series continued

Multivolume work, individual titles

32 James C. Crutchfield, ed., The Fisheries: Problems in Resource Management, vol. 1 of Studies on Public Policy Issues in Resource Management (Seattle: Univ. of Washington Press, 1965), 61–74.

(MLA arranges the note differently.)

32 James C. Crutchfield, ed., The Fisheries: Problems in Resource Management (Seattle: U of Washington P, 1965) 61–74, vol. 1 of Studies on Public Policy Issues in Resource Management.

Work in a series

33 Ernest L. Presseisen, Before Aggression: Europeans Prepare the Japanese Army, Monographs and Papers of the Association for Asian Studies, no. 21 (Tucson: Univ. of Arizona Press, 1965), 117.

(MLA omits the abbreviation *no.* and the preceding comma, as well as the comma before the page number.)

Multivolume work in a series

34 Adrian Morey and C. N. L. Brooke, Gilbert Foliot and His Letters, Cambridge Series in Medieval Life and Thought, n.s., vol. 2 (New York: Cambridge Univ. Press, 1965), 296.

(MLA abbreviates *new series* as *ns* [without periods] and omits the comma before the page number.)

Work in a series, proceedings

35 Walter L. Smith and William E. Wilkinson, eds., Proceedings of the Symposium on Congestion Theory, Probability and Statistics Monograph Series, no. 2 (Chapel Hill: Univ. of North Carolina Press, 1965), 401.

(MLA omits the abbreviation *no.* and the preceding comma, as well as the comma before the page number.)

Work in a series, author and editor

36 Henry Eno, Twenty Years on the Pacific Slope: Letters of Henry Eno from California and Nevada, 1848–1871, ed. W. Turrentine Jackson, Yale Western Americana Series, vol. 8 (New Haven: Yale Univ. Press, 1965), 14–44.

(MLA omits the abbreviation *vol.* and the preceding comma, as well as the comma before the page numbers.)

Work in a series, translator and editor

37 Jack F. Kilpatrick and Anna Gritts Kilpatrick, trans. and eds., The Shadow of Sequoyah: Social Documents of the Cherokees, 1862–1964, Civilization of the American Indian Series, no. 81 (Norman: Univ. of Oklahoma Press, 1965), 47–54.

(MLA omits the abbreviation *no.* and the preceding comma, as well as the comma before the page numbers.)

Note: See Appendix E for MLA policy on publishers' names.

BIBLIOGRAPHY (OR LIST OF WORKS CITED)

Multivolume Works and Series continued

Crutchfield, James C., ed. The Fisheries: Problems in Resource
    Management. Vol. 1 of Studies on Public Policy Issues in
    Resource Management. Seattle: Univ. of Washington Press,
    1965.
(MLA gives the total number of volumes and the inclusive dates of publication.)
Crutchfield, James C., ed. The Fisheries: Problems in Resource Management.
    Seattle: U of Washington P, 1965. Vol. 1 of Studies on Public Policy
    Issues in Resource Management. 12 vols. 1965–75.

Presseisen, Ernest L. Before Aggression: Europeans Prepare the
    Japanese Army. Monographs and Papers of the Association for
    Asian Studies, no. 21. Tucson: Univ. of Arizona Press, 1965.
(MLA omits the abbreviation *no.* and the preceding comma.)

Morey, Adrian, and C. N. L. Brooke. Gilbert Foliot and His
    Letters. Cambridge Studies in Medieval Life and Thought,
    n.s., vol. 2. New York: Cambridge Univ. Press, 1965.
(MLA abbreviates *new series* as *ns*, without periods.)

Smith, Walter, L. and William E. Wilkinson, eds. Proceedings of
    the Symposium on Congestion Theory. Probability and Statis-
    tics Monograph Series, no. 2. Chapel Hill: Univ. of North
    Carolina Press, 1965.
(MLA omits the abbreviation *no.* and the preceding comma.)

Eno, Henry. Twenty Years on the Pacific Slope: Letters of Henry
    Eno from California and Nevada, 1848–1871. Ed. W. Turrentine
    Jackson. Yale Western Americana Series, vol. 8. New Haven:
    Yale Univ. Press, 1965.
(MLA omits the abbreviation *vol.* and the preceding comma.)

Kilpatrick, Jack F., and Anna Gritts Kilpatrick, trans. and eds.
    The Shadow of Sequoyah: Social Documents of the Cherokees,
    1862–1964. Civilization of the American Indian Series,
    no. 81. Norman: Univ. of Oklahoma Press, 1965.
(MLA omits the abbreviation *no.* and the preceding comma.)

Note: See Appendix E for MLA policy on publishers' names.

NOTES
Journals

Basic form

38 Raymond Aron, "The Education of the Citizen in Industrial Society," <u>Daedalus</u> 91 (1962): 249–50.

Season or month necessary for identification

39 D. W. Harding, "Regulated Hatred: An Aspect of the Work of Jane Austen," <u>Scrutiny</u> 8 (Mar. 1940): 346.

Each issue paginated separately

40 Harry Bird, "Some Aspects of Prejudice in the Roman World," <u>University of Windsor Review</u> 10, no. 1 (1975): 64.
(In MLA style, a period and the issue number follow the volume number with no intervening space: 10.1 (1975): 64.)

Issues with numbers only

41 C. E. Nwezeh, "The Comparative Approach to Modern African Literature," <u>Yearbook of General and Comparative Literature</u>, no. 28 (1979): 22.
(MLA omits *no.* and the preceding comma.)

Series designation

42 Bernard M. Dwork, "On the Zeta Function of a Hyper-surface," <u>Annals of Mathematics</u>, 2nd ser., 83 (1966): 518.
(MLA omits the comma after the name of the journal and before the volume number.)

NOTES
Magazines

Weekly

43 Barbara W. Tuchman, "The Decline of Quality," <u>New York Times Magazine</u>, 2 Nov. 1980, 39.
(MLA omits the comma after the name of the magazine and puts a colon rather than a comma after the date.)

Monthly

44 Norman O. Brown, "Apocalypse: The Place of Mystery in the Life of the Mind," <u>Harper's</u>, May 1961, 27.
(MLA omits the comma after the name of the magazine and puts a colon rather than a comma after the date.)

Note: See Appendix E for MLA policy on publishers' names.

BIBLIOGRAPHY (OR LIST OF WORKS CITED)

Journals

Aron, Raymond. "The Education of the Citizen in Industrial
    Society." Daedalus 91 (1962): 249–63.

Harding, D. W. "Regulated Hatred: An Aspect of the Work of Jane
    Austen." Scrutiny 8 (Mar. 1940): 346–62.

Bird, Harry. "Some Aspects of Prejudice in the Roman World."
    University of Windsor Review 10, no. 1 (1975): 64–73.
(In MLA style, a period and the issue number follow the volume number with no intervening space:
10.1 (1975): 64–73.)

Nwezeh, C. E. "The Comparative Approach to Modern African
    Literature." Yearbook of General and Comparative Literature,
    no. 28 (1979): 22.
(MLA omits *no.* and the preceding comma.)

Dwork, Bernard M. "On the Zeta Function of a Hypersurface."
    Annals of Mathematics, 2nd ser., 83 (1966): 518–19.
(MLA omits the comma after the name of the journal and before the volume number.)

BIBLIOGRAPHY (OR LIST OF WORKS CITED)

Magazines

Tuchman, Barbara W. "The Decline of Quality." New York Times
    Magazine, 2 Nov. 1980. 38–45, 50, 53–57. (*or* 38–57.)
(To indicate that an article continues over several discontinuous pages, MLA enters a plus sign (+)
after the number of the first page of the article: Tuchman, Barbara W. "The Decline of
Quality." New York Times Magazine 2 Nov. 1980: 38+.)

Brown, Norman O. "Apocalypse: The Place of Mystery in the Life of
    the Mind." Harper's, May 1961, 27–35.
(MLA omits the comma after the name of the magazine and puts a colon rather than a comma after
the date.)

Note: See Appendix E for MLA policy on publishers' names.

NOTES

Magazines *continued*

Unsigned article

> 45 "Report on Hepatitis in Blood," U.S. News and World Report, 7 June 1976, 78.
> (MLA omits the comma after the name of the magazine and puts a colon rather than a comma after the date.)

Weekly column item

> 46 "Drummer," The Talk of the Town, New Yorker, 28 Oct. 1980, 45.
> (MLA omits the comma after the name of the magazine and puts a colon rather than a comma after the date.)

NOTES

Newspapers

Basic entry

> 47 Susan F. Rasky, "Senate Calls for Revisions in New Tax for Health Care," New York Times, 8 June 1989, A20.
> (MLA omits the comma after the name of the newspaper and puts a colon rather than a comma after the date.)

State interpolated

> 48 "Unknown Author of Wind Answers Crane Criticism," Sweetwater [Texas] Daily Reporter, 15 Dec. 1925, 6.
> (MLA omits the comma after the name of the newspaper and puts a colon rather than a comma after the date.)

City interpolated, with section number

> 49 Times [London], 19 May 1943, sec. 2, p. 5.
> (MLA omits the comma after *[London]*, puts a colon rather than a comma after *sec. 2*, and omits the abbreviation *p.*)

Author, title, edition

> 50 Wayne E. Green, "Cold-Fusion Development Spurs Hot Race for Patents," Wall Street Journal, 9 June 1989, eastern ed., B1.
> (MLA omits the comma after the name of the newspaper and puts a colon rather than a comma after *eastern ed.*)

Editorial

> 51 "Credit for All at the World Bank," editorial, New York Times, 1 Nov. 1980, A24.
> (MLA omits the comma after the name of the newspaper and puts a colon rather than a comma after the date.)

Note: See Appendix E for MLA policy on publishers' names.

BIBLIOGRAPHY (OR LIST OF WORKS CITED)

Magazines continued

"Report on Hepatitis in Blood." <u>U.S. News and World Report</u>,
 7 June 1976, 78.
(MLA omits the comma after the name of the magazine and puts a colon rather than a comma after the date.)

"Drummer." The Talk of the Town. <u>New Yorker</u>, 27 Oct. 1980, 45.
(MLA omits the comma after the name of the magazine and puts a colon rather than a comma after the date.)

BIBLIOGRAPHY (OR LIST OF WORKS CITED)

Newspapers

Rasky, Susan F. "Senate Calls for Revisions in New Tax for Health
 Care." <u>New York Times</u>, 8 June 1989, A20.
(MLA omits the comma after the name of the newspaper and puts a colon rather than a comma after the date.)

"Unknown Author of <u>Wind</u> Answers Crane Criticism." <u>Sweetwater</u>
 [Texas] <u>Daily Reporter</u>, 15 Dec. 1925, 6.
(MLA omits the comma after the name of the newspaper and puts a colon rather than a comma after the date.)

<u>Times</u> [London], 19 May 1943, sec. 2, pp. 5, 8.
(MLA enters a plus sign (+) after the opening page number to indicate that the article continues on discontinuous pages: <u>Times</u> [London] 19 May 1943, sec. 2: 5+.)

Green, Wayne E. "Cold-Fusion Development Spurs Hot Race for
 Patents." <u>Wall Street Journal</u>, 9 June 1989, eastern ed., B1.
(MLA omits the comma after the name of the newspaper and puts a colon rather than a comma after *eastern ed.*)

"Credit for All at the World Bank." Editorial. <u>New York Times</u>,
 1 Nov. 1980, A24.
(MLA omits the comma after the name of the newspaper and puts a colon after the date.)

Note: See Appendix E for MLA policy on publishers' names.

NOTES

Newspapers *continued*

Letter

> ⁵² Carlos Romero-Barcelò, letter, <u>New York Times</u>, 1 Nov. 1980, A25.
>
> (MLA omits the comma after the name of the newspaper and puts a colon rather than a comma after the date.)

Numbered sections, columns indicated, no title or author

> ⁵³ <u>San Francisco Sunday Examiner & Chronicle</u>, 26 June 1966, sec. 2, p. 4, cols. 1–3.
>
> (MLA omits the comma after the name of the newspaper, puts a colon rather than a comma after *sec. 2,* and omits the abbreviation *p.*)

NOTES

Reviews

Signed, with title, in magazine

> ⁵⁴ Alan M. Dershowitz, "Inside the Sanctum Sanctorum," review of <u>Independent Journey: The Life of William O. Douglas</u>, by James F. Simon, <u>New York Times Book Review</u>, 2 Nov. 1980, 9.
>
> (MLA abbreviates *review* as *rev.*, omits the comma before the date, and puts a colon rather than a comma after the date.)

Signed, untitled, in journal

> ⁵⁵ Robert E. Lott, review of <u>Emilia Pardo Bazán</u>, by Walter T. Pattison, <u>Symposium</u> 28 (1974): 382.
>
> (MLA abbreviates *review* as *rev.*)

Unsigned, untitled, in journal

> ⁵⁶ Review of <u>Married to Genius</u>, by Jeffrey Meyers, <u>Journal of Modern Literature</u> 7 (1979): 579.
>
> (MLA abbreviates *Review* as *Rev.*)

NOTES

Works of Literature

Without editing or commentary

> ⁵⁷ Malcolm Lowry, <u>Under the Volcano</u> (New York: Reynal and Hitchcock, 1947), 348.
>
> (MLA omits the comma before the page number.)

Note: See Appendix E for MLA policy on publishers' names.

BIBLIOGRAPHY (OR LIST OF WORKS CITED)

Newspapers continued

Romero–Barcelò, Carlos. Letter. New York Times, 1 Nov. 1980, A25.
(MLA omits the comma after the name of the newspaper and puts a colon after the date.)

San Francisco Sunday Examiner & Chronicle. 26 June 1966, sec. 2,
    p. 4, cols. 1–3.
(MLA puts a colon rather than a comma after *sec. 2* and omits the abbreviation *p.*)

BIBLIOGRAPHY (OR LIST OF WORKS CITED)

Reviews

Dershowitz, Alan M. "Inside the Sanctum Sanctorum." Review of
    Independent Journey: The Life of William O. Douglas, by James
    F. Simon. New York Times Book Review, 2 Nov. 1980, 9.
(MLA abbreviates *Review* as *Rev.*, omits the comma before the date, and puts a colon rather than a
comma after the date.)

Lott, Robert E. Review of Emilia Pardo Bazán, by Walter T.
    Pattison. Symposium 28 (1974): 382.
(MLA abbreviates *Review* as *Rev.*)

Review of Married to Genius, by Jeffrey Meyers. Journal of Modern
    Literature 7 (1979): 579–80.
(MLA abbreviates *Review* as *Rev.*)

BIBLIOGRAPHY (OR LIST OF WORKS CITED)

Works of Literature

Lowry, Malcolm. Under the Volcano. New York: Reynal and
    Hitchcock, 1947.

Note: See Appendix E for MLA policy on publishers' names.

NOTES

Works of Literature continued

Edited, emphasis on author

58 Joseph Conrad, Lord Jim, ed. Thomas C. Moser (New York: Norton, 1968), 65.
(MLA omits the comma before the page number.)

Edited, emphasis on editor or translator

59 Thomas G. Bergin, trans. and ed., The Divine Comedy, by Dante Alighieri (New York: Appleton-Century-Crofts, 1955), 19.
(MLA omits the comma before the page number.)

Edited, emphasis on writer of introduction

60 David Daiches, introduction to Pride and Prejudice, by Jane Austen (New York: Modern Library, 1950), vii.
(MLA omits the comma before the page number.)

Play: act, scene, line

61 William Shakespeare, Othello, in Shakespeare: Twenty-three Plays and the Sonnets, ed. Thomas Marc Parrott, 2nd ed. (New York: Scribner's, 1953), act 3, sc. 2, lines 1–5.
(First reference; MLA omits the comma before *act 3*.)

62 Othello 3.2.1–5.
(Subsequent reference, either in notes or within parentheses in the text)

or

63 Oth. 4.1.5–17.

Long poem: book or canto, line

64 John Milton, Paradise Lost, ed. Merritt Y. Hughes (New York: Odyssey, 1962), bk. 9, lines 342–75.
(First reference)

65 Paradise Lost 3.1–55.
(Subsequent reference, either in notes or in parentheses in the text)

or

66 PL 3.1–55.

Note: See Appendix E for MLA policy on publishers' names.

BIBLIOGRAPHY (OR LIST OF WORKS CITED)

Works of Literature continued

Conrad, Joseph. <u>Lord Jim</u>. Ed. Thomas C. Moser. New York: Norton, 1968.

Bergin, Thomas G., trans. and ed. <u>The Divine Comedy</u>, by Dante Alighieri. New York: Appleton–Century–Crofts, 1955.
(MLA puts a period after the title and capitalizes *by*.)

Daiches, David. Introduction to <u>Pride and Prejudice</u>, by Jane Austen. New York: Modern Library, 1950.
(MLA puts a period after *Introduction* and omits *to*, puts a period after the title, and capitalizes *by*.)

Parrott, Thomas Marc, ed. <u>Shakespeare: Twenty–three Plays and the Sonnets</u>. 2nd ed. New York: Scribner's, 1953.

Milton, John. <u>Paradise Lost</u>. Ed. Merritt Y. Hughes. New York: Odyssey, 1962.

Note: See Appendix E for MLA policy on publishers' names.

NOTES

Works of Literature continued

Short poem: stanza, line

67 Walt Whitman, "Song of Myself," in <u>The American Tradition in Literature</u>, ed. George Perkins et al., vol. 2, 6th ed. (New York: Norton, 1985), sec. 6, lines 131–35.
(First reference; MLA omits the comma before *sec. 6.*)

68 "Song of Myself," 7.145–48.
(Subsequent reference)

Biblical citation: chapter, verse

69 1 Sam. 14:6–9.

Classical translation: book, chapter

70 Aristotle, <u>Poetics</u>, trans. S. H. Butcher, ed. Francis Fergusson (New York: Hill and Wang, 1961), bk. 7, chap. 2.
(First reference; MLA omits the comma before *bk. 7.*)

71 <u>Poetics</u> 7.2.
(Subsequent reference)

Classical translation: numbered divisions

72 Plato, <u>The Republic</u>, trans. Desmond Lee (Harmondsworth: Penguin, 1955), 562E–C.
(First reference; MLA omits the comma before *562E-C.*)

73 <u>Republic</u> 562E–C.
(Subsequent reference)

NOTES

Reference Works

Encyclopedia entry, unsigned

74 "Huygens, Christiaan," <u>Encyclopaedia Britannica</u>, 13th ed.

Dictionary entry

75 "Advertisement," <u>Webster's Third International Dictionary</u>.
(Because the number of the edition appears in the title, the date is not needed.)

Note: See Appendix E for MLA policy on publishers' names.

BIBLIOGRAPHY (OR LIST OF WORKS CITED)

Works of Literature continued

Perkins, George, Sculley Bradley, Richmond Croom Beatty, E. Hudson
    Long, eds. The American Tradition in Literature. 2 vols.
    6th ed. New York: Norton, 1985.

The Bible. Revised Standard Version.

Aristotle. Poetics. Trans. S. H. Butcher. Ed. Francis Fergusson.
    New York: Hill and Wang, 1961.

Plato. The Republic. Trans. Desmond Lee. Harmondsworth: Penguin.
    1955.

BIBLIOGRAPHY (OR LIST OF WORKS CITED)

Reference Works

"Huygens, Christiaan." Encyclopaedia Britannica. 13th ed.

"Advertisement." Webster's Third International Dictionary.
(Because the number of the edition appears in the title, the date is not needed.)

Note: See Appendix E for MLA policy on publishers' names.

NOTES

Reference Works continued

Atlas entry

> ⁷⁶ "Hidden Face of the Moon," <u>Times Atlas of the World</u>, 1971 ed.

General encyclopedia, signed entry

> ⁷⁷ William Markowitz, "Time, Measurement and Determination of," <u>Encyclopedia Americana</u>, 1965 ed.

General encyclopedia, initialed article, name supplied

> ⁷⁸ J[oe] B[en] W[heat], "Cliff Dwellings," <u>Encyclopaedia Britannica</u>, 1964 ed.

Dictionary not widely known

> ⁷⁹ Horace B. English and Ava Champney English, <u>A Comprehensive Dictionary of Psychological and Psychoanalytical Terms</u> (New York: McKay, 1958), 77.
> (**MLA** omits the comma before the page number.)

Reference work not widely known, signed article

> ⁸⁰ Benjamin S. Bloom and Ernest A. Rakow, "Higher Mental Processes," in <u>Encyclopedia of Educational Research</u>, ed. Robert L. Ebel, 4th ed. (New York: Macmillan, 1969), 595–96.
> (**MLA** omits the word *in* and the comma before the page numbers.)

NOTES

Public Documents

Congressional hearing, House

> ⁸¹ U.S. Congress, House, Committee on Agriculture, Subcommittee on Dairy and Poultry, <u>Federal Loan for Poultry Processing Plant in New Castle, Pa.</u>, hearing, 89th Cong., 1st sess., 19 Oct. 1965 (Washington: GPO, 1966), 47.
> (**MLA** begins the note as follows: ⁸¹ United States. Cong., . . . **MLA** omits the comma before the page number.)

Congressional Record

> ⁸² <u>Congressional Record</u>, 89th Cong., 2nd sess., 1966, vol. 72, pt. 5, p. 12161.
> (**MLA** abbreviates *Congressional Record* as *Cong. Rec.* and puts a colon rather than a comma after *pt. 5.*)

Constitution

> ⁸³ Constitution of the United States, art. 3, sec. 1.

Note: See Appendix E for MLA policy on publishers' names.

BIBLIOGRAPHY (OR LIST OF WORKS CITED)

Reference Works continued

"Hidden Face of the Moon." <u>Times Atlas of the World.</u> 1971 ed.

Markowitz, William. "Time, Measurement and Determination of."
     <u>Encyclopedia Americana</u>. 1965 ed.

W[heat], J[oe] B[en]. "Cliff Dwellings." <u>Encyclopaedia Britannica</u>.
     1964 ed.

English, Horace B., and Ava Champney English. <u>A Comprehensive</u>
     <u>Dictionary of Psychological and Psychoanalytical Terms</u>. New
     York: McKay, 1958.

Bloom, Benjamin S., and Ernest A. Rakow. "Higher Mental
     Processes." In <u>Encyclopedia of Educational Research</u>.
     Ed. Robert L. Ebel. 4th ed. New York: Macmillan, 1969.
     (MLA omits the word *In*.)

BIBLIOGRAPHY (OR LIST OF WORKS CITED)

Public Documents

U.S. Congress. House. Committee on Agriculture. Subcommittee on
     Dairy and Poultry. <u>Federal Loan for Poultry Processing Plant</u>
     <u>in New Castle, Pa</u>. Hearing. 89th Cong., 1st sess.,
     19 Oct. 1965. Washington: GPO, 1966.
     (MLA spells out *United States* and abbreviates *Congress* as *Cong.*)

<u>Congressional Record</u>. 89th Cong., 2nd sess., 1966. Vol. 72,
     pt. 5, pp. 12161–214.
     (MLA shortens this type of entry: <u>Cong. Rec.</u> 17 Nov. 1980: 3852.)

Constitution of the United States.

Note: See Appendix E for MLA policy on publishers' names.

NOTES

Public Documents continued

Congressional hearing

84 U.S. Congress, Senate, Committee on Environment and Public Works, <u>Construction and Repair Programs to Alleviate Unemployment</u>, hearing, 97th Cong., 2nd sess., 1 Dec. 1982 (Washington: GPO, 1983), 8.

(MLA begins the note 84 United States, Cong., . . . and omits the comma before the page number.)

Act of Congress

85 U.S. Congress, Senate, Committee on Commerce, Science, and Transportation, Subcommittee on Surface Transportation, <u>Household Goods Transportation Act of 1980</u> (Washington: GPO, 1983), 2.

(MLA begins the note 85 United States, Cong., . . . and omits the comma before the page number.)

Congressional report prepared by another agency

86 U.S. Congress, House, Committee on Post Office and Civil Service, <u>Background on the Civil Service Retirement System</u>, report prepared by the Congressional Research Service (Washington: GPO, 1983), 17.

(MLA begins the note 86 United States, Cong., . . . and omits the comma before the page number.)

Executive document

87 U.S. President, Proclamation, <u>Martin Luther King Day</u>, 15 Jan. 1988.

(MLA spells out *United States* and puts a comma after it.)

Executive report

88 U.S. Department of Commerce, Bureau of the Census, <u>Aircraft Propellers</u> (Washington: Bureau, 1979), 13.

(MLA spells out *United States*, puts a comma after it, and omits the comma before the page number.)

Treaty

89 U.S. Department of State, "Nuclear Weapons Test Ban," 15 Aug. 1990, TIAS no. 1943, <u>United States Treaties and Other International Agreements</u>, vol. 34, pt. 6, p. 7.

(MLA spells out *United States* and puts a comma after it, puts a colon rather than a comma after *pt. 6*, and omits the abbreviation *p*.)

Note: See Appendix E for MLA policy on publishers' names.

BIBLIOGRAPHY (OR LIST OF WORKS CITED)

Public Documents *continued*

U.S. Congress. Senate. Committee on Environment and Public Works. Construction and Repair Programs to Alleviate Unemployment. Hearing. 97th Cong., 2nd sess., 1 Dec. 1982. Washington: GPO, 1983.
(**MLA** spells out *United States* and abbreviates *Congress* as *Cong.*)

U.S. Congress. Senate. Committee on Commerce, Science, and Transportation. Subcommittee on Surface Transportation. Household Goods Transportation Act of 1980. Washington: GPO, 1983.
(**MLA** spells out *United States* and abbreviates *Congress* as *Cong.*)

U.S. Congress. House. Committee on Post Office and Civil Service. Background on the Civil Service Retirement System. Report prepared by the Congressional Research Service. Washington: GPO, 1983.
(**MLA** spells out *United States* and abbreviates *Congress* as *Cong.*)

U.S. President. Proclamation. Martin Luther King Day. 15 Jan. 1988.
(**MLA** spells out *United States*.)

U.S. Department of Commerce. Bureau of the Census. Aircraft Propellers. Washington: Bureau, 1979.
(**MLA** spells out *United States*.)

U.S. Department of State. "Nuclear Weapons Test Ban," 15 Aug. 1990, TIAS no. 1943. United States Treaties and Other International Agreements, vol. 34.
(**MLA** spells out *United States*.)

Note: See Appendix E for MLA policy on publishers' names.

NOTES

Public Documents *continued*

Individual authors, work in a series

90 G. Halsey Hunt and Stanley R. Mohler, <u>Aging: A Review of Research and Training Grants Supported by the National Institutes of Health</u>, U.S. Public Health Service Publication, no. 652 (Bethesda: National Institutes of Health, 1958), iii–iv.
(MLA omits *no.* and the preceding comma, as well as the comma before the page numbers.)

Labor union agreement, unpublished

91 "Automobile, Aerospace and Agricultural Implement Workers of America: International Union, United, AFL–CIO, and the Ford Motor Company, Agreement between," 20 Oct. 1961, 184–85.
(MLA puts a colon rather than a comma after the date.)

Labor union document, unpublished

92 Stone Cutters Association of North America, Journeymen, "Constitution and By-Laws," 1926, 4.
(MLA puts a colon rather than a comma after the date.)

Convention proceedings

93 Longshoremen's and Warehousemen's Union, International, CIO, <u>Proceedings of the Seventh Biennial Convention of San Francisco, 7 Apr. to 11 Apr. 1947</u> (San Francisco: Trade Pressroom, n.d.), 83.
(MLA omits the comma before the page number.)

State statutes

94 California, <u>Education Code</u>, Sec. 13444 (1963).

NOTES

Unpublished Sources

Manuscript, letter

95 Robert Cockburn, letter to Lord Melville, 17 May 1819, Manuscript Collection, Rutgers University, New Brunswick, N.J., group 125.
(MLA uses the abbreviation *U* for *University* and omits the name of the state.)

Manuscript, nature identified

96 Zaccheus Towne, diary, July 1776–Feb. 1777, Manuscript Collection, Rutgers University, New Brunswick, N.J., group 615.
(MLA uses the abbreviation *U* for *University* and omits the name of the state.)

Note: See Appendix E for MLA policy on publishers' names.

BIBLIOGRAPHY (OR LIST OF WORKS CITED)

Public Documents *continued*

Hunt, G. Halsey, and Stanley R. Mohler. <u>Aging: A Review of</u>
<u>Research and Training Grants Supported by the National</u>
<u>Institutes of Health</u>. U.S. Public Health Service Publication,
no. 652. Bethesda: National Institutes of Health, 1958.
(MLA omits *no.* and the preceding comma.)

"Automobile, Aerospace and Agricultural Implement Workers of
America: International Union, United, AFL-CIO, and the Ford
Motor Company, Agreement between." 20 Oct. 1961.

Stone Cutters Association of North America. Journeymen.
"Constitution and By-Laws." 1926.

Longshoremen's and Warehousemen's Union, International, CIO.
<u>Proceedings of the Seventh Biennial Convention of San</u>
<u>Francisco, 7 Apr. to 11 Apr. 1947</u>. San Francisco: Trade
Pressroom, n.d.

California. <u>Education Code</u>. 1963.

BIBLIOGRAPHY (OR LIST OF WORKS CITED)

Unpublished Sources

Cockburn, Robert. Letter to Lord Melville. 17 May 1819. Group
125, Manuscript Collection, Rutgers University, New Brunswick,
N.J.
(MLA puts periods after *125* and *University* [abbreviated as *U*], and omits the name of the state.)

Towne, Zaccheus. Diary. July 1776–Feb. 1777. Group 615,
Manuscript Collection, Rutgers University, New Brunswick, N.J.
(MLA puts periods after *615* and *University* [abbreviated as *U*], and omits the name of the state.)

Note: See Appendix E for MLA policy on publishers' names.

NOTES

Unpublished Sources continued

Manuscript, title supplied

97 Papers on Industrial Espionage, Report of Agent 106, 17 July 1919, University of Washington, Seattle.
(MLA uses the abbreviation *U* for *University*.)

Manuscript, handwritten

98 Dorothy Scarborough, "The Wind," MS, Dorothy Scarborough Papers, The Texas Collection, Baylor University, Waco, Tex., 2.
(MLA uses the abbreviation *ms.* for *manuscript*, abbreviates *University* as *U*, and omits the name of the state.)

Typescript

99 The Oral Memoirs of J. R. Smith, TS, Oral History Division, Butler College, Butler, N.Y., 75.
(MLA uses the abbreviation *ts.* for *typescript* and omits the name of the state.)

Photocopied work

100 James Yaffe, "A Report on the [University of Nebraska] Summer Writing Institute: 1979," photocopy, n.d., 4.
(MLA uses the abbreviation *U* for *University*.)

NOTES

Dissertations

Dissertation

101 Marilyn Rosenthal, "Poetry of the Spanish Civil War" (Ph.D. diss., New York University, 1972), 21.
(In MLA style, the title is followed by a comma, and the facts of publication are given as diss., New York U, 1972, 21. The abbreviation *Ph.D.* is omitted.)

Dissertation published by microfilm service

102 Laura Elizabeth Rhodes Casari, <u>Malcolm Lowry's Drunken Divine Comedy</u>, Ph.D. Diss., University of Nebraska, 1967 (Ann Arbor: UMI, 1967), 77.
(MLA identifies the work as diss., U of Nebraska, 1967. The abbreviation *Ph.D.* is omitted.)

Abstract of dissertation

103 Catherine Pastore Blair, "Mark Twain, Anatomist," <u>DAI</u> 41 (1981): 4388A.
(In MLA style, the page reference is followed not by a period but by the name of the university granting the degree, enclosed in parentheses. A period ends the entry.)

Note: See Appendix E for MLA policy on publishers' names.

BIBLIOGRAPHY (OR LIST OF WORKS CITED)

Unpublished Sources continued

Papers on Industrial Espionage. Report of Agent 106.
17 July 1919. University of Washington, Seattle.
(MLA uses the abbreviation *U* for *University*.)

Scarborough, Dorothy. "The Wind." MS. Dorothy Scarborough
Papers. The Texas Collection, Baylor University, Waco, Tex.
(MLA puts a comma after the title, abbreviates *manuscript* as *ms.*, uses the abbreviation *U* for *University*, and omits the name of the state.)

The Oral Memoirs of J. R. Smith. TS. Oral History Division.
Butler College, Butler, N.Y.
(MLA puts a comma after the title, abbreviates *typescript* as *ts.*, and omits the name of the state.)

Yaffe, James. "A Report on the [University of Nebraska] Summer
Writing Institute: 1979." Photocopy. N.d.
(MLA uses the abbreviation *U* for *University*.)

BIBLIOGRAPHY (OR LIST OF WORKS CITED)

Dissertations

Rosenthal, Marilyn. "Poetry of the Spanish Civil War." Ph.D.
diss., New York University, 1972.
(MLA gives the facts of publication as Diss. New York U, 1972. The abbreviation *Ph.D.* is omitted.)

Casari, Laura Elizabeth Rhodes. Malcolm Lowry's Drunken Divine
Comedy: Under the Volcano and Shorter Fiction. Ph.D. Diss.,
University of Nebraska, 1967. Ann Arbor: UMI, 1967.
67-15812.
(MLA identifies the work as Diss. U of Nebraska, 1967. The abbreviation *Ph.D.* is omitted.)

Blair, Catherine Pastore. "Mark Twain, Anatomist." DAI 41 (1981):
4387A-88A.
(MLA includes after the page reference the name of the university granting the degree, followed by a period.)

Note: See Appendix E for MLA policy on publishers' names.

NOTES

Nonprint Sources

Film

104 Phil Alden Robinson, dir., <u>Field of Dreams</u>, with Kevin Costner, Amy Madigan, and James Earl Jones, Universal, 1989.

Performance, musical theater

105 Jerome Robbins, dir. and chor., <u>Jerome Robbins' Broadway</u>, Imperial Theatre, New York, 14 June 1989.

Performance, orchestra

106 Zubin Mehta, dir., New York Philharmonic, Avery Fisher Hall, Lincoln Center, New York, 25 Nov. 1980.

Performance, ballet

107 Jiri Kylian, <u>Return to the Strange Land</u>, with Cynthia Anderson and Michael Bjerknes, Joffrey Ballet, City Center, New York, 19 Nov. 1980.

Performance, drama, emphasis on author of play

108 Lillian Hellman, <u>The Little Foxes</u>, dir. Austin Pendleton, with Elizabeth Taylor, Martin Beck Theatre, New York, 23 May 1981.

Musical composition

109 Wolfgang Amadeus Mozart, Piano Concerto in B-flat major, K. 595.

Musical composition, with title

110 Franz Schubert, Symphony No. 8 (<u>Unfinished</u>).

Recording, emphasis on composer

111 Claudio Monteverdi, <u>L'Orfeo</u>, dir. Nikolaus Harnoncourt, with Lajos Kozma, Concentus Musicus Wien, Telefunken, SKH 21/1-3, n.d.

Recording, emphasis on conductor

112 Herbert von Karajan, cond., Brahms' Symphony No. 1 in C minor, op. 68, Vienna Philharmonic Orchestra, London Records, STS 15194, 1960.

Note: See Appendix E for MLA policy on publishers' names.

BIBLIOGRAPHY (OR LIST OF WORKS CITED)

Nonprint Sources

Robinson, Phil Alden, dir. <u>Field of Dreams</u>. With Kevin Costner,
    Amy Madigan, and James Earl Jones. Universal, 1989.

Robbins, Jerome, dir. and chor. <u>Jerome Robbins' Broadway</u>.
    Imperial Theatre, New York, 14 June 1989.
(MLA puts a period after *New York*.)

Mehta, Zubin, dir. New York Philharmonic, Avery Fisher Hall,
    Lincoln Center, New York, 25 Nov. 1980.
(MLA puts a period after *New York*.)

Kylian, Jiri. <u>Return to the Strange Land</u>. With Cynthia Anderson
    and Michael Bjerknes. Joffrey Ballet, City Center, New York,
    19 Nov. 1980.
(MLA puts a period after *New York*.)

Hellman, Lillian. <u>The Little Foxes</u>. Dir. Austin Pendleton. With
    Elizabeth Taylor. Martin Beck Theatre, New York, 23 May 1981.
(MLA puts a period after *New York*.)

Mozart, Wolfgang Amadeus. Piano Concerto in B-flat major, K. 595.

Schubert, Franz. Symphony No. 8 (<u>Unfinished</u>).

Monteverdi, Claudio. <u>L'Orfeo</u>. Dir. Nikolaus Harnoncourt.
    With Lajos Kozma. Concentus Musicus Wien. Telefunken,
    SKH 21/1-3, n.d.

Karajan, Herbert von, cond. Brahms' Symphony No. 1 in C minor,
    op. 68. Vienna Philharmonic Orchestra. London Records, STS
    15194, 1960.

Note: See Appendix E for MLA policy on publishers' names.

NOTES

Nonprint Sources continued

Recording, emphasis on performer

     113 The Beatles, "The Long and Winding Road," Let It Be, Apple Records, n.d.

Recording, spoken

     114 Dylan Thomas, "Fern Hill," Dylan Thomas Reading, vol. 1, Caedmon, TC 1102, n.d.

Cassette

     115 Anne Paolucci, Dante and Machiavelli, audiocassette (Deland, Fla.: Everett/Edwards, n.d.).

Work of art

     116 Thomas Gainsborough, The Morning Walk, National Gallery, London.

Work of art, reproduction in book

     117 Anne Vallayer-Coster, The White Soup Bowl, private collection, Paris; plate 52 in Women Artists: 1550–1950, by Ann Sutherland Harris and Linda Nochlin (New York: Knopf, 1977), 82.
(MLA omits the comma before the page number.)

Television program

     118 The Stranger in the Empty Chair, writ. Paul Kresh, dir. Jack Kuney, prod. Bernice Belth, with Richard Kiley, WPIX-TV, 26 Apr. 1981.

Television program, episode in a series

     119 Norm Gorin, prod., "The Cop, the Kid, and the Knife," narr. Morley Safer, Sixty Minutes, CBS, New York, 16 Nov. 1980.

Letter to author

     120 Arthur Pearl, letters to author, 7 Feb. to 22 Mar. 1968.

Interview, telephone

     121 Thomas Purcell, telephone interview with author, 25 Oct. 1980.

Interview, in person

     122 Edward Teller, interview with author, 12 July 1962.

Note: See Appendix E for MLA policy on publishers' names.

BIBLIOGRAPHY (OR LIST OF WORKS CITED)

Nonprint Sources *continued*

The Beatles. "The Long and Winding Road." <u>Let It Be</u>. Apple
    Records, n.d.

Thomas, Dylan. "Fern Hill." <u>Dylan Thomas Reading</u>. Vol. 1.
    Caedmon, TC 1102, n.d.

Paolucci, Anne. Audiocassette. <u>Dante and Machiavelli</u>. Deland,
    Fla.: Everett/Edwards, n.d.

Gainsborough, Thomas. <u>The Morning Walk</u>. National Gallery, London.

Vallayer-Coster, Anne. <u>The White Soup Bowl</u>. Private Collection,
    Paris. Plate 52 in <u>Women Artists: 1550–1950</u>, by Ann
    Sutherland Harris and Linda Nochlin. New York: Knopf, 1977.
(MLA puts a period after the book title and capitalizes *by*.)

<u>The Stranger in the Empty Chair</u>. Writ. Paul Kresh. Dir. Jack
    Kuney. Prod. Bernice Belth. With Richard Kiley. WPIX–TV,
    26 Apr. 1981.
(MLA puts a period after *TV*.)

Gorin, Norm, prod. "The Cop, the Kid, and the Knife." Narr.
    Morley Safer. <u>Sixty Minutes</u>. CBS, New York, 16 Nov. 1980.
(MLA puts a period after *New York*.)

Pearl, Arthur. Letters to author. 7 Feb. to 22 Mar. 1968.

Purcell, Thomas. Telephone interview. 25 Oct. 1980.

Teller, Edward. Personal interview. 12 July 1962.

Note: See Appendix E for MLA policy on publishers' names.

NOTES

Nonprint Sources continued

Paper read at a meeting

> 123 J. R. Nichols, "Opiates as Reinforcing Agents: Some Variables Which Influence Drug–Seeking in Animals," paper delivered at the American Psychological Association, Washington, 7 Sept. 1967.
> (MLA omits *paper delivered at the.*)

NOTES

Microform Materials

Information service

> 124 James J. Groark, <u>Utilization of Library Resources by Students in Non–residential Degree Programs</u> (ERIC, ED 121 236, 1974), 7.
> (MLA puts a colon rather than a comma after the date.)

Microform, identification of type

> 125 Allardyce Nicoll and George Freeley, eds., <u>American Drama of the Nineteenth Century</u>, micro–opaque (New York: Readex Microprint, 1965–).

NOTES

Computer Materials

Computer software

> 126 <u>Visispell: Fut.heuristix</u>, computer software, version 1.00 (San Jose: Visicorp, 1983), disk.

Material from a computer service

> 127 "Johnson, Susannah Carrie," <u>American Men and Women of Science</u>, 15th ed. (New York: Bowker, 1983), DIALOG file 257, item 0105622.

CD-ROM

> 128 <u>Million Dollar Dictionary</u> CD–ROM (New York: Dun's Marketing Service, 1988).

Note: See Appendix E for MLA policy on publishers' names.

BIBLIOGRAPHY (OR LIST OF WORKS CITED)

Nonprint Sources continued

Nichols, J. R. "Opiates as Reinforcing Agents: Some Variables Which Influence Drug-Seeking in Animals." Paper delivered at the American Psychological Association. Washington, 7 Sept. 1967.
(MLA omits *Paper delivered at the.*)

BIBLIOGRAPHY (OR LIST OF WORKS CITED)

Microform Materials

Groark, James J. Utilization of Library Resources by Students in Non-residential Degree Programs. ERIC, 1974. ED 121 236.

Nicoll, Allardyce, and George Freeley, eds. American Drama of the Nineteenth Century. Micro-opaque. New York: Readex Microprint, 1965-.

BIBLIOGRAPHY (OR LIST OF WORKS CITED)

Computer Materials

Visispell: Fut.heuristix. Computer software. Version 1.00. San Jose: Visicorp, 1983. Disk.

"Johnson, Susannah Carrie." American Men and Women of Science. 15th ed. New York: Bowker, 1983. DIALOG file 257, item 0105622.

Million Dollar Dictionary. CD-ROM. New York: Dun's Marketing Service, 1988.

Note: See Appendix E for MLA policy on publishers' names.

6 TABLES, FIGURES, AND COMPUTER MATERIALS

Graphic representations of data can help make the results of your research comprehensible to your reader. Tables and figures (graphs, maps, diagrams, and photographs) can buttress your argument by revealing complex relationships in a way that prose alone often cannot.

TABLES

The data that you collect constitute the evidence on which your inferences and conclusions are based. Large quantities of statistics or numerical data should be tabulated in the interest of both brevity and clarity. Not all statistical matter, however, need be presented in tabular form. If statistics fit smoothly into the text, so much the better. For example, you would not tabulate the following numbers if you had no additional data: "The 607 delegates, representing seventeen nations, voted 402 to 205 in favor of the resolution." A simple array of data may be presented informally in the text:

```
and the class members were about evenly divided on the

candidates, as is shown in these results:
```

	Boys	Girls	Total
For Smith	17	16	33
For Brown	13	15	28
Total	30	31	61

Long series of numbers in the body of a paper can interfere with the development of an argument. Readers who are interested more in summaries and conclusions than in details may be distracted by masses of statistics in the text. Although complete and original data should be available in an appendix (see pages 202 and 203 for an example of a master data sheet), tables in the text itself should contain only quantified information such as totals and subtotals, rank-order relationships, and results of statistical analyses.

Clarity and unity in tables

A table should not try to present too many kinds of data or show too many relationships. It should have a clear and unified purpose. Of course, a table may present a large quantity of data, but the data should be organized so that they are easily assimilable. Tables within the body of the text should be as brief as clarity permits. Very long and complex tables usually belong in an appendix.

Relation of Tables and Text

To help your reader comprehend the data in a table, you should provide a clear introduction. The introduction might explain the principles governing the table or state the significance of the data. It definitely should explain how the data support your thesis.

Independence of tables and text

Two general rules apply to the relationship between tables and text. First, a table should be so constructed that it may be read and understood without reference to the text. For those readers who wish to study only the statistical data, tables should be organized logically and explained fully in a caption, or title. Second, the text should be so complete that readers can follow the argument without referring to the tables. You should incorporate into the body of the paper enough analytical and summary statements derived from each table to provide a coherent and valid report of actual findings.

References to tables

Tables should be placed as close as possible to the discussion of the facts or data in the text. If a table appears within the two or three pages following the first reference to it, only the number of the table need be given in the text ("Table 3 shows . . . "). Tables that are farther away from their initial mention in the text should be referred to by table number and page number ("Table 4 on page 13 shows . . . "). Avoid using imprecise phrases like "in the following table" and "in the table above," which may be confusing when the table is not immediately visible.

Tables on separate pages

You may wish to place some tables on separate pages. When you have a table that occupies more than half of a page or when you wish to place a table broadside, or lengthwise, you will want to devote a separate page to it. Also, when you generate a table on software other than your word-processing program, you probably will want to enter it on a separate page. Placing a table on a separate page makes revision easy because retyping or reprinting the text does not affect the table.

Captions

Each table must have a caption, or title, that tells concisely and clearly what the table contains. (The table of contents in the preliminary pages should list tables by number and caption.) The caption should not repeat material from the table column headings or interpret the data presented in the table. Rather, it should be a descriptive phrase:

```
Table 4.  Coastal Vertical Movement of Rocks at Las Cruces
```

not

```
Table 4.  Coastal Vertical Movement of Rocks at Las Cruces
before and after the 3 March 1985 Earthquake
```
(This caption unnecessarily repeats headings from the table.)

Use participial constructions rather than relative clauses.

```
Numbers of Minority Students Attending College, 1980—88
```

not

```
Numbers of Minority Students Who Attended College, 1980—88
```
(This caption contains a wordy construction, the relative clause.)

Even though you may use abbreviations in table columns, you should not use them in captions.

Place the caption above the table. You may use one of three formats for table captions: inverted pyramid, block style, and paragraph style.

Inverted-pyramid captions

Captions in the inverted-pyramid format generally use uppercase and lowercase letters, though all uppercase letters may be used. The rules for the capitalization of such captions are the same as the rules for capitalizing other titles: capitalize the first word, the last word, and all principal words, with the exception of articles (*a, an, the*), coordinate conjunctions (*and, but, or, for, nor, yet, so*), prepositions (*to, at, before, between,* for example), and the word *to* in an infinitive (when these words fall in the middle of the title). The caption should not have end punctuation. The caption is centered between the left and right margins. Additional lines are centered below the first line.

Table 7

Distribution of American Tax Dollars among
Local, State, and Federal Governments,
1912 and 1988

or

TABLE 7

DISTRIBUTION OF AMERICAN TAX DOLLARS AMONG
LOCAL, STATE, AND FEDERAL GOVERNMENTS,
1912 AND 1988

Block-style captions

Alternatively, you may use the block style, which places captions flush with the left margin of the table.

Table 7. Distribution of American Tax Dollars among
Local, State and Federal Governments, 1912 and 1988

Paragraph-style captions

The paragraph format indents the first word of the caption five spaces and brings the following line back to the left margin of the table.

   Table 7. Distribution of American Tax Dollars among
Local, State, and Federal Governments, 1912 and 1988

Use throughout your paper whichever format you adopt.

Numbering

Tables should be numbered with arabic numerals (not roman numerals). Tables, including those that appear in appendixes, may be numbered consecutively throughout the paper. If the last table in the text is Table 23, the first table in Appendix A would be Table 24. Alternatively, tables may be double-numbered by chapter. The numbers, separated by a period, represent the chapter number and the number of the table in that chapter, respectively. Table 3.7 would be the seventh table in Chapter 3; Table 4.1 would be the first table in Chapter 4. This system is particularly useful when you have many tables.

Some individuals and institutions prefer to use all capital letters for the word *table*, as in TABLE 7.

Columns and Rows

The body of a table consists of vertical columns and horizontal rows. Computer programs with the capacity to generate spreadsheets, adjust columns, or generate rules may help you create formats for your tables. If you are using a typewriter, you can devise table formats by using the underline key for horizontal lines and adding vertical lines by hand. If your table can be read easily, vertical rules may be omitted.

Descriptive column headings

Columns should have appropriate descriptive headings (called *boxheadings* when they are enclosed by vertical and horizontal rules). Column headings may have subheads, placed in parentheses. If two or more levels of headings are needed, then *decked heads* must be used. In a decked head, two or more related columns are positioned beneath a *spanner head*. A horizontal rule separates the spanner and column heads. In the following example of decked heads, the spanner heads are "Avg. wages in mfg." and "Avg. federal income tax," and the column heads are "Men," "Women," and "Total."

Avg. wages in mfg.			Avg. federal income tax		
Men	Women	Total	Men	Women	Total

Punctuation and capitalization of column heads

Capitalize the first word of a table heading, as well as any other word that requires capitalization in a sentence (proper nouns, for example). All other words should be in lowercase. Headings do not take end punctuation. You may use abbreviations, provided their meaning is obvious, to create well-proportioned tables. Possibly ambiguous abbreviations should be clarified with a note or key.

When a table consists of numerous columns or when frequent reference will be made to specific columns, number the columns from left to right. Enclose each column number in parentheses: (1), (2), (3), and so forth (see page 197). Then in the text you may refer to columns by number.

Horizontal rules

Closely spaced, double horizontal rules (or a single rule) should be placed at the top of the table. A single horizontal rule goes below the column headings—at least one-half space below so as not to look like underlining—and double or single rules go at the bottom of the table. When a table continues on to a second page, the bottom rule appears only at the end of the table, not at the end of each page.

Footnotes for Tables

Tables and figures (see pages 196 through 211) may require footnotes that reveal the source of the data or give explanatory information.

Independent notes for each table Each table should have an independent series of footnotes, regardless of whether the table is located in the text or in a separate section. Footnotes should be placed at the end of the table, even if the paper contains endnotes or footnotes. Each table should be self-contained.

Superscripts in tables Lowercase letters or standard reference symbols may be used as superscripts in tables. Lowercase letters should begin with [a] and proceed alphabetically, as in superscript[a] and superscript[b]. When superscript letters might be confusing, as in tables consisting of mathematical or chemical equations, standard reference symbols should be used. The customary order of symbols is asterisk ($*$), dagger ($\dagger$), double dagger ($\ddagger$), section mark ($\S$), parallels ($\parallel$), two asterisks ($**$), two daggers ($\dagger\dagger$), and so on. If your typewriter or printer does not have these symbols, you should draw them neatly by hand. Symbols should appear as a self-contained series on each page, as well as with each table.

A note that applies to the table as a whole or to the title of the table is not indicated by a superscript. The word *Note*, followed by a colon, should be placed below the table.

Oversize Tables

Long tables Some tables are too large to fit on one page. When tables are too long, you have three options. You may use photography or xerography to reduce the table. (Be sure that the reduced version is legible.) You may divide the table and place sections side by side on a broadside page (see page 200). Or you may spread the table over two or more pages. When a table continues beyond one page, you do not need to repeat the caption. Repeat only the table number, followed by a comma and the word *continued*: `Table 4.7,` `continued` (see the example on pages 198 and 199). The column headings and subheadings should be repeated on every page. Only the final page of the table should have a bottom rule.

Wide tables When tables are too wide and cannot be divided into two or more separately numbered tables, you have three options. Preferred practice is to turn a wide table broadside, or lengthwise, on the page, so that the left side of the table is at the bottom of the page and the right side is at the top (see the table on page 200). No text should appear on any page with a broadside table; the page number appears in the usual place.

If the table will not fit broadside, you may present the table across two facing pages. Half of the table goes on a left-hand page, half on a right-hand page (see pages 198 and 199). The right-hand page preceding the first page of the table should be left blank. The horizontal rules at the top of a two-page table should align perfectly across the two pages. If your software or printer cannot generate tables on facing pages, you may want to create the table in two sections and photocopy one section to use in your final copy.

Another option is to fold the page containing an overly wide table, following the instructions on pages 188 and 189.

Tables too long and too wide When tables are too long and too wide, you may consider several solutions. Material may be placed broadside and continued onto one or more pages. Material may be reduced photographically or xerographically so that it fits within the standard margins, or six-by-nine inches. Or the page containing the table may be folded (see pages 188 and 189 for folding instructions).

FIGURES

The term *figure* usually refers to any kind of graphic representation or illustration, whether in the text or in an appendix. Figures include graphs, charts, drawings, diagrams, maps, photographs, blueprints, and some kinds of computer print-outs. Pages containing only photographs may be designated as either plates or figures. If you plan to use illustrations, be sure that you possess or have access to the skills and materials required for a satisfactory finished product. You should investigate the problems and expense of illustrations before you plan a paper around them. Software programs allow you to generate numerous kinds of figures and graphics on a computer. In addition to information and suggestions that may be obtained from commercial advertisers, suppliers, lithographers, and printers, the assistance of faculty in departments such as architecture, computer science, graphic arts, and industrial arts may be valuable.

Relation of Figures and Text

The reader is most likely to understand the concepts and information contained in a figure if you provide an appropriate introduction in the text. The introduction may be a description of the figure or a statement of its significance. You need to show your reader that the content of the figure contributes to your argument.

Independence of figures and text

Like tables, figures should be designed so that they can be read and understood without reference to the text. Captions should be fully descriptive. Moreover, the text should be so complete that the reader can follow the argument without examining the figures. The text, however, should refer to each figure and explain or analyze its content.

References to figures

If a figure appears within the two or three pages following the first reference to it, only the number of the figure need be given in the text ("Figure 4 shows . . . "). When you refer to a figure that is farther away from its initial mention, you should provide both figure number and page number ("Figure 5 on page 19 shows . . . ").

Captions

Each figure must have a caption, or title, that tells concisely and clearly what the figure contains. Avoid wordy introductory phrases such as "Graph showing" or "Chart representing." Captions should be placed below the figure. The table of contents should list figures by number and caption.

When you have a typed or printed figure, you may wish to type or print the caption as well. If the figure is a drawing or photograph, you may print the caption in India ink or use transfer letters. The format and punctuation of captions for figures are the same as those for tables (see page 182).

Numbering

Figure, like tables, should be numbered with arabic numerals (not roman numerals). Figures, including those that appear in appendixes, may be numbered consecutively throughout the paper. If the last figure in the text is Figure 9, the first figure in Appendix A would be Figure 10. Alternatively, figures, like tables, may be double-numbered by chapter (see pages 183 and 184). Figure 1.1 would be the first figure in Chapter 1; Figure 2.2 would be the second figure in Chapter 2.

If the total number of illustrations in your paper is small, then each illustration may be labeled and numbered as a figure regardless of whether it is a map, a graph, a diagram, or whatever. If your paper has more than ten illustrations of any one type (more than ten graphs or more than ten maps, for example), you should identify each type and give it a separate sequence of numbers. A series of maps would be numbered as Map 1, Map 2, . . . , Map 12, and so on. A series of photographs would be numbered as Photo 1, Photo 2; a series of graphs as Graph 1, Graph 2, . . . , Graph 20. (If you number by chapter, the sequences would be Map 1.1, Map 1.2, Map 2.1, Map 2.2, and so on.)

Hand-drawn and Computer-generated Graphs

Line, bar, area, and volume graphs effectively convey quantitative and proportional data. They may be drawn by hand, but it is also possible to generate them with computer software.

Line graphs   **DESIGN OF GRAPHS**   A line graph shows the relationship between two or more variables. The data have a range of some kind, such as time, age, distance, or weight. Line graphs may be plotted on rectangular coordinate paper or generated on a computer. The graphs at the top and bottom of page 205 are line graphs.

Bar graphs   Bar graphs consist of a series of heavy lines or bars arranged to show the relationships among certain data or groups of data (see the middle figure on page 205). Bar graphs may be divided into two categories. One type consists of bars of different lengths and allows direct comparison of quantities or percentages. Each bar may be shaded to show varying degrees of component elements. The other type consists of bars of the same length. The bars usually represent 100 percent or some other unit and are shaded to allow comparison of component elements.

Area and volume graphs   Area and volume graphs show relationships between or among quantities. The so-called pie chart or circle graph is the best-known example. The entire pie represents 100 percent, and the size of each slice indicates the appropriate proportion of the whole. A common method of emphasizing one element is to arrange the pie to look as though a slice (the factor to be stressed) has been cut and slightly withdrawn (see the pie charts on page 208).

PRESENTATION OF NUMERICAL DATA IN GRAPHS   Whatever the design or technology you use to generate a graph, you will want to observe the conventions pertaining to the presentation of numerical data.

1. Scales of numerical value read from left to right and usually from bottom to top.
2. If one or both scales have a zero point, it should be indicated, even if a break in the continuity of the scale must be drawn.
3. Scales that are based on percentages should indicate clearly the basis of comparison.
4. Scale values should be placed toward the outside of the figure; normally, this is to the left of the vertical scale and below the horizontal scale.
5. The exact numerical data from which a graph is produced should be included either in the figure or in an accompanying table.
6. A key or legend must be included when symbols or distances are not otherwise explained.

Mounted Illustrations

A photograph, map, or printed form smaller than the regular page should be mounted on thesis paper or on heavier paper, depending on the thickness and weight of the illustration. Use rubber cement or dry mounting tissue and allow the page to dry or set thoroughly.

Plates

Pages consisting of or containing only photographs are frequently referred to as *plates*. The plate number and caption may be placed at the top of the page or, in the case of a full-page photograph, centered on the preceding left-hand page (see pages 206 and 207). Departmental practice and preference should be followed consistently in the preparation, placement, and labeling of plates. A list of plates ordinarily follows the table of contents in the preliminaries.

Captions

Captions for mounted illustrations may be typed, lettered by hand, or made from dry-transfer letters. Captions should be entered on the page before the illustrations are mounted.

Oversize Figures

Photographic reduction

A figure that is too large to fit on a standard page may be folded or photographically reduced. Reduction is generally preferable as long as the material remains easily readable.

Folding large figures and tables

If you decide to fold an overly wide figure or table, you must make the fold or folds in such a way that the figure cannot be accidentally caught up in the binding. A wide figure should be folded from right to left—that is, the left side should be fixed in the binding and the right side should be folded in. Take the right side of the figure and fold it to the left, placing the right edge one-and-one-half inches from the left margin. If more than one fold is necessary, bring the next fold over to two-and-one-half inches from the left side of the page. Additional folds should follow one inch to the right of the previous one.

An overly long figure or table should be folded from bottom to top. Follow the instructions above for horizontal folding. The bottom fold should be at least one inch from the bottom of the other pages in the text. You will need to cut a strip one inch wide from the left side of the folded section so that it will miss the binding.

Avoid folding oversize figures and tables in two directions.

Supplies for Creating Figures

Illustrations pose special problems, so you may want to seek technical advice. Perhaps a college or university duplicating service, an instructional media center, or a department of architecture, art, graphic arts, or industrial arts may be able to assist you.

Paper The paper you use for figures should be similar in weight to the paper used for the text. Advisers generally want to approve any variation from the prescribed thesis paper. You would not expect objections to the use of full-size photographs or photostats. The inclusion of graphs on cross-ruled paper, however, may not be acceptable. If it is not, the figure may be prepared on graph paper and then photocopied, a process that generally makes the ruling invisible.

If your thesis or dissertation is to be microfilmed, you should investigate the advantages and limitations of various kinds of paper and materials. For example, India ink reproduces far better than ball-point pen, and blue ink does not reproduce well at all.

Aids for creating figures In planning for illustrations, you should find out which of the various technical or commercial aids will best suit your needs. You may need to investigate and decide among one or more of the following: computer-generated material, hand-drawn or commercially prepared symbols and figures, dry-transfer or direct-application tape, translucent or opaque figures or tape, reproducible or nonreproducible copies, use of thesis paper only or inclusion also of sensitized paper and/or transparent film for the preparation of overlays. Computer-generated graphics can make most kinds of graphs and tables. Dry-transfer lines, shadings, and cross-hatching are readily available from artist supply houses and graphic arts companies (blueprinters, lithographers, printers). Dry-transfer figures and designs are applied directly to the paper by rubbing the upper surface of the material to which they adhere.

You will also have to decide whether the master copies of illustrations are to be photocopied, photostated, or xerocopied for inclusion in each copy of the paper, or whether an original illustration is to be drawn or otherwise prepared for each copy. If only one set of illustrations is to be prepared, the master copies need to be done with paper and ink that reproduce well.

COMPUTER MATERIALS

The increasing use of computers in research requires special attention to the location and availability of computer programs, original data, and computer output.

Computer Programs

If published programs are used, the source note for the figure should include not only the usual citation but also the name of the machine used, the configuration, and the source language. If the program is available only locally or if it was prepared especially for your investigation, it should be reproduced by computer print-out (see page 210 for an example). Page numbers, captions, explanations, and notes as needed should be added by typewriter.

Computer Output

Print-outs are the output category of computer material. You will have to decide which tables, flow charts, maps, and other computer output are to be incorporated into the text and which are best placed in an appendix. Factors such as accuracy, appearance, feasibility, and size should be considered when you decide whether to use print-outs, reproduced copies of print-outs, or typescript copies for material included in the text.

TYPING, PRINTING, AND LAYOUT INSTRUCTIONS

Tables

SMALL TABLES   The following guidelines apply to placing within the text tables that are one page or less in length:

1. Place each small table on one page.
2. Include textual material on the page with a table that occupies less than half of the page.
3. Quadruple-space from the text to a table and from a table to the text.
4. Place the table between complete paragraphs. Avoid inserting a table into the middle of a paragraph, even if you have to leave some extra space on the page.

LARGE TABLES   For tables that are too large to fit on one page, apply the following guidelines as appropriate:

1. If a table is too long but can be satisfactorily contained in a space no wider than three inches, place two equal parts side by side and separate them with a double rule. If a table can be contained in a space ranging from three to four and one-half inches, double it up as just described and place it broadside on the page (see page 200).
2. If a table is too long for one page and too wide to be doubled up, continue it on one or more pages. At the top of each new page, repeat the table number, followed by a comma and the word *continued*; omit the table caption; and repeat all the column headings. Put the bottom rule on only the last page of the table (see the table on pages 198 and 199).
3. If a table is too wide or too long and too wide, look for ways to divide it into two or more tables; otherwise, give serious consideration to reducing the table photographically. The final reduced copy should measure about six-by-nine inches and be completely legible. The reduced copy should not include the caption or any of the surrounding text.
4. If a table is between six and nine inches wide, and you prefer not to reduce it photographically, place it broadside on the page with the top of the table to the left, toward the binding of your paper (see page 200). Continue the table broadside on subsequent pages as necessary.
5. As a last resort, place the table either vertically or broadside on a sheet no longer than eleven inches from top to bottom and fold (for folding instructions, see pages 188 and 189). When the sheet has been folded, place the page number in its regular location.

MARGINS   The width of a table depends on its content. If a table is less than six inches wide, center it between the margins. Try to leave at least one-inch margins; three-fourths of an inch should be the minimum. Remember that a one-and-one-half-inch margin must be maintained on the left.

PAGINATION Place the page number in its usual position in the upper right-hand corner on all pages containing tables. If the margins have been decreased, adjust the placement of the page number accordingly.

CAPTIONS There are three formats for table captions: inverted pyramid, block style, and paragraph style. Determine your department's preference (if any) and then use the chosen format consistently. Single-space captions and place them above the table. Single-space from the caption to the top rule of the table. Begin the table with a single horizontal rule or two closely spaced horizontal rules extending the width of the table.

Inverted-pyramid format

The following examples show the inverted-pyramid format. Follow these guidelines when using it:

1. Center the table number and caption between the margins.
2. Double-space from the table number to the caption.
3. When a caption is longer than one line, make each succeeding line shorter than the line above it and center it on the line above.

Table 14

Intelligence Scores of Fathers and Sons

Table 7

Commodity Value Added by Sector (1879 Prices)
Average Decennial Rates of Change

Table 1.3

MULTIPLE CORRELATIONS AND REGRESSION EQUATIONS
INVOLVING GPA, ACT, AND STUDY HOURS FOR
THE FINAL SAMPLE DURING NONSTRESS WEEK

Block-style format

Block-style captions start flush with the left margin of the table, which might not coincide with the left margin of the page.

Table 3. Multiple Correlations and Regression Equations
Involving GPA, ACT, and Study Hours for the Final Sample
during Nonstress Week

Paragraph-style format

The first line of a caption in the paragraph-style format is indented five spaces from the left margin of the table, which might not be the same as the left margin of the page.

Table 9.3 Means, Variances, Standard Deviations, and Expected Probabilities of the Outcome

Column headings

SPACING   The spacing and proportion of the column headings and body of a table should contribute to its clarity. Follow these guidelines for spacing column headings:

1. Leave a blank space above and below all column headings; single-space within headings; and leave at least one space on either side of the longest heading.
2. Center headings between the vertical rules that enclose them or, if there are no vertical rules, in the space allowed for each column. Enclose subheadings in parentheses and center them below the main heading.
3. Align the bottom lines of all column headings on the same plane.
4. Type or print a horizontal rule (use the underscore key) one single space below the column headings.
5. If the top headings are too long, they may be typed either vertically or with a vertical slant up to the right (see pages 202 and 203).
6. If you number the columns, place the numerals in parentheses on the next line below the lowest order of column headings (see page 197).

Table body

Follow these guidelines for spacing items in the body of a table:

1. Leave enough space between columns so that each entry stands out as a separate item that can be read easily.
2. If columns are divided by vertical rules, leave at least one space on each side of the longest entry.
3. Align columns of words on the left.
4. Align columns of numbers on their decimal points.

```
Number of samples included       324
Number of titrations made          6
Average of findings             32.6
Mean variation of findings     2.456
```

5. In mixed columns of numbers and other items, align the numbers on their decimal points and center other items in the column.
6. Single-space within items and use one-and-one-half spaces or a double space between items, unless space availability or restrictions indicate a more desirable spacing.

FOOTNOTES   Double-space below the bottom rule of the table or, if the table continues on to additional pages, below the last line of material. Indent table footnotes five spaces from the left margin of the table. Space them as you space footnotes in the text.

Figures

The following guidelines, listed in order of priority, apply to the placement of figures in the text:

1. Confine each figure to one page if possible. Leave the usual margins.
2. Include textual material on the page with a figure that occupies no more than half of the page (but see item 4 below). Begin the page with textual material. Quadruple-space from the text to a figure and from a figure to the text.
3. Place a figure between complete paragraphs. Do not interrupt a paragraph with a figure.
4. Some figures may be placed on separate pages. These include figures requiring special artwork that would be difficult to insert in a typed or printed manuscript and figures that must be increased or reduced in scale. A series of small figures discussed together in the text may be grouped together on one page (see page 205).
5. If photographic reduction is not practical, fold a figure that is too large for one page (see pages 188 and 189 for folding instructions).

PAGINATION Place the assigned page number in its usual position in the upper right-hand corner on all pages containing figures. Type or print the page number on a folded figure after the page has been folded.

CAPTIONS Place the caption one quadruple space or more below the figure, centered between the margins. Choose a format from among the formats for captions shown on page 182.

FOOTNOTES If a footnote is needed, double-space below the caption and insert the note. Alternatively, you may place a footnote in an open space within the figure, as long as the footnote does not interfere with the clear presentation of your illustration.

TABLES, FIGURES, AND COMPUTER MATERIALS

Sample Pages

Table 3

A Comparison of DAT Subtest Scores and Ninth-
Grade Semester Grades for Algebra

DAT subtest	N	r	Percentage of efficiency	Mean	S.D.
Verbal Reasoning	129	.31[a]	4.61	25.85	8.46
Numerical Ability	132	.51[a]	13.40	19.10	7.06
Abstract Reasoning	124	.29[a]	4.00	34.00	8.44
Space Relations	123	.20[b]	2.02	47.85	19.94

[a] Correlation significant at the .01 level.

[b] Correlation significant at the .05 level.

Table 4 shows correlations of the Differential Aptitude Test
subtest scores with grades in Spanish. The correlations of .57
(Verbal Reasoning), .43 (Spelling), and .58 (Sentences) were
significant at the .01 level.

Table 4

A Comparison of DAT Subtest Scores and Ninth-
Grade Semester Grades for Spanish

DAT subtest	N	r	Percentage of efficiency	Mean	S.D.
Verbal Reasoning	74	.57[a]	17.15	22.10	8.46
Spelling	68	.43[a]	9.72	44.95	22.53
Sentences	72	.58[a]	18.54	26.80	13.17

[a] Correlation significant at the .01 level.

Two short tables on a page with text

Table 1.4

Annual Earnings Forgone while Attending High School and
College and University, Adjusted and Not Adjusted for
Unemployment, 1900 to 1956, in Current Prices

Year (1)	Average weekly earnings, all manufacturing (dollars) (2)	Annual earnings forgone per student while attending			
		High school		College and university	
		Unadjusted (dollars) (3)	Adjusted for unemployment (dollars) (4)	Unadjusted (dollars) (5)	Adjusted for unemployment (dollars) (6)
1900	8.37	92	84	209	192
1910	10.74	118	113	269	259
1920	26.12	287	275	653	626
1930	23.25	256	224	581	509
1940	25.20	277	236	630	537
1950	59.33	653	626	1,483	1,422
1956	80.13	881	855	2,003	1,943

Sources:

Column 2: Economic Report of the President, January, 1957,
Table E-25, and U.S. Department of Labor; and Historical Statistics
of the United States, 1789-1945, a Supplement to Statistical
Abstract of the United States, 1949, Series D, 134-44.

Column 3: For high school students, Col. (2) multiplied by 11.

Column 5: For college and university students, Col. (2)
multiplied by 25.

Columns 4 and 6: The percent unemployed is based on Clarence D.
Long, The Labor Force under Changing Income and Employment
(Princeton: Princeton Univ. Press, 1958), Appendix C, Table C-1,
and for 1956, Table C-2.

**Single-page table with vertical rules, column numbers, source of
information, and spanner headings**

Table 13

Accident Reports in Government Shops and in the Iron and
Steel and the Machine-Building Industries

Week in which disability terminated	Government shops		Iron and steel (1910)	Machine building (1912)
	Arsenals (1912)	Navy yards (1912)		
(No. of 300-day workers	3,992	15,608	65,147	15,703)

No. of disabilities terminating in specified week

	Arsenals	Navy yards	Iron and steel	Machine building
First week	89	535	9,889	7,680
Second week	27	153	4,433	2,048
Third week	57	339	1,915	869
Fourth week	57	257	1,014	512
Fifth week	15	129	807	272
Sixth week and later	55	320	1,251	621
Total	300	1,733	19,309	12,002

Percentages

	Arsenals	Navy yards	Iron and steel	Machine building
First week	30	31	51	64
Second week	9	9	23	17
Third week	19	20	10	7
Fourth week	19	15	5	5
Fifth week	5	7	4	2
Sixth week and later	18	18	7	5
Total	100	100	100	100

Table 13, continued

Week in which disability terminated	Government shops		Iron and steel (1910)	Machine building (1912)
	Arsenals (1912)	Navy yards (1912)		

Percentages (excluding all under the third week)

Third week	31	32	39	38
Fourth week	31	25	20	23
Fifth week	8	12	16	12
Sixth week and later	30	31	25	27
Total	100	100	100	100

Accident frequency rates (per 1,000 300-day workers)

First week	22	34	152	66
Second week	7	10	68	18
Third week	14	22	29	8
Fourth week	14	17	16	4
Fifth week	4	8	12	2
Sixth week and later	14	21	19	5
Total	75	112	296	103

Long table on facing pages

APPENDIX D

Table 19. Spelling Scores of the DAT and First Semester Grades in Spanish for 68 Freshmen at Roosevelt High School (r = .43)

Raw Score	No. receiving grade of					Total students
	F	D	C	B	A	
90–94						
85–89				1		1
80–84			1	2		3
75–79			1	2	2	5
70–74				1		1
65–69				3	1	4
60–64			4	1	1	6
55–59	1	1		1	2	5
50–54	1	2	1	2	1	7
45–49			2		1	3
40–44	1		3	1	1	6
35–39		2	1	1		4
30–34		1	3	2		6
25–29	1		1		1	3
20–24		2	1			3
15–19		1		1		2
10–14	1		2			3
5– 9	1	1		1		3
0– 4	1	2				3

Broadside table with doubled-up columns separated by two vertical lines

Table 3

Representative Microprobe Analyses of Amphibole and Chlorite

Weight % oxides

	1	2	3	4	5	6
SiO_2	39.1	41.4	40.8	39.9	33.2	33.58
TiO_2	0.10	0.08	0.32	0.34	0.04	0.064
Al_2O_3	20.8	21.8	14.4	20.0	12.7	13.5
FeO	12.0	15.04	18.4	12.3	4.72	9.21
MnO	0.50	0.45	0.31	0.43	0.07	0.21
MgO	9.20	6.80	7.28	8.83	30.3	28.9
CaO	7.50	7.04	9.90	7.47	0.12	0.18
Na_2O	6.27	6.83	4.37	6.20	0.00	0.002
K2O	0.37	0.49	0.18	0.31	0.08	-
Total	95.8	99.9	95.9	95.7	81.3	85.65

Cations for 23 Oxygens

(24 oxygens for chlorite)

	1	2	3	4	5	6
Si	5.86	5.99	6.30	5.97	5.76	5.66
${}^{iv}Al$	2.14	2.01	1.70	2.03	2.24	2.34
Ti	0.012	0.009	0.037	0.038	0.005	0.009
Al	1.52	1.70	0.92	1.50	0.36	0.35
Fe	1.50	1.82	2.37	1.54	0.68	1.30
Mn	0.064	0.055	0.040	0.054	0.008	0.032
Mg	2.05	1.47	1.68	1.97	7.84	7.26
Sum C	5.15	5.05	5.04	5.10		
Ca	1.20	1.09	1.64	1.20	0.024	0.032
Na_B	0.65	0.86	0.32	0.70	0.000	0.000
Sum B	2.00	2.00	2.00	2.00		
Na_A	1.17	1.06	0.99	1.10		
K	0.070	0.090	0.036	0.060	0.016	
Total	16.24	16.15	16.03	16.16	16.94	16.98

1. magnesio-alumino taramite, MVJ84-9C.
2. alumino taramite, MVJ84-9B.
3. ferroan pargasite, LACMNH 20370.
4. magnesio-alumino taramite, R-15.
5. clinochlore, MVJ84-42-2.
6. clinochlore, R-10.

	Subject			Seat		Grades				Otis Test					Book List		Spy system
Case number	Age	Sex	Class	Seat row	Seat number	Course grade	University grade	Changed grade	Added	Marked wrong	Error in total	True score	Number checked	Fictitious	Case 1H	Case 2H	Case 3H
CLASS #1.																	
1	19	M	Fr.	4	5	3.3	2.8					45					
2	19	F	Fr.	1	2	3.3	3.3					33	19				
3	17	F	Fr.	1	4	1.0	1.0					38	12				
4	22	M	Jr.	1	7	2.7	1.5					37	12				
5	20	M	Jr.	1	6	5.0	4.9					54	22				
6	19	F	So.	1	8	2.0	2.6	1				42	13				
7	19	F	Fr.	1	9	1.0	1.0	1				37	18				
8	21	M	Fr.	1	10	3.3	3.0					50	23				
9	17	F	Fr.	1	11	2.0	2.0					36					
10	19	F	Fr.	2	1	1.0	1.0	(E corrected)				33	15				
11	18	F	Fr.	2	3	2.0	2.0					42	18				
12	18	F	So.	2	4	3.0	1.8	1	2			51	22				
13	21	M	So.	2	5	4.0	4.0				1	56	30	4			
14	18	F	Fr.	2	7	5.0	4.6					50	22	1			
15	25	M	Fr.	2	8	2.0	2.5					57	26				
16	20	F	Jr.	2	9	3.7	4.0					52	25				
17	20	M	Fr.	2	10	1.0	1.0	(E corrected)				47	23			X	X
18	21	M	So.	3	1	2.0	2.8					34	14			X	X
19	19	F	Fr.	3	3	3.0	3.0					50	9				
20	18	F	So.	3	4	1.0	1.0				1	39	27	1			
21	17	F	So.	3	5	1.0	1.7	1				45	16				
22	18	F	Fr.	3	6	3.0	3.0				1	35	9				
23	22	M	So.	3	7	3.0	2.8					51					
24	18	M	Fr.	3	8	3.0	3.4					52	27	1			
25	40	F	So.	3	9	4.0	4.0					49	27				
26	18	M	Jr.	3	10	4.7	4.8					47	28				
27	19	F	Fr.	1	1	3.0	2.1	7	11			39	32	6	X	X	X
28	21	F	Fr.	1	2	2.0	2.8	1		2		46	26	3	X	X	X
29	20	M	Jr.	4	5	1.0	2.8					35	22				
30	20	F	So.	1	3	4.0	3.6	2	7			37					
31	21	F	Jr.	1	5	4.0	3.0	2				60	20				
32	19	M	Fr.	1	7	1.0	2.8					49	5				
33	18	F	Fr.	1	9	2.0	2.0	1	1	1		43	20	1			
34	18	F	Jr.	1	10	3.0	3.7					53	28	1			
35	17	F	Fr.	2	1	4.0	3.1				1	47	26				
36	23	M	Jr.	1	11	1.0	1.8	2		1	1	29	12				
37	19	F	Fr.	2	2	1.0	2.0					36	18				
38	18	F	Fr.	2	3	2.0	2.8					41	16				
39	18	M	Fr.	2	6	1.7	1.7	(E corrected)				46	13				

Master data sheet on facing pages (this arrangement may not be acceptable in theses or dissertations; a data sheet of this size could be folded or reduced)

mental Group

2-2	2-0	2-	1-2	1-0	1-	0-2	0-0	0-	Own score	True score	Q#1	Q#2	Q#3	Q#4	Q#5	Q#6	Q#7	Q#8	Q#9
											N	N	Y	N	N	N	N	Y	Y
9	5	1	2	3	0	2	0	18	35	26	N	N	N	N	N	N	Y	Y	Y
5	9	0	1	4	2	0	0	19	35	12	Y	N	Y	N	N	N	N	N	Y
11	6	0	9	2	6	1	1	4	51	42	N	N	N	N	N	N	Y	Y	Y
26	6	0	1	1	0	2	4	0	6	58	N	N	N	N	N	N	N	N	Y
											Y	N	N	N	N	N	N	N	Y
5	5	0	10	5	4	1	2	8	39	32									
16	7	0	6	7	0	0	2	2	59	44	N	N	N	N	N	N	N	N	Y
											N	N	Y	N	N	N	Y	Y	Y
10	8	0	3	3	0	0	1	15	42	26	Y	N	N	N	N	N	N	N	Y
10	3	2	4	15	0	0	0	6	49	28	Y	N	N	Y	c	N	N	N	N
14	7	0	4	8	0	1	0	6	54	38	N	N	N	Y	acd	N	N	N	N
21	6	0	1	5	0	1	0	6	60	46	N	N	N	N	N	N	N	Y	Y
11	3	0	5	3	2	0	0	16	38	32	N	N	N	N	N	N	N	N	N
25	2	0	1	2	3	1	0	6	60	54	N	N	Y	N	N	N	Y	Y	Y
18	2	0	7	2	2	0	0	9	51	50	Y	N	N	N	N	N	N	N	Y
24	4	0	3	1	0	0	0	8	60	54	Y	N	Y	N	N	N	N	Y	Y
10	2	0	9	6	1	0	0	12	40	38	N	N	N	Y	N	N	N	N	N
24	3	0	3	3	1	0	0	6	61	54	Y	N	N	N	N	N	N	N	N
8	7	3	3	2	6	2	2	7	47	26	N	N	N	N	N	N	N	N	Y
11	10	1	2	4	3	0	0	9	53	26	N	N	N	N	N	N	N	N	Y
10	5	0	1	2	5	3	10	4	38	28	Y	N	N	Y	N	N	N	Y	Y
											Y	Y	Y	N		N	N	N	N
16	4	0	9	3	1	3	0	4	53	56	Y	N	Y	N	N	N	N	Y	Y
20	4	0	6	0	0	0	0	10	54	52	N	N	Y	N	a-e	Y	N	N	Y
18	5	0	2	4	0	1	0	10	52	42	Y	N	N	Y	N	N	N	Y	Y
17	12	1	3	5	0	0	1	1	68	40	Y	Y	N	N	N	N	N		Y
12	11	2	0	1	0	0	2	12	51	24	Y	Y	N	N	N	N	N	Y	N
13	12	0	1	5	2	1	2	4	58	30	N	N	N	N	N	N	N	Y	Y
10	4	0	7	7	3	0	0	9	45	34	N	N	N	Y	N	N	N	Y	N
10	1	0	0	5	0	0	0	24	27	20	N	N	Y	N	N	N	Y	Y	Y
7	6	1	6	0	1	0	0	19	36	26	Y	Y	N	N	ab	N	Y	Y	Y
20	2	1	6	3	3	0	0	5	58	52	N	N	N	N	ac	N	Y	Y	N
8	6	2	1	1	3	1	5	13	37	20	N	N	N	N	N	N	N	N	Y
12	7	1	0	2	1	0	7	10	43	24	Y	Y	N	N	Y	N	N	Y	N
6	8	2	2	2	1	0	0	19	37	16	N	N	N	Y	Y	N	N	Y	Y
6	6	0	4	2	0	0	0	22	30	20	Y	N	N	Y	N	N	N	Y	Y
16	7	1	0	0	0	1	2	13	48	34	Y	Y	Y	N	N	N	N	Y	N

In 1930, Folling discovered that phenylketonuria was actually a metabolic error. Figure 2 is a pictorial representation of competition for amino acid uptake into the brain.

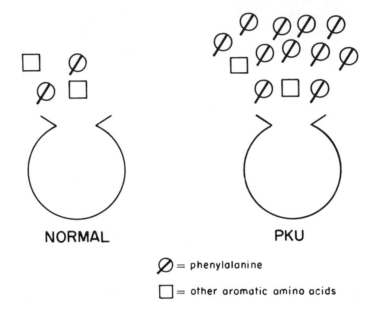

NORMAL   PKU

⊘ = phenylalanine

☐ = other aromatic amino acids

Figure 2

Competition for Uptake of
Amino Acids by Brain

Source: John A. Anderson and Kenneth F. Swaiman, eds., Phenylketonuria and Allied Metabolic Diseases, U.S., Department of Health, Education, and Welfare, Children's Bureau (Washington: GPO, 1967), 3.

The drawing at the left shows equal amounts of phenylalanine and other amino acids being taken up into the brain under normal conditions. If, as shown on the right, the system is loaded with huge amounts of phenylalanine, this reduces the opportunity for uptake of other amino acids that utilize the same catalytic site.

Hand-drawn illustration on a page with text

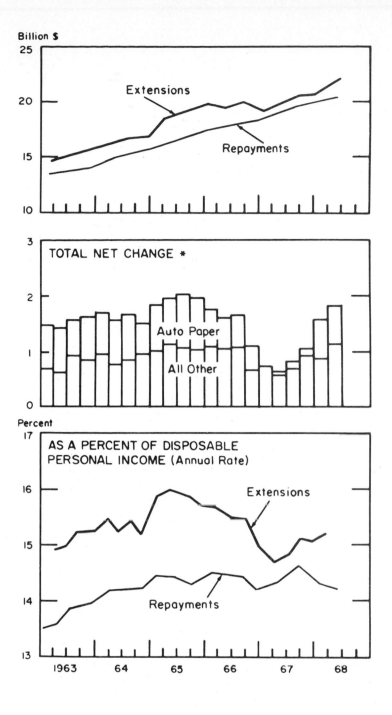

Chart 3

Consumer Installment Credit—Quarterly,
Seasonally Adjusted

*Extensions minus repayments

PLATE 2

RELATIVE LOCATIONS AND SURROUNDING TOPOGRAPHIES
OF LAKES A, B, AND C

Caption page for a plate

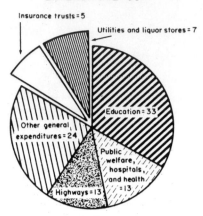

REVENUE=98

Utilities and liquor stores = 7

From Federal Government = 13

Property taxes = 25

Insurance trusts = 8

Sales and gross receipts taxes = 19

Charges and misc. = 13

Other taxes = 13

EXPENDITURE = 95

Insurance trusts = 5

Utilities and liquor stores = 7

Education = 33

Other general expenditures = 24

Public welfare, hospitals, and health = 13

Highways = 13

Figure 2.4

Distribution of State and Local Government
Revenue and Expenditure in 1966
(in Billions of Dollars)

FIGURE 2.4

DISTRIBUTION OF STATE AND LOCAL GOVERNMENT
REVENUE AND EXPENDITURE IN 1966
(IN BILLIONS OF DOLLARS)

Figure 2.4 Distribution of State and Local Government Revenue and
Expenditure in 1966 (in Billions of Dollars)

Figure 2.4 Distribution of State and Local Government Revenue
and Expenditure in 1966 (in Billions of Dollars)

**Pie charts with segments separated for emphasis and sample
caption formats**

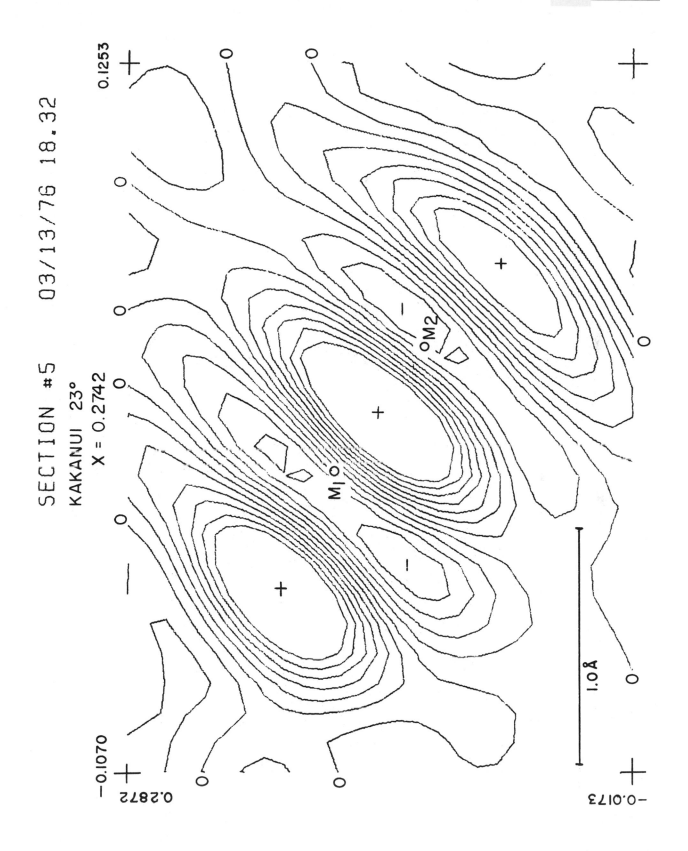

SECTION #5   03/13/76 18.32
KAKANUI 23°
X = 0.2742

0.1253

0.2872   −0.1070

−0.0173

1.0 Å

```
                PROGRAM DUST
C               TO CONVERT PARTICLE VOLUME DISTRIBUTION DATA INTO
C               PARTICLE COUNT ESTIMATE PER CHANGE OF STANTON DATA
                REAL*4 AREA(5),VOL(5,8),LABEL(15),SLABEL(15),PART(5,8),
              1 LENGTH(8),WIDTH(5)
                INTEGER*2 IPART(8)
                BYTE FILNAM(15)
                DATA WIDTH,LENGTH/1.5,3.75,7.5,15.0,30.0,1.5,3.75,7.5,15.0,30.0,
              1 60.0,120.0,240.0/
C
                IN=3
                OUT=6
                PI=3.14159
                DO 100 I=1,5
                AREA(I)=PI*(WIDTH(I)*0.5)**2
                DO 100 J=1,8
                VOL(I,J)=AREA(I)*LENGTH(J)
100             CONTINUE
C               OPEN INPUT DATA FILE BY ENTERING FILNAM
105             TYPE 1
1               FORMAT(' INPUT DATA FILE NAME: ',$)
                ACCEPT 2,FILNAM
2               FORMAT(15A1)
                I=ILEN(FILNAM,15)
C               REJECT IF FILNAM IF LENGTH IS 0 OR NEGATIVE
                IF(I.LE.0) GO TO 105
                CALL ASSIGN(IN,FILNAM,I,'OLD','NC')
C
                READ(IN,3) LABEL
3               FORMAT(15A4)
                WRITE(OUT,4) LABEL
4               FORMAT('1',15A4)
                READ(IN,5) ND
5               FORMAT(I3)
                DO 300 M=1,ND
                SUM=0.
                READ(IN,3) SLABEL
                WRITE(OUT,6) SLABEL
6               FORMAT('0',15A4)
                WRITE(OUT,7) LENGTH
7               FORMAT(' AVERAGE LENGTH:',8F13.2/' WIDTH')
                DO 200 I=1,5
                READ(IN,8) IPART
8               FORMAT(10I3)
                DO 200 J=1,8
                DART=IPART(J)/VOL(I,J)
                SUM=SUM+DART
                PART(I,J)=DART
200             CONTINUE
                SUM=100./SUM
                DO 240 I=1,5
                DO 220 J=1,8
                PART(I,J)=PART(I,J)*SUM
220             CONTINUE
                WRITE(OUT,9)WIDTH(I),(PART(I,J),J=1,8)
9               FORMAT(' ',F10.2,6X,8F13.3)
240             CONTINUE
300             CONTINUE
                TYPE 10
10              FORMAT(' ANOTHER DATA SET (1) OR STOP (0)? ',$)
                ACCEPT 5,I
                IF(I.GT.0) GOTO 105
                STOP
                END
```

Oversize computer program reduced photographically to fit on one page

Table 17

Crystal Structure of Mt. Gibele Anorthoclase, Quadripartite Sites
Bond Distances between 2.00 and 3.30 Angstroms

ATOM 1	X	Y	Z	ATOM 2	X	Y	Z	DISTANCE	NUMBER
T1O	0.00852	0.17107	0.21851						1
				T1M	-0.00600	0.18357	-0.22709	3.13991	6
				T2M	0.30948	0.12017	0.65035	3.07848	12
T1O	0.50852	-0.32893	0.21851						2
				T2M	0.69052	-0.12017	0.34965	2.99342	10
T1O	-0.00852	-0.17107	-0.21851						3
				T1M	0.00600	-0.18357	0.22709	3.13991	4
				T2O	0.30672	-0.11149	-0.32887	3.13515	8
T1M	0.00600	-0.18357	-0.22709						4
				T1O	-0.00852	-0.17107	-0.21851	3.13991	3
				T2O	0.30672	-0.11149	0.67113	3.14067	9
T1M	0.50600	0.31643	0.22709						5
				T2O	0.69328	0.11149	0.32887	3.02022	7
T1M	-0.00600	0.18357	-0.22709						6
				T1O	0.00852	0.17107	0.21851	3.13991	1
				T2M	0.30948	0.12017	-0.34965	3.19361	11
T2O	0.69328	0.11149	0.32887						7
				T1M	0.50600	0.31643	0.22709	3.02022	5
				T2M	0.69052	-0.12017	0.34965	3.00633	10
T2O	0.30672	-0.11149	-0.32887						8
				T1O	-0.00852	-0.17107	-0.21851	3.13515	3
				T2M	0.30948	0.12017	-0.34965	3.00633	11
T2O	0.30672	-0.11149	0.67113						9
				T1M	0.00600	-0.18357	0.22709	3.14067	4
				T2M	0.69052	-0.12017	0.65035	3.00633	12
T2M	0.69052	-0.12017	0.34965						10
				T1O	0.50852	-0.32893	0.21851	2.99342	2
				T2O	0.69328	0.11149	0.32887	3.00633	7
T2M	0.30948	0.12017	-0.34965						11
				T1M	-0.00600	0.18357	-0.22709	3.19361	6
				T2O	0.30672	-0.11149	-0.32887	3.00633	8

Oversize computer output reduced photographically to fit on one page

7 STYLE AND MECHANICS

Accuracy and clarity in your prose are as essential as precision in your research. If your ideas and conclusions are to make a contribution to knowledge, you must communicate them to as large an audience as possible. For this purpose you need to follow the conventions of style and mechanics readily understood and widely accepted in the academic community.

This chapter surveys the issues of style and mechanics that you are most likely to confront when writing a research paper, thesis, or dissertation. For other questions about grammar, diction, mechanics, and usage, you should have at hand and consult frequently a dictionary, a thesaurus, a handbook of grammar, and a textbook on composition and rhetoric. (A listing of such reference works begins on page 231 at the end of this chapter.) If you are required to follow a local or professional style sheet, you will want to refer to it also.

STYLE

Style is not mere decoration; it cannot be separated from meaning. Stylistic choices are not made apart from consideration of your ideas and definition of the audience with whom you wish to communicate. Your choices about sentence structure, diction, and tone together create the style of your writing. Because the audience for a research paper, thesis, or dissertation is usually the academic community, your writing should be formal in diction and tone.

Diction

The diction, or word choice, in a research paper, dissertation, or thesis should be formal rather than colloquial. Contractions and abbreviations should be avoided, and in nontechnical papers numbers generally should be spelled out.

Tone

Your tone, or attitude toward your subject, should be serious, not ironic or flippant. Humorous, casual, or conversational approaches are inappropriate. Because they defy your audience's expectations for this kind of writing, these tones generally fail to have the intended effect. Since your purpose is to promote understanding of your subject, you will not want to use a tone that can easily be misinterpreted.

Personal Pronouns

Most research papers, theses, and dissertations should be written in the third person—that is, with nouns or third-person pronouns (*he, she, they,* or *it*) as subjects of the sentences.

Using a first-person pronoun (*I, we, me, us, my, our, mine, ours*) to call attention to the fact that a statement is your opinion often weakens the assertion by implying uncertainty. The reader assumes that statements in your paper, unless otherwise attributed, are your opinion and represent your point of view. The first-person pronoun is appropriate when you relate a personal experience, such as your own process of research, or when you wish to call particular attention to your opinion as distinguished from the views of others. In papers that call for a subjective response to texts, ideas, or situations (some kinds of literary criticism and anthropological studies, for example), you will want to use first-person pronouns. Whatever choice of pronouns you make for the text, you may freely use the first person in the preface and acknowledgments.

Because your reader will assume that you are addressing him or her, second-person pronouns (*you, your*) rarely belong in a research paper. Commands (implied second person, as in "Observe that . . . ," the subject of which is actually *you*) should be avoided. In very informal papers or in creative writing you may address your reader directly.

The edited sentences below demonstrate ways of eliminating unnecessary first- and second-person constructions.

Original   `In my opinion, presidential candidates should debate in an`

`uncontrolled forum.`

Revised   `Presidential candidates should debate in an uncontrolled`

`forum.`

Original   `I firmly believe that previous researchers have`

`misinterpreted the evidence.`

Revised   `Previous researchers have misinterpreted the evidence.`

Original   `Notice that these statistics substantiate the previous`

`study.`

Revised   `These statistics substantiate the previous study.`

Tense

You should cast verbs in the tense or tenses appropriate to the time of the events under discussion. A few general guidelines apply, however. Events in literary works are discussed in the present tense.

`After passing up the opportunity to kill the kneeling`

Claudius, Hamlet enters his mother's bedchamber, where he

kills Polonius.

Discussions of literature generally use the present tense.

In What Maisie Knew, Henry James portrays a child . . .

The past tense is appropriate for discussions about works of theory or philosophy.

In his Critique of Pure Reason, Immanuel Kant speculated

that . . .

The present tense, however, may also be used in such discussions to indicate that a given work continues to present the same ideas.

In his Critique of Pure Reason, Kant demonstrates that . . .

When you report the results of research, use the past tense to describe the result of a particular experiment. Use the present tense for generalizations or conclusions.

Scores on standardized tests did not correlate with the

ability to write.
(Reporting the results of a particular study)

Scores on standardized tests do not correlate with the

ability to write.
(Generalization based on one or more studies)

Sentence Structure

Sentences in a research paper, thesis, or dissertation should be active, forceful, and varied, reinforcing your meaning. With your sentence structure you will want to explore the full range of possibilities for expressing the logical relationships of ideas. You will want to use compound and complex sentences and parallel constructions, as required by your subject. Because meaning, or content, cannot be separated from its expression in language, weak or inappropriate sentence structure often reveals faulty logic or undeveloped thought. Careful attention to your sentences can help you refine your ideas as you write.

ACTIVE AND PASSIVE VOICE   Active voice is a stronger construction than passive voice. In the active voice, the actor is the subject of the sentence, whereas in the passive voice, the object or receiver of the action is the subject. Sentences should be active except when you specifically want to emphasize that the subject was acted upon, as in "The Lindbergh baby was kidnaped." Changing a sentence from passive to active may result not only in the use of a stronger form of the verb but also in the elimination of wordiness, as in this example:

Passive   The Worldly Philosophers was written by Robert Heilbroner.

Active   Robert Heilbroner wrote The Worldly Philosophers.

POSTPONED SUBJECTS   Expletive constructions—*there are, there is, it is*—result in weak sentences. You can avoid this construction, thereby condensing and strengthening your sentence, by determining the subject of the sentence and supplying a verb.

Original   There is no valid reason for calculating the standard deviation of such a distribution.

Revised   No valid reason exists for calculating the standard deviation . . .

Original   It was in the Poetics that Aristotle analyzed Greek tragedy.

Revised   In the Poetics Aristotle analyzed Greek tragedy.

Parallelism

Elements in an outline or list, as well as chapter titles, subtitles, and headings, should be parallel—that is, they should take the same grammatical form. If you use a noun or noun phrase (such as "Effective Regulations") for one chapter title, the next chapter title should also be a noun phrase ("Adequate Screening" rather than, for example, "To Provide Adequate Screening," an infinitive phrase). Similarly, in a sentence outline, all entries must be complete sentences.

The entries in the following outline are not parallel. Entry I is a complete sentence. Entry I.A is a noun phrase. Entry I.B is a participial phrase.

Topic outline with nonparallel entries

I. Nuclear Opponents Cite Dangers

    A. Nuclear Accidents Involving Leakage

    B. Disposing of Nuclear Waste

    C. Groups That Threaten Sabotage

 II. Protecting against Nuclear Accidents

    A. Sound Design and Construction

    B. Monitoring Systems

    C. Automatic Devices for Correcting Problems

The entries in the following outline are parallel; they are all noun phrases:

Topic outline with parallel entries

 I. Dangers of Nuclear Power Plants

    A. Leakage of Radiation

    B. Disposal of Nuclear Waste

    C. Sabotage by Terrorist Groups

 II. Safety Features of Nuclear Power Plants

    A. Sound Design and Construction

    B. Monitoring Systems

    C. Automatic Correction Devices

You may use other constructions in an outline as long as each entry takes the same form. In the next outline, each entry is a complete sentence.

Sentence outline

 I. Emerson expounded a political theory close to

    anarchism.

    A. He believed that individuals should govern

       themselves.

    B. He believed that the state should not be

       concerned with property.

 II. Emerson disapproved of the educational system.

    A. He found fault with methods of instruction.

    B. He criticized the curriculum.

III. Emerson sought to abolish established religion.

Logical Consistency

The requirement for parallelism is not exclusively a grammatical one, but a logical one as well. Grammatical inconsistencies often signal problems in logic. Logical consistency requires headings at the same level of an outline to have approximately equivalent importance and to refer to similar categories of ideas. For example, three headings designating historical periods and a fourth at the same level designating procedural difficulties would not be logically consistent. Moreover, each heading at a given level should represent the same degree of generalization and refer to approximately the same kind of information. The following set of headings is logically unbalanced:

Outline without parallel logic

I. U.S. secondary schools during the nineteenth century

II. Changes in secondary school programs in Pennsylvania from 1890 to 1930

III. Nature of secondary school curricular changes from 1930 to 1970

IV. Percentages of teen-agers enrolled in high schools

The fourth heading is considerably narrower in focus than the others and calls for purely statistical information rather than interpretation. In addition, the scope of the inquiry changes from national in the first heading to local in the second.

Coherence

A paper that is coherent presents ideas, observations, or generalizations in a logical and consistent sequence. Problems with integrating a section of your argument may be a sign that the section belongs somewhere else in the paper or should be omitted.

Transitional expressions

Once you have organized your paper logically, you can use transitional expressions to help your reader see the relationships among sentences and paragraphs. Transitional expressions are words or phrases that indicate contrast (*but, however*), comparison (*similarly, just as*), the introduction of additional information (*also, likewise, in addition*), the presentation of examples (*for example, for instance*), and conclusions (*in short, in conclusion, therefore*). Such words or phrases do not substitute for organizational and logical development. Clear statements of purpose and the demonstration of logical relations with each paragraph, section, and chapter ensure the continuity and coherence of the paper. However, transitional expressions can help the reader follow your argument by emphasizing the connections between your sentences and among your ideas. You may wish to consult a handbook of grammar for a listing of expressions and information about how to use them.

MECHANICS

Grammatical and mechanical correctness are essential to effective communication. This section deals with problems that arise frequently during the writing of research papers, theses, and dissertations. You can resolve other questions concerning mechanics and grammar by consulting a handbook or textbook from the listing at the end of this chapter.

Spelling

When you are in doubt about the spelling of a word or when variant spellings exist, consult a standard dictionary (see the list on page 231) and select the preferred American spelling. Consistently use throughout your paper the form you select. For the correct spelling of proper names not found in a dictionary, refer to an authority such as a biographical dictionary or an encyclopedia. If you decide to use an unusual spelling (such as an archaism or an Anglicism) either once or throughout your paper, you should specify the reason for your decision in a note. When you find a misspelled word in a passage that you wish to quote directly, enter the word exactly as you find it and indicate that the error is not yours by entering *sic* (Latin for "thus") in brackets immediately after the word.

Hyphenation

Types of compound words

Hyphens are used to create compound words and to indicate the division of a word at the end of a line. Compounds that function as nouns may be open (*school year*), hyphenated (*self-concept*), or closed (*schoolroom*). The current trend is away from the use of the hyphen; it is usually dropped when a compound becomes common.

The following types of compound words should be hyphenated:

1. Prefixes followed by a capitalized word: *pro-American, post–World War II*.
2. Prefixes followed by a numeral: *post-1980, pre-1900*.
3. Prefixes followed by a hyphenated compound: *pro-city-state*.
4. Compound adjectives preceding nouns (when confusion about which word is the noun might result): *Australian-ballot controversy*, but *a controversy over the Australian ballot; nineteenth-century poet*, but *a poet of the nineteenth century*.
5. Compound adjectives with *self-, half-, quasi-,* and *all-: self-serving, quasi-scientific, all-powerful*.
6. Compound adjectives with *well-, ill-, better-, best-, little-,* and *lesser-* when they precede the noun: *ill-gotten gains*, but *his gains were ill gotten; a little-known composer*, but *a composer who was little known*.
7. Compounds when mispronunciation might occur without the hyphen: *co-opt, co-worker*.
8. Fractional numbers written out: *one-fourth, two and two-thirds*.

9. Combinations of words including a prepositional phrase: *stick-in-the-mud*.
10. Compound nouns with *self-*, *great-* (relatives), *-in-law*, and *-elect*: *self-concept*, *great-grandfather*, *sister-in-law*, *president-elect*.

Webster's Third New International Dictionary is the best source of information on hyphenation.

Hyphens also indicate the division of a word at the end of a line of typescript. The division of words between syllables is discussed on pages 238 and 239 in Chapter 8.

Titles of Works

Punctuation for a title depends on the nature of the source material. Some titles should be underlined to indicate italics; others should be put in quotation marks; some are neither italicized nor put in quotation marks.

ITALICIZED TITLES   Italic is a typeface in which the letters slant to the right. *This sentence is printed in italic type.* Italic is indicated in manuscripts and typescripts with underlining even if your typewriter or printer can produce italics. <u>The underlining in this typed sentence tells a printer that the sentence should appear in italics.</u>

The titles of the following types of works should also be italicized—that is, underlined in your typescript—wherever they appear:

Books: <u>Eros and Civilization: A Philosophical Inquiry into Freud</u>

Pamphlets: <u>Regional Dances of Mexico</u>

Journals: <u>Critical Inquiry</u>

Newspapers: <u>Los Angeles Times</u>

Plays: <u>Much Ado about Nothing</u>

Long poems: <u>The Prelude</u>

Magazines: <u>Atlantic Monthly</u>

Films: <u>Field of Dreams</u>

Television programs: <u>Wall Street Week</u>

Ballets: <u>Nutcracker</u>

Operas: <u>Don Giovanni</u>

Record albums, tapes, or CDs: <u>André Watts: Live in Tokyo</u>

Paintings: <u>View of Toledo</u>

Sculptures: Pietà

Musical compositions identified by name (rather than by key or type of work): Pastoral Symphony

Legal cases: Truax v. Corrigan

Names of vehicles: H.M.S. Mauretania; space shuttle Atlantis

Underline all marks of punctuation and spaces in a title. If a title appears at the end of a sentence, do not underline the final period.

Shakespeare's Proverbial Language: An Index.

Comparative Literature as Academic Discipline: A Statement of Principles, Praxis, Standards.

The Plays of Samuel Beckett: Waiting for Godot and Endgame.

The Four-Gated City: The Summer before the Dark.

Notice that titles within titles are left without underlining.

QUOTATION MARKS WITH TITLES   The titles of the types of works listed below should be put in quotation marks.

Articles in a journal: "The Father and the Bride in Shakespeare"

Articles in a magazine: "The Sporting Scene"

Articles in a newspaper: "Sahara Engulfs Much of Chad"

Articles in an encyclopedia: "Huntington, Collis Potter"

Articles in a compilation: "The Schizophrenic and Language"

Short stories: "The Magic Barrel"

Short poems: "Fern Hill"

Songs: "I Dream of Jeannie"

Chapters in books: "Emergence of the Polis"

Lectures: "Résumé Writing and Effective Interviewing"

Unpublished dissertations: "The Ambiente of Latin America in Five Novels by Graham Greene"

TITLES WITHOUT UNDERLINING OR QUOTATION MARKS   The titles of sacred works, series, editions, and societies and words referring to the divisions of a book are neither underlined nor put in quotation marks.

Sacred writings: Holy Bible.   Mark.   New Testament.   Koran.

Series: New Accents.   The Brain.   Approaches to Teaching Masterpieces of World Literature.

Editions: Library of America.   Norton Critical Edition.

Societies: American Psychological Association. Association of American Petroleum Geologists.

Divisions of a book: foreword; preface; introduction; appendix; glossary; chapter; act; volume; scene.

TITLES WITHIN TITLES   Titles often include another title. When a title marked by quotation marks appears within an italicized title, retain and underline the quotation marks.

Coleridge's "Kubla Khan"
("Kubla Khan" is a short poem included here as part of the title of a book.)

When a title ordinarily marked by quotation marks appears within another title ordinarily marked by quotation marks, change the interior quotation marks to single quotation marks.

"A Reading of Coleridge's 'Kubla Khan'"
("Kubla Khan" is a short poem mentioned in the title of an article.)

When a title that is ordinarily underlined appears within another underlined title, it is left without underlining or quotation marks.

Virginia Woolf's The Waves
(*The Waves* is a novel mentioned in the title of a book of criticism.)

An underlined title that appears within a title in quotation marks remains underlined.

"A Principle of Unity in Between the Acts"
(*Between the Acts* is a novel mentioned in the title of an article.)

Capitalization

The prose in a research paper, thesis, or dissertation follows standard rules and conventions for capitalization. The frequent use of capitalization in documentation, however, requires particular attention.

Capitalize the first and last words in titles and all other words with the exception of articles (*a, an, the*), coordinate conjunctions (*and, but, or, for, nor, yet, so*), prepositions (*to, at, before, between,* etc.), and the word *to* in an infinitive. Always capitalize the first and last words of a subtitle, the first word after a colon, and both elements of a hyphenated compound when the second word is a noun or a proper adjective (*Pro-American,* for example). Original capitalization may be changed to conform to these rules. Original spelling and internal punctuation should not be changed.

Style: An Anti-Text

Two Years before the Mast

The Ship Sails On

Emily Dickinson: The Mind of the Poet

The Roll-Call

Far from the Madding Crowd

'On Actors and Acting'

'The Lotus-Eaters'

College Composition and Communication

University of Toronto Quarterly

References to divisions of research materials or divisions of your paper should be capitalized when they are used as a kind of title:

Chapter 7

Section 3

Appendix C

General references to a type of division are not capitalized:

the final chapter

an index

the preface

the glossary

this section

Nearly every foreign language has its own rules for capitalization of titles and names. See *The Chicago Manual of Style,* the *MLA Handbook for Writers of Research Papers,* or a dictionary for the language in question.

Italics

Emphasis

Italics (defined on page 220) may be used to provide emphasis within your own work or in direct quotations. This use of italics should be kept to a minimum because an overabundance of emphasized words reduces the impact of them all, as in this sentence:

An hour into the marathon he was in second place, and she

was in last place. Yet she eventually won the race.

When you use italics to add emphasis in direct quotations, indicate your alteration of the original with a note enclosed in brackets: [my emphasis] or [emphasis mine]. Similarly, if you want to point out that the original contains italics, you may do so within brackets: [original emphasis] or [italics in original]. For a detailed discussion of interpolation see pages 84 and 85 in Chapter 3.

Words as words

Italics may be used in references to words as words, letters as letters, and terms to be defined.

She spelled the word laxiflorous.
(Word as word)

That word begins with a capital A.
(Letter as letter)

The term virgule means solidus or slanted line.
(Term to be defined)

Foreign words and phrases

Foreign words and phrases should be underlined except when they have become Anglicized—that is, accepted as English words.

Abbreviations

Do not use abbreviations in the text of a research paper, thesis, or dissertation. Exceptions to this general rule include abbreviations of social titles such as *Mr., Messrs., Mrs., Ms.,* and their foreign equivalents; professional and honorary titles such as *Dr., Prof., Rev.,* and *Hon.* preceding proper names; identifications such as *Esq.* (to designate an attorney), *Ph.D., S.T.B.* (Bachelor of Sacred Theology), *Sr.* and *Jr.* following proper names; familiar abbreviations of names of countries (*USSR*), cities (*St. Louis*), and organizations (*UNESCO, YWCA*); and abbreviations for units of time, such as *a.m., p.m., A.D., B.C.* In technical writing, abbreviations of units of measurement such as *mm, cc, ft,* and *in* can be used freely. Names of states, reference works, universities, publishers, and books of the Bible should be spelled out in the text unless you designate an alternative, either in the text or in a note: (Oxford English Dictionary, hereafter OED). Consistently use any abbreviations that you select.

The general warning against abbreviations does not apply to material included in notes, appendixes, bibliographies, and, most particularly, tables and figures, where abbreviations are not only permissible but often preferable and where the accepted style, especially in the sciences and mathematics, allows exceedingly abbreviated forms. Consult your adviser or instructor if you have any questions about the extent to which your subject requires the use of abbreviations.

Punctuation

Punctuate your writing in accordance with the conventions described in the handbook of grammar you are using. This section focuses on the punctuation marks (other than periods and commas) most often required in the text and documentation of research papers: quotation marks, the colon, brackets, parentheses, ellipsis points, and the virgule.

QUOTATION MARKS   Whether in the text, notes, or bibliographic entries, titles of the following types of works should be put in double quotation marks: articles, essays, parts of a collection, newspaper articles, journal and magazine articles, short stories, short poems, unpublished dissertations, and lectures. Single quotation marks indicate the inclusion of one quotation inside another. Quotations that are run into the text should be enclosed in quotation marks. See pages 68 through 71 in Chapter 3 for information about the use of quotation marks with quoted material.

THE COLON   Within the text, the colon may be used to introduce quotations whether long or short, whether run in or set off. (See pages 71 through 75 in Chapter 3 for information on ways to introduce quotations.) In addition, the colon may follow a complete sentence for the purpose of introducing material that amplifies or concludes it. One space follows the colon.

In some election years four different political parties

may exert influence in the state: Democratic, Republican,

Conservative, and Liberal.

Becker maintains, "None of this is unusual: it is just

interesting gossip about a great man."[1]

In note and bibliography entries, the colon is used to separate the title from the subtitle and the place of publication from the name of the publisher. One space follows the colon.

---

[1] Ernest Becker, *The Denial of Death* (New York: Free Press, 1973), 101.

BRACKETS   Brackets are used to enclose material interpolated into a direct quotation. Interpolations may be made to clarify the antecedent of a pronoun, indicate the source of an error with the word *sic* (meaning "thus" in Latin), and insert explanatory material. (See pages 84 and 85 for a discussion of interpolation.) In addition, brackets within a parenthetical expression function like parentheses, as illustrated below.

The moral direction of the argument in Elaine Pagels'

latest book (<u>Adam, Eve, and the Serpent</u> [New York: Random

House, 1988]) recalls the quality of her earlier book on

the Gnostic Gospels, according to one reviewer.

PARENTHESES   Parentheses are used to enclose incidental, explanatory, or qualifying remarks in a sentence. Parenthetical material should not be crucial to the meaning of a sentence; the omission of parenthetical material should leave the meaning of the sentence intact.

Hollander reported, "Sam, Saul, Shep, Sebastian, and

Sandra (as I shall call them) all spoke about this

'tableau.'"2

Parentheses function like commas in many circumstances but enclose supplemental material more emphatically than do commas. Parentheses also enclose publication information in notes, bibliographies, and works cited lists (as detailed in chapters 4 and 5) and letters and numbers in enumerations in the text (see page 229).

ELLIPSIS POINTS   Three ellipsis points (spaced periods) are used to indicate an omission from quoted material. The ellipsis should be preceded and/or followed by punctuation that completes the meaning of the quoted sentence. (See pages 79 through 83 in Chapter 3 for a discussion of the use of ellipsis.) Ellipsis points should not be used in your own writing to extend sentences or to mean *etc.*

THE VIRGULE   A virgule (/) with a space on each side is used between lines of poetry that are run into the text.

King Lear immediately gives his youngest daughter another

chance to voice her love for him and thereby receive a

---

2 Norman N. Hollander, *Five Readers Reading* (New Haven: Yale Univ. Press, 1975), 1.

portion of his kingdom: "How, how, Cordelia! Mend your

speech a little, / Lest you may mar your fortunes."[3]

The virgule is also used, without space on either side, to indicate alternatives, as in *pass/fail, either/or,* and *and/or.* The virgule also separates elements of a date expressed entirely in numbers, as in *2/20/88.*

Numbers

Numbers expressed in words

In formal nonscientific writing, numbers from one to one hundred and numbers that can be expressed in one or two words—for example, *seventy-five, three thousand, fifteen,* and *seven billion*—should be spelled out. Use numerals for dates; page, street, serial, and telephone numbers; fractions accompanied by a whole number, decimals, and percentages; and quantities combined with abbreviations and symbols. In writing that presents numbers for calculation, express all numbers in numerals.

A sentence should not begin with a numeral. If a number must begin a sentence, spell it out. The word *and* connects a digit in the hundreds to a digit in the tens, as in *two hundred and fifty,* but is omitted above the tens, as in *three thousand fifty* or *two million two hundred thousand.*

If possible, a sentence that starts with a number should be rewritten.

Original Five hundred and seventeen people visited the gallery last

week.

Rewritten Last week 517 people visited the gallery.

Punctuation of numerals

Numbers consisting of four or more digits, except most dates and all street, telephone, and page numbers, must have commas inserted at the thousands and millions points. In dates of five digits, insert a comma to mark the thousands.

Built in 1916, the elementary school at 10916 Main Street

had a play area comprising 4,729 square feet of concrete

and 57,128 square feet of lawn. Maintenance of the yard

cost $56,157 last year.

The illustration is on page 1078.

The fossil dates from 10,000 B.C.

---

[3] William Shakespeare, *King Lear,* in *The Riverside Shakespeare,* ed. G. Blakemore Evans (Boston: Houghton Mifflin, 1974), act 1, sc. 1, lines 93–94.

Fractions A fraction should be spelled out in the text when it is not accompanied by a numeral. Fractions are hyphenated when spelled out, as in *two-thirds of the voters*. Numerals in a fraction are separated by a slanted line, as in 2/3 or 27 3/4.

Decimals and percentages Numbers with decimal points and percentages are written in numerals. The word *percent* (spelled as one word) accompanies the number. In formal nonscientific writing, the percent symbol (%) should be used only in tables and figures. In scientific or technical papers, the use of the percent symbol preceded by a numeral is standard practice. In the absence of a number, the word *percentage* is used.

```
Sales have increased 37 percent this year.

The current rate of inflation is 4.3 percent.

The percentage of nonvoters has increased significantly.
```

Numbers in tables Textual reference to numbers taken from figures and tables should be in the form of numerals, even if the numbers might otherwise be written out.

```
Table 1 indicates that only 2 of the 33 tests were valid.
```

Numbers with abbreviations Numbers combined with abbreviations are expressed in numerals: *6 ft, 27 mm.*

Dates Dates in the text may be written in one of two ways, depending on your preference:

```
On 22 July 1989 the group met for the first time.

On July 22, 1989, the group met for the first time.
```

Notice that commas enclose the year when the month precedes the day, but no commas are needed when the day precedes the month. Use consistently the form that you choose.

When you are referring to a month or season and a year, commas to set off the year are optional.

```
In January 1981 New York City declared a drought

emergency.

In January, 1981, New York City declared a drought

emergency.
```

B.C. and A.D. The abbreviation *B.C.* (meaning "before Christ") follows the year. The abbreviation *A.D.* (*anno Domini* in Latin, or "in the year of our Lord") precedes the year. The designations *B.C.E.* ("before the Christian [or common] era") and *C.E.* (Christian [or common] era) follow the year.

```
Agricultural methods changed little between 1900 B.C. and

A.D. 1400.

Agricultural methods changed little between 1900 B.C.E.

and 1400 C.E.
```

Inclusive pages   When citing inclusive pages, enter only the final two digits if all other numbers remain the same: 121–48, 300–07, 1813–16, 23976–78. Enter any numbers that have changed: 2989–3016, 23976–4801. Never use fewer than two digits, except for numbers below ten: 5–8, 1–2, but not 501–2. For numbers below one hundred, enter both digits even if the number in the tens place remains the same: 47–48, 55–69, 70–71.

Inclusive years   In references to inclusive years, give only the final two digits when the century remains the same: 1975–78, 1939–45, 1901–09, 1515–82, 711–17. When the century changes, include the entire set of digits: 1890–1950, 400–1000, 1700–1900.

Arabic and roman numerals   Current usage discourages roman numerals except for designating individuals in a series, such as Henry VIII and Philip II, and for numbering outlines. Otherwise, use arabic numerals throughout research papers, theses, and dissertations.

Enumeration

Lists within text   You may wish to give some items special emphasis through enumeration. When the list of items is short enough to be run smoothly into the text, identifying numerals or letters are enclosed in parentheses.

```
The steps in writing a research paper include (1) choosing

a topic, (2) preparing a working bibliography,

(3) outlining the paper, (4) collecting information, and

(5) writing the paper.
```

Such enumeration in the text may also be introduced with a colon.

```
Writing a research paper includes the following steps:

(1) choosing a topic . . .
```

Displayed lists   When the length or number of items to be enumerated would create a cumbersome or confusing sentence if the list were run into the text, set the list off from the text. When the items to be listed are complete sentences, use the following format:

The authors made three recommendations for keeping

European markets open:

    1. Companies must step up their strategic planning in

Europe.

    2. Business leaders outside Europe must realize that

there is strength in numbers.

    3. Non-European companies must enlist their

governments' help at the highest levels.

If the listed items are words or phrases that are a grammatical part of the lead-in statement, they should be punctuated as a series and a period should be put at the end of the last item.

The syllabus for the seminar included sessions on

    1. new systems of discourse,

    2. the rhetorical inheritance,

    3. literacy, and

    4. measurement of writing ability.

Displayed outlines   When your list of items is subdivided, use either the number-letter sequence recommended for outlines (see page 20 in Chapter 1) or the decimal sequence for outlines (see pages 20 and 21).

If you need to include an outline within the text, the outline should follow the conventional format and sequence (see pages 20 and 21). When items enumerated in an outline are longer than one line, align the second and succeeding lines with the first word in the line above.

I. Carol Gilligan has attempted to distinguish the moral

   development of women from that of men.

   A. Gilligan has designated male morality as "the

      morality of justice."

B. Gilligan has designated female morality as "the

morality of care."

EDITING AND PROOFREADING

Your paper should be scholarly and accurate in every way, including style and mechanics. After you have revised your paper, paying attention to the interaction of content and style, you should edit it thoroughly, making corrections in mechanics and grammar, consulting reference books when necessary, and proofreading carefully.

Because writers are often too close to their work to view it objectively, an effective way to measure your audience's reaction is to read the paper to someone else. Reading the paper aloud to yourself can also be helpful. The passages over which you hesitate or stumble probably need revision. Finishing the final draft a few days ahead of your deadline will give you an opportunity to read and proofread and then set the paper aside so that you can return to it with a fresh perspective and a keen eye ready to detect rough spots and errors.

SELECTED REFERENCE WORKS

Dictionaries

The American Heritage Dictionary. 2nd college ed. Boston: Houghton Mifflin, 1982.

The American Heritage Dictionary of the English Language. Boston: Houghton Mifflin, 1969.

The American Heritage Illustrated Encyclopedic Dictionary. Boston: Houghton Mifflin, 1987.

The Oxford English Dictionary. 13 vols. Oxford: Clarendon Press, 1888–1933. 4-vol. supplement, 1972–86. Available on CD-ROM disk.

The Oxford English Dictionary. 13 vols. 1888–1933. Reprinted in 2-vol. small-print ed. New York: Oxford Univ. Press, 1971. Available on CD-ROM disk.

The Oxford English Dictionary. 2nd ed. 20 vols. New York: Oxford Univ. Press, 1989.

The Random House Dictionary of the English Language. 2nd ed., unabridged. New York: Random House, 1987.

Webster's New World Dictionary of the English Language. New York: Simon and Schuster, 1988.

Webster's Ninth New Collegiate Dictionary. Springfield: Merriam-Webster, 1988.

Webster's Third New International Dictionary, Unabridged: The Great Library of the English Language. Springfield: Merriam-Webster, 1961.

Webster's II New Riverside University Dictionary. Boston: Houghton Mifflin, 1984.

Thesauruses

The Random House Thesaurus: College Edition. New York: Random House, 1984.
Roget's International Thesaurus. 4th ed. New York: Crowell, 1977.
Roget's Thesaurus of English Words and Phrases. London: Longman, 1982.
Roget's II: The New Thesaurus. Expanded ed. Boston: Houghton Mifflin, 1988.
Webster's Collegiate Thesaurus. Springfield: Merriam-Webster, 1976.
Webster's New Dictionary of Synonyms. Springfield: Merriam-Webster, 1984.

Reference Works on Usage

Copperud, Roy H. *American Usage and Style: The Consensus.* New York: Van Nostrand, 1979.
Creswell, Thomas J. *Usage in Dictionaries and Dictionaries of Usage.* Eds. Virginia McDavid and James B. McMillan. Publication of American Dialect Society, nos. 63–64. University: Univ. of Alabama Press, 1975.
Follett, Wilson. *Modern American Usage: A Guide.* Ed. Jacques Barzun. New York: Hill and Wang, 1966.
Fowler, H. W. *A Dictionary of Modern English Usage.* 2nd rev. ed. New York: Oxford Univ. Press, 1987.
Morris, William, and Mary Morris. *Harper Dictionary of Contemporary Usage.* New York: Harper and Row, 1975.

Handbooks of Grammar

Fowler, H. Ramsey, and Jane E. Aaron. *The Little, Brown Handbook.* 4th ed. Glenview: Scott, Foresman, 1989.
Hacker, Diana. *Rules for Writers: A Concise Handbook.* 2nd ed. New York: St. Martin's, 1988.
Hodges, John D., and Mary E. Whitten with Suzanne S. Webb. *Harbrace College Handbook.* 10th ed. New York: Harcourt, 1986.
Kirszner, Laurie G., and Stephen R. Mandell. *The Holt Handbook.* 2nd ed. Fort Worth: Holt, 1989.
Lunsford, Andrea, and Robert Connors. *The St. Martin's Handbook.* New York: St. Martin's, 1989.
Troyka, Lynn Quitman. *Simon and Schuster Handbook for Writers.* Englewood Cliffs: Prentice-Hall, 1987.
Watkins, Floyd C., and William B. Dillingham. *Practical English Handbook.* 8th ed. Boston: Houghton Mifflin, 1989.

Books on Rhetoric and Composition

Axelrod, Rise B., and Charles R. Cooper. *The St. Martin's Guide to Writing.* 2nd ed. New York: St. Martin's, 1988.

Baker, Sheridan, and Robert E. Yarber. *The Practical Stylist with Readings*. 4th ed. New York: Harper and Row, 1986.

Bazerman, Charles. *The Informed Writer: Using Sources in the Disciplines*. 3rd ed. Boston: Houghton Mifflin, 1988.

Cook, Claire Kehrwald. *Line by Line: How to Improve Your Own Writing*. Boston: Houghton Mifflin, 1989.

Elbow, Peter. *Writing with Power: Techniques for Mastering the Writing Process*. New York: Oxford Univ. Press, 1981.

Kennedy, X. J., and Dorothy M. Kennedy. *The Bedford Guide for College Writers*. New York: St. Martin's, 1987.

Kuriloff, Peshe. *Rethinking Writing*. New York: St. Martin's, 1989.

Trimmer, Joseph F., and James M. McCrimmon. *Writing with a Purpose*. 9th ed. Boston: Houghton Mifflin, 1988.

Strunk, William, Jr., and E. B. White. *The Elements of Style*. 3rd ed. New York: Macmillan, 1979.

Williams, Joseph M. *Style: Ten Lessons in Clarity and Grace*. 3rd ed. Glenview: Scott, Foresman, 1989.

Guides to Avoiding Biased Language

American Psychological Association. "Guidelines for Nonsexist Language in APA Journals." *American Psychologist* 32 (1977): 487–94.

Frank, Francine Wattman, and Paula A. Treichler. *Language, Gender, and Professional Writing: Theoretical Approaches and Guidelines for Nonsexist Usage*. New York: Modern Language Association, 1989.

Miller, Casey, and Kate Swift. *The Handbook of Nonsexist Writing*. New York: Lippincott, 1980.

8 THE FINISHED COPY

This chapter provides information about producing the finished copy of your research paper, thesis, or dissertation. Whether you plan to use a typewriter or a computer printer, your goal is to produce a clean, legible copy. (You may want to review the typing and printing instructions at the end of chapters 2, 3, 4, 5, and 6.)

THE FINAL DRAFT

Before you begin to think about producing the finished copy, you should have a completely accurate, thoroughly polished final draft. The final draft should correctly observe the conventions regarding capitalization, punctuation, spelling, compound words, hyphenation, and paragraphing. It should reveal thoughtful word choices and attention to detail in the use of quotations. Even though your paper is still in draft form, it should follow the format requirements for front and back matter, margins, indention, notes and bibliography, placement of documentation, spacing, and so on. This groundwork is particularly important if someone else will type your paper, but it is also necessary if you plan to type or print the paper yourself. Advisers generally wish to approve the final draft of a thesis or dissertation before you prepare the finished copy.

EQUIPMENT AND SUPPLIES

The equipment you need to produce the finished copy includes a typewriter or word processor and printer with appropriate software; the supplies may include paper, a typewriter ribbon, and materials for making corrections. Before you decide to acquire any of these supplies, you should ascertain departmental or institutional requirements.

The Typewriter or Computer Printer

Typewriters

Computer printers

You will want to use a machine that produces clean, clear copy. An electric or electronic typewriter is preferable to a manual machine because it produces a better copy. Computer printers can generally be divided into two classes: dot-matrix printers (of varying qualities, including near letter quality) and letter-quality printers such as daisy-wheel, ink-jet, and laser printers. Because this technology has been developing rapidly, requirements and standards for reports, theses, and dissertations likewise have been changing. Dot-matrix printing may not be acceptable, particularly for a dissertation that will be photocopied rather than set into type. It is a good idea to show your adviser some sample pages before you prepare the finished copy.

Type

Most machines allow you to choose between two sizes of type: *elite type,* which contains twelve spaces or letters to the inch, and *pica type,* which contains ten spaces or letters to the inch. Elite type increases by about one-fifth the amount of material that fits on each page. Your choice of type size may depend either on individual or institutional preference.

Some electronic typewriters and computer printers offer smaller or larger type, as well as an array of different typefaces. These should not be used for theses or dissertations, and they rarely are acceptable in reports written for academic credit. For information on creating a facsimile of type-set material with a computer, see *The Art of Desktop Publishing: Using the Personal Computer to Publish It Yourself,* eds. Tony Bove, Cheryl Rhodes, and Wes Thomas, 2nd ed. (Toronto: Bantam, 1987).

Software

If you plan to produce computer graphics or to print your finished copy on a computer printer, you will need appropriate software programmed to send the correct instructions to the printer. If you plan to submit your text on a diskette, you should make certain that your reader has a word-processing program compatible with the one you use. For information on submitting manuscripts on diskettes to publishers, consult *Chicago Guide to Preparing Electronic Manuscripts for Authors and Publishers* (Chicago: Univ. of Chicago Press, 1987).

Special Symbols

Special symbols are a practical necessity in some subjects and professional fields. Special-purpose typewriters are available, and special keys may be purchased for most ordinary typewriters. Some typewriters have interchangeable elements for different languages and disciplines. Similarly, many printers have fonts that allow you to use special letters and symbols. In some cases you must enter instructions in your word-processing program in order to send such symbols to your printer.

Special symbols most often needed, even in general subject matter, include accent marks, both grave (`) and acute (´), and square brackets ([ ]). Most other symbols are particular to a specialized subject. Any symbol not available on your typewriter or printer should be neatly handwritten on the page in black ink.

Ribbon

A black typewriter or printer ribbon should be used. The ribbon may be either cloth or carbon, as appropriate. In cloth ribbons, nylon is preferable to cotton, which smears easily. A cloth ribbon should be changed as often as necessary to produce a consistent copy. A carbon ribbon is used only once.

Paper

Most colleges and universities require the writer to present the original copy of a research paper, thesis, or dissertation on a good-quality bond paper of twenty-pound weight, eight and one-half by eleven inches in size. A rag content of 25 or 50 percent is ordinarily required (the higher the percentage, the more durable the paper). Erasable bond and onion skin generally are not acceptable because they smear easily. These requirements hold whether you use a typewriter or a computer printer.

Copies

Any copies that must be submitted with the original should be photocopies. Keep at least one copy of your paper for yourself in case some mishap befalls the original and other photocopies. All pages of each photocopy should be identical in weight, color, and texture of paper.

Materials for Correction

You can reduce the need for corrections by quickly proofreading each page before removing it from the typewriter or running the computer printer. On a typewriter, simple corrections can usually be made at this time so that they are hardly noticeable. After the sheets have been removed from the machine, the discovery of errors often requires the retyping of the entire page. After retyping, you should proofread again.

Correcting typed copy — Typed letters may be removed with correction fluid (Liquid Paper is one well-known brand), white carbon paper, an erasing ribbon, or correction tape. Whichever material you use, make certain that the letter or word is completely removed or covered before you type over it. If your typewriter has an erasing ribbon, you probably will want to use it. Correction fluid, if applied carefully, can be used to make an acceptable correction.

Correcting on a word processor — You should also proofread carefully when you use a word processor. Some programs include a spell checker, which helps you to detect typographical errors as well as misspelled words but does not pick up an error if you type the wrong word, such as *the* for *he*, but spell it correctly. Once you have located an error in a computer-generated text, you may use the "find-and-replace" function, available in most word-processing programs, to search for and correct all instances of the error.

SPACING

Consistently use throughout your paper any spacing that you select. Rules governing spacing exist to make your paper readable.

Spacing with a typewriter — If you use a typewriter, the guide sheet on page 243 will help you space your page consistently. Place the sheet behind the page being typed. You can then see where to begin the first line and how much space remains on the page. You may devise a guide sheet with different margins or for another size of paper by drawing the appropriate lines on a piece of thin paper. Some typewriters have a device that indicates at any point how many more lines may be typed on the page. You can calculate the amount of space that footnotes will take by typing them on a separate piece of paper. You can then allow the appropriate number of lines for footnotes at the bottom of the page.

Most word-processing programs automatically space the pages and place notes at the bottom of each page or at the end of each chapter, according to the specifications you select. To be certain that your printer is spacing the pages correctly, you should look at several sample pages before printing the entire paper.

Margins

Recommended margins are one and one-half inches for the left margin and one inch for the right, top, and bottom margins (see the typing and printing instructions in Chapter 2 for information concerning placement of page numbers). Larger or smaller margins may be required by a local style sheet.

Some typewriters and printers produce margins that are justified—that is, aligned on the right as well as on the left, as in a printed book. When justifying, most typewriters and printers leave noticeably large spaces between words; as a result, typed material with justified margins can be difficult to read. Because of the precise spacing needed in notes and bibliographies, many advisers discourage the use of justified margins in research papers, theses, and dissertations.

Centered Material

Any material to be centered on a page, such as first-level headings and set-off poetry, should be centered between margins, not between the edges of the page.

When the recommended margins are used, the center point is four and one-half inches from the left edge of the paper. The six-inch line of typed matter (eight and one-half inches minus the two margins) holds seventy-two elite or sixty pica characters. The closest approximation to the center is found by moving in thirty-six elite spaces or thirty pica spaces from the correct left margin.

Most computer programs and electronic typewriters allow you to center a line automatically by pressing a combination of function keys before or after typing the line.

Line Length

Lines in a typescript that does not have justified right margins are not of equal length. You may want to try to make lines as nearly equal as possible by breaking words where appropriate. It is preferable to leave lines a little short rather than to run them past the right margin.

Division of Words, Numbers, and Lines of Text

When the division of a word is necessary, the break should come between syllables. Standard dictionaries indicate the proper places to break words. Many word-processing programs hyphenate words automatically.

At the end of a line, one-letter and two-letter divisions, such as *a-ble, a-tone, de-velop, consecrat-ed,* or *entire-ly,* are not acceptable. The word should be written on one line, or another division point should be used—for example, *conse-crated.* As a general rule, compound words should be divided between the elements that make up the compound—for example, *volley-ball* rather than *vol-leyball.* When the appearance of a part of a word would lead to confusion about pronunciation (as in *wo-men*), the word should not be broken. Divide words that are already hyphenated only at the hyphen.

The writer must indicate for the typist the nature of hyphens at the end of lines in the draft. In some cases, the hyphen at the end of a line should be omitted when the word is typed on one line. In the case of a hyphenated word, however, the hyphen at the end of the line should be retained when the word is typed on one line; the retention of the hyphen is indicated by a small line drawn just below the hyphen.

Compound words

Hyphenated words

```
                                              volley-
ball
```
[Word typed on one line: *volleyball*]

```
                                                self=
centered
```
[Word typed on one line: *self-centered*]

Indivisible elements

The following elements should never be divided: letters that are the names of radio or television stations, government agencies, institutions, or companies; the name of the month and the day; years; hours of the day; monetary expressions; and parts of an equation.

```
KWLZ          RFC          March 2        6x + 4y = 27
```

$$C + O_2 = CO_2 \qquad \$1{,}378.50 \qquad 525 \text{ B.C.} \qquad 4{:}00 \text{ a.m.}$$

In the case of proper names, the given name and surname or initials and surname should be on the same line when possible; very long names are an exception.

Long formulas and equations

Very long formulas or equations may be set on centered lines by themselves, if necessary, to avoid breaking. If an equation is so long and complex that it must be run over to another line, the break should come if possible before the equality sign (in algebraic equations) or after the arrow (chemical equations).

When a word cannot be included in its entirety or properly divided and hyphenated within the established margin, the entire word should be placed on the next line. No more than two successive lines should end with hyphenated words. Words should not be broken between pages. Avoid carrying over just one line of a paragraph to the following page.

Divisions between pages

Alignment of Numerals

When numerals are arranged in vertical lists, both arabic and roman numerals should be aligned on the right side. This alignment makes the left side uneven, but it is the accepted form. Due allowance must be made when starting a column to provide space for the longest number to be listed. Columns of figures should appear as follows:

```
     I.              1
    II.              7
   III.             18
   XIV.            296
 XXXIII.         26,173
XXXVIII.      1,008,957
```

Numbers with decimals are aligned on the decimal points.

```
  7.9

123.657

 54.4

  7.3333
```

Leaders

In large tables and on pages containing the table of contents and the list of figures, you may wish to use leaders, or spaced periods. They must be arranged so that the periods are aligned perpendicularly and will end at the same point on the right-hand side—usually about two or three spaces before the material to which the leader guides the reader's eye. A simple way to accomplish this alignment is to place all the periods on the even numbers of the typing scale.

Punctuation

Periods, colons, commas, question marks, and semicolons follow the previous letter without spacing. Two spaces follow a period. One space follows a colon, a semicolon, and a comma. Dashes are indicated by two consecutive hyphens (—). Neither hyphens nor dashes have space on either side of them.

```
She needs the following materials: one saw, one hammer,

and one nail.
```
(One space after a colon in text)

```
New York: Random House
```
(One space after a colon in facts of publication)

```
Writing the Research Paper: A Guide and Sourcebook
```
(One space after a colon between title and subtitle)

```
To err is human; to forgive, divine.
```

```
1976; New York: Holt, 1983.
```
(One space after semicolon, whether in text or notes)

```
The stock——American Can——was selling above par.
```
(No space on either side of a dash)

```
Two—thirds of the members attended.
```
(No space on either side of a hyphen)

THE TYPIST

Unless you type quite proficiently and have sufficient time, you should employ a typist to produce the finished copy either on a typewriter or on a word processor. The graduate office or placement bureau can often supply the names of professional typists. An expert will charge more per page than a less-experienced person, but in the long run the work of the professional may cost less because extensive retyping may be avoided.

Before the typing begins, you and your typist should have a clear understanding about your respective responsibilities. You should discuss with the typist your requirements for the final paper in complete detail. Your agreement with the typist should be explicit with respect to the cost (of each page, of extra copies, and of tables), the typewriter or printer to be used, the time schedule, and any unusual requirements.

The writer makes decisions on matters such as the weight of paper to be used, the size of type, and the number of copies (if any). The typist usually provides the supplies, such as the typewriter or printer, paper, ribbons, and correction materials.

You can expect your typist to prepare a true or exact copy of the draft you submit and to reproduce capitalization, punctuation, spelling, and wording exactly as they appear in your draft. Your typist should space material according to standard specifications, such as those found in this manual, even if the final draft copy is not spaced precisely. You may expect your typist to hyphenate words correctly when hyphenation is necessary at the ends of lines. Because any errors in the final draft will probably appear in the finished copy, you should proofread carefully before submitting your paper to a typist.

PROOFREADING

No matter how many times a paper is checked for errors, at least one always seems to escape notice. The goal, of course, is to reduce errors to a minimum. Even though your typist should proofread each page, you are responsible for one or more final proofreadings to make certain that your paper is correct. Careful proofreading before the typing begins can save both money and time. If a particular kind of error appears more than once, look through the entire paper for that error. All direct quotations and statistical data should be checked against the originals, and computations should be checked and cross-checked to guarantee accuracy. The sequence of page numbers and citation numbers and the correspondence of captions and numbers of tables and figures in the text with the listings in the front matter should be examined. Every title in the bibliography must be compared with the title page of the book or article. Headings and page numbers in the text should be compared with the table of contents.

If your proofreading turns up errors, you will have to decide how to correct them. Although one or two corrections per page in black ink are usually acceptable in research papers, any page with very noticeable or distracting corrections should be retyped. Corrections in dissertations must be made on the typewriter. When you use a computer printer, which allows you to correct and print individual corrected pages, you should not need to insert any corrections by hand.

first line of text begins here

Typewriter Spacing Guide Sheet

(See page 237 for instructions on using this guide.)

1½ inches]   [1 inch]

18
17
16
15
14
13
12
11
10
9
8
7
6
5
4
3
2
1   last line of text here

[1 inch]

APPENDIX A

Latin Abbreviations

Latin abbreviations for subsequent references are now rarely used. Most writers who do use the Latin forms treat them as Anglicized words and therefore do not underline them to indicate italics; previously, these abbreviations were italicized. The Latin abbreviations most common in subsequent-reference notes—*ibid.*, *op. cit.*, and *loc. cit.*—are used as follows.

Ibid.   In consecutive references to the same source, the abbreviation *ibid.* ("in the same place") may be used to avoid repetition. If the second reference is to the same page as the initial reference, *ibid.* is used alone. It may also be used to indicate a different page in the same source.

> 15 Loren Eiseley, <u>The Immense Journey</u> (New York: Random House, 1961), 91–94.

> 16 Ibid.

> 17 Ibid., 100.

Ibid. may be used to refer to a second article by the same author in the same book or issue of a periodical, but not to a different book by the same author. The following examples illustrate references to two contributions by the same author to a book of readings.

> 18 Frank Moore Colby, "Trials of an Encyclopedist," <u>Reading I've Liked</u>, ed. Clifton Fadiman (New York: Simon and Schuster, 1945), 278.

> 19 Colby, "Confessions of a Gallomaniac," ibid., 288–89.

Ibid. should not be used to refer to a work in an immediately preceding multiple note, and in footnotes *ibid.* should not be used more than two pages after the original citation.

Op. cit.   When references to the same work follow each other closely but not consecutively and when they refer to different pages in that work, *op. cit.* ("in the work cited") may be used in place of the title and facts of publication. The author's surname, without given name or initials unless another author with the same surname has been cited, must be repeated (in order to identify the work cited). The name is followed by the abbreviation *op. cit.* The volume or page reference closes the citation.

[20] Martin Luther King, Jr., Why We Can't Wait (New York: New American Library, 1964), 78–80.

[21] Powell Davies, The Meaning of the Dead Sea Scrolls (New York: New American Library, 1956), 50.

[22] King, op. cit., 108–09.

[23] Davies, op. cit., 81.

[24] Ibid.

(The references to King are not consecutive, and different pages in his work are cited. Footnote 24 refers to Davies, 81.)

Loc. cit.   For a second but nonconsecutive reference to the exact material (that is, the same volume and page) previously cited, substitute *loc. cit.* ("in the place cited") for *op. cit.* The author's name, usually without given name or initials, must appear to identify the work. Page numbers never follow the form *loc. cit.* because they are unnecessary.

[25] Loren Eiseley, The Immense Journey (New York: Random House, 1961), 91–94.

[26] Eugene Burdick and Harvey Wheeler, Fail–Safe (New York: Dell, 1962), 257.

[27] Eiseley, loc. cit.

(This abbreviation is used because the reference is to pages 91 through 94. Citation of any other page or pages would have called for the use of *op. cit.*, followed by page number[s].)

APPENDIX B

American Psychological Association Style for References

The American Psychological Association (APA), like the Modern Language Association (MLA), uses parenthetical documentation within the text. But instead of putting the author's last name and a page number in parentheses, APA style places in parentheses the author's last name and the year of publication. Complete information about each source cited in the text is then given in an alphabetical reference list at the end of the research paper, thesis, or dissertation.

PARENTHETICAL REFERENCE CITATIONS IN TEXT

Author not cited in text

When you do not mention the author's name in your text, that name, followed by a comma and the date of publication, appears in parentheses at the end of your sentence.[1]

```
Darwin's three principal metaphors for the workings of

nature were the tangled bank, the tree of life, and the

face of nature (Gould, 1989).
```

Use the last name only in both first and subsequent citations, except when you have more than one author with the same last name.

---

[1] See the reference list on pages 250 and 251 for bibliographical information on the works cited in this section.

Author cited in text

If you mention the author's name in your text, cite only the date of publication in parentheses, immediately after the author's name.

```
Gould (1989) attributes Darwin's success to his gift for

the appropriate metaphor.
```

Author and date cited in text

If you use both the name of the author and the date in the text, parenthetical reference is not necessary.

```
In a 1989 article Gould explains Darwin's most successful

metaphors.
```

Quotation with name of author

When your sentence contains a quotation and includes the name of the author, place the publication date and page number in parentheses. Abbreviate page or pages (*p.* or *pp.*). The publication date should follow the name of the author; the page number should follow the end of the quotation.

```
Gould (1989) explains that Darwin used the metaphor of the

tree of life "to express the other form of

interconnectedness--genealogical rather than ecological--

and to illustrate both success and failure in the history

of life" (p. 14).
```

Quotation without name of author

When you quote but do not identify the author in the sentence, the name of the author, date of publication, and page number appear in parentheses at the end of the sentence.

```
Darwin used the metaphor of the tree of life "to express

the other form of interconnectedness--genealogical rather

than ecological" (Gould, 1989, p. 14).
```

Work by two authors

When you refer to a work by two authors, cite both names each time the reference appears.

```
Sexual-selection theory has been used to explore patterns

of insect mating (Alcock & Thornhill, 1983). . . . . Alcock

and Thornhill (1983) also demonstrate . . .
```

Work by two through five authors

For a work by more than two authors but fewer than six authors, cite all names in the first reference. In subsequent references, cite only the name of the first author and use *et al.*

DeLong, Wickham, and Pace (1989) devised a new staining

method of cell identification. . . . The new staining

method (DeLong et al., 1989) allows for identification . . .

Work by more than six authors

For a work by six or more authors, give only the last name of the first author followed by *et al.* in first and subsequent references.

Authors with the same last name

When you cite works by two or more authors with the same last name, use initials to identify the authors in the text even if their dates of publication differ.

J. V. Smith (1989) has confirmed the findings of H. G.

Smith (1987) . . .

Work identified by title

When a work is listed in the reference list by title alone, a shortened version of the title is used in the text to identify the work. The title of a book is underlined; the title of an article appears within quotation marks.

The National Endowment for the Humanities supports

"theoretical and critical studies of the arts" but not

work in the creative or performing arts (Guidelines, 1988,

p. 1).

Changes in the Medical College Admissions Test to begin in

1991 should encourage more students to pursue general

studies in the humanities, natural sciences, and social

sciences ("New Exam," 1989).

Corporate author

When you cite a work by a corporate author, use the name of the organization as the author.

Retired officers retain access to all of the university's

educational and recreational facilities (Columbia

University, 1987, p. 54).

You may use well-known abbreviations of the name of a corporate author in subsequent parenthetical references. For example, you might use NSF for National Science Foundation and NEH for National Endowment for the Humanities.

Reference to more than one work

Parenthetical references may mention more than one work. Multiple citations should be arranged as follows:

- List two or more works by the same author in order of date of publication: (Gould, 1987, 1989).
- Differentiate works by the same author and with the same publication date by adding an identifying letter to each date: (Bloom, 1987a, 1987b). The letters also appear in the reference list, where the works are alphabetized by title.
- List works by different authors in alphabetical order by last name, and use semicolons to separate the references: (Gould 1989; Smith, A. D. 1983).

References

Alcock, J., & Thornhill, R. (1983). The evolution of insect mating systems. Cambridge: Harvard University Press.

Bloom, H. (Ed.). (1987a). Eugene O'Neill. New York: Chelsea.

Bloom, H. (Ed.) (1987b). John Dryden. New York: Chelsea.

Columbia University. (1987). Faculty Handbook. New York: Author.

Darwin, C. (1964). On the origin of the species: A facsimile of the first edition (Introd. Ernst Mayer). Cambridge: Harvard University Press. (Original work published 1859)

DeLong, E. F., Wickham, G. S., & Pace, N. R. (1989). Phylogenetic stains: Ribosomal RNA—based probes for the identification of single cells. Science, 243, 1360—1362.

Gould, S. J. (1987). Time's arrow, time's cycle: Myth

and metaphor in the discovery of geological time.
Cambridge: Harvard University Press.

Gould, S. J. (1989). The wheel of fortune and the wedge of progress. Natural History, 89(3), 14, 16, 18, 20–21.

Guidelines and application form for directors, 1990 summer seminars for school teachers. (1988). Washington, DC: National Endowment for the Humanities.

New exam for doctor of future. (1989, March 15). The New York Times, p. B–10.

Smith, A. D. (1983). Theories of nationalism. London: Duckworth.

Smith, A. L. (1977). Churchill's German army: Wartime strategy and cold war politics, 1943–47. Beverly Hills: Sage.

REFERENCE LIST

A reference list at the end of the paper, the equivalent of a bibliography, includes all works cited. In APA style, this list of sources is entitled "References." The first line of the entry begins flush left; the second and successive lines are indented three spaces from the left. Entries appear in alphabetical order according to the last name of the author; two or more works by the same author appear in chronological order by date of publication, beginning with the earliest; two or more works by the same author and with the same publication date appear in alphabetical order by title. When you have two or more books or articles by the same author, repeat the name of the author in each entry.

Books

Basic entry   The entry for a book begins with the last name of the author, followed by a comma and the author's initials followed by periods. The date of publication follows in parentheses, followed by a period. Only the first word of the book title, the first word of the subtitle, and proper names within both are capitalized. The entire title is underlined and followed by a period. Facts of publication include the city of publication. If the city might be confused with another location, use U.S. Postal Service abbreviations (listed in Appendix D) to identify the state. The name of the location is followed by a colon and the name of the publisher. The entry ends with a period.

Alvarez, A. (1970). <u>The savage god: A study of suicide</u>.

New York: Random House.

Book by more than one author   For a book by more than one author, invert and list the names of all the authors, regardless of the number. Use commas to separate surnames and initials. Place an ampersand (&) before the name of the last author.

Forsyth, A., & Thornhill, R. (1983). <u>The evolution of

insect mating</u>. Cambridge: Harvard University Press.
(In APA style, the names of university presses are spelled out.)

Campbell, W. G., Ballou, S. V., & Slade, C. (1990). <u>Form

and style: Theses, reports, term papers</u> (8th ed.).

Boston: Houghton Mifflin.

For a book with more than six authors, list the first six only, followed by *et al.*, an abbreviation for "and others."

Edition other than first   Identify an edition other than the first or a specific volume with parentheses following the title without any intervening punctuation.

Cochran, J. A. (1975). <u>Money, banking, and the economy</u>

(3rd ed.). New York: Macmillan.

Edited volume   Indicate that a book is an edited volume by placing the abbreviation for editor (Ed.) or editors (Eds.) within parentheses in the author position.

Stanton, D. C. (Ed.). (1987). <u>The female autograph:

Theory and practice of autobiography from the tenth to

the twentieth century</u>. Chicago: University of Chicago

Press.

Book without author or editor

Enter and alphabetize a book without an author or editor by title alone.

Guidelines and application form for directors, 1990 summer

seminars for school teachers. (1988). Washington, DC:

National Endowment for the Humanities.

Multivolume work

For a multivolume work published over several years, place in parentheses the first and last year separated by a hyphen.

Bowsky, W. M. (Ed.). (1963–1967). Studies in Medieval

and Renaissance history (Vols. 1–4). Lincoln:

University of Nebraska Press.

To refer to a single volume in a multivolume series, include only the relevant date and volume number.

Bowsky, W. M. (Ed.). (1967). Studies in Medieval and

Renaissance history (Vol. 4). Lincoln: University of

Nebraska Press.

Translation

Indicate the name of a translator within parentheses following the title.

Derrida, J. (1976). Of grammatology (G. Spivak, Trans.).

Baltimore: Johns Hopkins University Press. (Original

work published 1967)

The parenthetical reference in the text should indicate the original date of publication as well as the date of the translation: (Derrida, 1967/1976).

Work in a series

The entry for an individually titled work in a series provides both the volume and the series titles.

Crutchfield, J. C. (Ed.). (1965). The fisheries:

Problems in resource management: Vol. 1. Studies on

public policy issues in resource management. Seattle:

University of Washington Press.

Reprinted work   The entry for a reprinted work indicates the original date of publication within parentheses.

```
Darwin, C.  (1964).  On the origin of the species: A

    facsimile of the first edition (Introd. Ernst Mayer).

    Cambridge: Harvard University Press.  (Original work

    published 1859)
```

The parenthetical reference in the text includes both dates: (Darwin 1859/1964).

Periodicals

Basic entry   The basic entry for an article in a periodical begins with the last names and initials of all authors, inverted. The year of publication follows in parentheses; for magazine and newspaper articles, give the month and day (if any). Next come the title of the article, not enclosed in quotation marks; the title of the periodical, underlined; the volume number, underlined; and inclusive page numbers. A period follows the author entry and the title of the article. The name of the periodical, the volume number, and page numbers are separated by commas. Only the first word of the article title, the first word of the article subtitle, and proper names within both are capitalized. All words except articles and prepositions are capitalized in the title of the periodical, and the title is underlined. All digits are repeated in page citations. The abbreviation *p.* or *pp.* is used in references to magazines and newspapers but not to journals.

```
Malkiel, B. G.  (1989).  Is the stock market efficient?

    Science, 3, 1313-1318.
```
(In APA style, the closing page number is not shortened.)

Article by more than one author
```
Dornbusch, S. M., Carlsmith, J. M., Bushwall, S. J.,

    Ritter, P. L., Leiderman, H., Hastorf, A. H., & Gross,

    R. T.  (1985).  Single parents, extended households,

    and the control of adolescents.  Child Development, 56,

    326-341.
```

Journal paginated by issue   If each issue of a journal begins with page 1, give the issue number in parentheses after the volume number.

Olson, G. A., & Moxley, J. M. Directing freshman

composition: The limits of authority. College

Composition and Communication, 40(1), 51–60.

Magazine article   The entry for an article in a magazine without volume numbers includes the month and day (if any), as well as the year, and the abbreviation *p.* or *pp*.

Grover, Ronald. (1988, September 19). A megawatt power

play in California. Business Week, pp. 34–35.

Newspaper articles   An entry for a newspaper (or magazine) article without a by-line begins with the headline or title in the author position without underlining or quotation marks.

New exam for doctor of future. (1989, March 15). The New

York Times, p. B–10.

When a newspaper article appears on discontinuous pages, give all page numbers and separate the numbers with commas.

Broad, W. J. (1989, March 14). Flight of shuttle begins

flawlessly. The New York Times, pp. A–1, C–7.

If appropriate, indicate the nature of an article in brackets following the article title.

Rotbert, R. I. (1989, March 15). Writers' anonymity aids

journal's integrity [Letter to editor]. The Chronicle

of Higher Education, p. B–6.

Special issue   In an entry for a special issue of a journal, identify the editors (if any) of the issue and the title of the issue. If the issue does not specify its editors, the title of the issue occupies the author position.

Woods, R. D. (Ed.). (1988). Mexican autobiography

[Special issue]. Auto/Biography Studies, 3(4).

Monograph   In an entry for a monograph, identify the nature of the material within brackets and give the volume number of the issue. Place additional identifying numerals, such as issue and serial (or whole) numbers in parentheses after the volume number.

Shumaker, W. (1954). English autobiography: Its

emergence, materials, and form [Monograph]. University

of California English Studies, B.

Kreutzer, M. A., Leonard, C., & Flavell, J. H. (1975).

An interview study of children's knowledge about

memory. Monographs of the Society for Research in

Child Development, 40(Whole No. 1).

Abstract   If you wish to cite only the abstract of a published article, provide a complete entry for the published article and cite the source of the abstract, if different, in parentheses.

Dorin, J. R., Inglis, J. D., & Porteous, D. J. (1989).

Selection for precise chromosomal targeting of a

dominant marker by homologous recombination. Science,

243, 1357–1360. (From Science Abstracts, 1989, 75,

Abstract No. 1153)

Book review   Indicate the subject of a book review within brackets following the title.

Broyard, A. (1989, January 22). Fiction: A user's manual

[Review of The company we keep: An ethics of fiction].

The New York Times Book Review, pp. 3, 27.

If the review does not have a title, use the material within brackets as the title.

Article in press   When an article has been accepted for publication, the expression *in press* takes the date position, and the name of the journal (but not the volume or page numbers) is given.

Chapters and Articles in Books

Article in an edited collection

In a reference to a chapter or article in an edited book, place the author of the chapter in the author position. The second part of the entry identifies the book in which the article appears. The name of the editor is not inverted. The page numbers for the individual chapter or article appear in parentheses after the title of the book.

Olney, J. (1980). Autobiography and the cultural moment:

A thematic, historical, and bibliographical

introduction. In J. Olney (Ed.), Autobiography: Essays

theoretical and critical (pp. 3–27). Princeton:

Princeton University Press.

Previously published article

When an article in a collection was published previously, give the original citation in parentheses. The parenthetical citation in the text includes both publication dates.

Howarth, H. L. (1980). Some principles of autobiography.

In J. Olney (Ed.) Autobiography: Essays theoretical and

critical (pp. 84–114). Princeton: Princeton University

Press. (Reprinted from New Literary History, 1974, 5,

363–381)

Translated article

In an entry for a translated article, the original title may be given in brackets.

Gusdorf, G. (1980). Conditions and limits of

autobiography [Conditions et limites de

l'autobiographie]. In J. Olney (Ed.), Autobiography:

Essays theoretical and critical (pp. 28–48).

Princeton: Princeton University Press. (Reprinted from

Reichenkron, G., & Haase, E. [Eds.]. [1956]. Formen

der selbstdarstellung [Forms of self-representation].

Berlin: Duncker and Humblot)

Technical and Research Reports

Basic form

Entries for technical and research reports should follow the basic format for a book entry. The series or number of the report should be identified in parentheses immediately after the title.

Hunt, G. H., & Mohler, S. R. (1958). Aging: A review of

research and training grants supported by the National

Institutes of Health (U.S. Public Health Service

Publication No. 652). Bethesda: National Institutes of

Health.

Report from an information service

For a report that comes from an information service, such as the National Technical Information Service (NTIS) or Educational Resources Information Center (ERIC), identify the service and document number in parentheses at the end of the entry.

Groak, J. J. (1974). Utilization of library resources by

students in non-residential degree programs.

Washington, DC: U.S. Government Printing Office. (ERIC

Document Reproduction Service No. ED 121 236)

Author as publisher

When the author of a report is also the publisher, as in the case of many newsletters, list *Author* as publisher.

Teachers Insurance and Annuity Association, College

Retirement Equities Fund. (1989). The participant.

New York: Author.

Proceedings of Meetings

Published proceedings

When contributions to a meeting appear in book form, the entry follows the format for a book.

Ferrua, P. (Ed.). (1979). Proceedings of the first

international symposium on letterism. Paris:

Avant-Garde.

Bentley, S.   (1978).   Introduction.   In G. E. Carter, J.

R. Parker, and S. Bentley (Eds.), <u>Minority literature</u>

<u>and the urban experience</u>.   LaCrosse: Institute for

Minority Studies, University of Wisconsin.   Fourth

Annual Conference on Minority Studies, April 1976,

University of Wisconsin, LaCrosse.

Unpublished proceedings
     For an unpublished contribution to a conference or symposium, indicate the place and date of the meeting.

Peltonen, K.   (1989, June 16).   Colors in <u>Ulysses</u>.   Paper

presented at the James Joyce Conference, Curtis

Institute of Music, Philadelphia.

Doctoral Dissertations

Microfilm of dissertation
     When you use the microfilm of a dissertation as the source, give the microfilm number as well as the volume and page numbers in *Dissertation Abstracts International*.

Baker, C. A.   (1985).   Multiple alliance commitments: The

role of the United States in the Falklands war.

<u>Dissertation Abstracts International</u>, <u>45</u>, 4445B.

(University Microfilms No. 85–77, 123)

Typescript of dissertation
     When you use the typescript copy of a dissertation, give the university and year as well as the volume and page numbers in *Dissertation Abstracts International*. If the dates are different, provide the date of the dissertation after the name of the university.

Moskop, W. W.   (1985).   The prudent politician: An

extension of Aristotle's ethical theory (Doctoral

dissertation, George Washington University).

<u>Dissertation Abstracts International</u>, <u>45</u>, 4445B.

Unpublished dissertation

Treat a dissertation that does not appear in *Dissertation Abstracts International* as an unpublished work. Underline the title.

Rosenthal, M. (1976). <u>Poetry of the Spanish civil war</u>.

Unpublished doctoral dissertation, New York University.

Unpublished Materials

Completed material

When unpublished material is in completed form, underline the title and indicate the unpublished status at the end of the entry.

Johnson, S. J. <u>The teaching of twelfth-grade advanced</u>

<u>placement biology</u>. Unpublished manuscript.

When an unpublished manuscript has been submitted for publication, indicate that fact at the end of the entry.

Bell, J. C. <u>Forms of childhood autism</u>. Manuscript

submitted for publication.

Draft material

When unpublished material remains in draft or unorganized tabular form, put the name of the topic in brackets in the title position; do not underline the topic. Indicate the status of the material at the end of the entry.

Hansen, A. L. (1987). [Survival rates of Scandinavian

immigrants, 1890–1920]. Unpublished raw data.

Nonprint Media

In entries for nonprint media, place the name of the principal organizer or creator in the author position, and in parentheses identify the function of the organizer or creator. The nature of the medium should be indicated in brackets immediately after the title. Enter the place and date of publication as for a book.

Film Redford, R. (Director). (1980). <u>Ordinary people</u> [Film].

Paramount.

Cassette Lake, F. L. (Author and speaker). (1989). <u>Bias and</u>

<u>organizational decision-making</u> [Cassette].

Gainesville: Edwards.

Toronto Stock Exchange (Producer). (1989). Canadian

stock options [Machine-readable database]. Toronto:

I. P. Sharp.

Numbered material   When you have a number for a cassette or other material, include it with the description within parentheses.

Hunter, K. (Speaker). (1989). Family counseling

[Cassette Recording No. 1175]. Washington, DC:

American Psychological Association.

Computer software   In an entry for computer software, include the name of the author or producer, the year of development or publication, the title underlined, the facts of publication, and any additional information necessary for locating and running the program.

International Software, Lingo Fun (Producer). (1987).

German Context, Levels 1 and 2 [Computer software].

Westerville, OH: International Software. (Network

version)

Harlow, George E. (Author). (1989). Program for

cataloging the mineral collection, American Museum of

Natural History [Computer program]. (Available from

[name and address]).

For information about other aspects of the APA format, see the *Publication Manual of the American Psychological Association,* 3rd ed. (Washington, DC: American Psychological Association, 1983).

APPENDIX C

Author-Number System of References

The author-number system, like the APA and MLA styles, uses parenthetical references within the text. The parenthetical references, however, do not contain an author's name.

In the author-number system, a numbered bibliography of references with entries arranged in alphabetical order or in order of citation in the text appears at the end of the paper. The number of each entry in the bibliography is placed within parentheses in the text to indicate the identity of a source. Page numbers, separated from the source number by a colon, follow when needed. Each entry is listed only once in the bibliography, but the number for an entry may be used repeatedly in the text.

Differences of opinion exist about returning to the gold standard. Collins (1) does not believe that the move would help the economy, while backers of the idea such as Kemp (2) see the gold standard as the key to a stable economy. As Collins puts it, gold is "as beautiful as ever but no cure for what ails us" (1:19). Most commentators agree that gold is a secure investment (1:19, 2:32).

References

1. Collins, Lora S. "An Assay of Gold." Across the Board, 5 Jan. 1982: 19–20.

2. Kemp, Jack. "The Renewal of Western Monetary Standards." Wall Street Journal, 7 Apr. 1982: 32.

APPENDIX D

Abbreviations of State Names

Usually, the name of the city is all that is needed to identify the place of publication in a note or a bibliographical reference. If one city might be confused with another (such as Lexington, Kentucky, and Lexington, Massachusetts) or if the location of a city is not well known, include the name of the state, using abbreviations. Use these abbreviations only in bibliographical references or in tables; do not use them in the text.

STATE NAME	TRADITIONAL ABBREVIATION (*CHICAGO MANUAL*)	U.S. POSTAL SERVICE ABBREVIATION (MLA AND APA)
Alabama	Ala.	AL
Alaska	Alaska	AK
American Samoa	Amer. Samoa	AS
Arizona	Ariz.	AZ
Arkansas	Ark.	AR
California	Calif.	CA
Canal Zone	C.Z.	CZ
Colorado	Colo.	CO
Connecticut	Conn.	CT
Delaware	Del.	DE
District of Columbia	D.C.	DC
Florida	Fla.	FL
Georgia	Ga.	GA
Guam	Guam	GU
Hawaii	Hawaii	HI
Idaho	Idaho	ID
Illinois	Ill.	IL
Indiana	Ind.	IN
Iowa	Iowa	IA
Kansas	Kans.	KS
Kentucky	Ky.	KY

STATE NAME	TRADITIONAL ABBREVIATION (*CHICAGO MANUAL*)	U.S. POSTAL SERVICE ABBREVIATION (MLA AND APA)
Louisiana	La.	LA
Maine	Maine	ME
Maryland	Md.	MD
Massachusetts	Mass.	MA
Michigan	Mich.	MI
Minnesota	Minn.	MN
Mississippi	Miss.	MS
Missouri	Mo.	MO
Montana	Mont.	MT
Nebraska	Nebr.	NE
Nevada	Nev.	NV
New Hampshire	N.H.	NH
New Jersey	N.J.	NJ
New Mexico	N.Mex.	NM
New York	N.Y.	NY
North Carolina	N.C.	NC
North Dakota	N.Dak.	ND
Ohio	Ohio	OH
Oklahoma	Okla.	OK
Oregon	Oreg.	OR
Pennsylvania	Pa.	PA
Puerto Rico	P.R.	PR
Rhode Island	R.I.	RI
South Carolina	S.C.	SC
South Dakota	S.Dak.	SD
Tennessee	Tenn.	TN
Texas	Tex.	TX
Utah	Utah	UT
Vermont	Vt.	VT
Virginia	Va.	VA
Virgin Islands	V.I.	VI
Washington	Wash.	WA
West Virginia	W.Va.	WV
Wisconsin	Wis.	WI
Wyoming	Wyo.	WY

APPENDIX E

MLA-Style Shortened Forms of Publishers' Names and Imprints

In MLA style, publishers' names are shortened. When the name of the publisher is that of a person (J. B. Lippincott), cite the last name only (Lippincott). When the name of the publisher includes more than one surname (Houghton Mifflin), cite only the first (Houghton). Abbreviate *University* as *U*, and *Press* as *P*. The following is a selected list of shortened names.

SHORT FORM	COMPLETE NAME
Abrams	Harry N. Abrams, Inc.
ALA	American Library Association
Allen	George Allen and Unwin Publishers, Inc.
Allyn	Allyn and Bacon, Inc.
Appleton	Appleton-Century-Crofts
Ballantine	Ballantine Books, Inc.
Bantam	Bantam Books, Inc.
Barnes	Barnes and Noble Books
Basic	Basic Books
Beacon	Beacon Press, Inc.
Benn	Ernest Benn, Ltd.
Bobbs	The Bobbs-Merrill Co., Inc.
Bowker	R. R. Bowker Co.
Cambridge UP	Cambridge University Press
Clarendon	Clarendon Press
Columbia UP	Columbia University Press
Cornell UP	Cornell University Press
Dell	Dell Publishing Co., Inc.
Dodd	Dodd, Mead, and Co.

SHORT FORM	COMPLETE NAME
Doubleday	Doubleday and Co., Inc.
Dover	Dover Publications, Inc.
Dutton	E. P. Dutton, Inc.
Farrar	Farrar, Straus and Giroux, Inc.
Free	The Free Press
Funk	Funk and Wagnalls, Inc.
Gale	Gale Research Co.
GPO	Government Printing Office
Harcourt	Harcourt Brace Jovanovich, Inc.
Harper	Harper and Row Publishers, Inc.
Harvard Law Rev. Assn.	Harvard Law Review Association
Harvard UP	Harvard University Press
Heath	D. C. Heath and Co.
Holt	Holt, Rinehart and Winston, Inc.
Houghton	Houghton Mifflin Co.
Humanities	Humanities Press, Inc.
Indiana UP	Indiana University Press
Johns Hopkins UP	The Johns Hopkins University Press
Knopf	Alfred A. Knopf, Inc.
Lippincott	J. B. Lippincott Co.
Little	Little, Brown and Co.
Macmillan	Macmillan Publishing Co., Inc.
McGraw	McGraw-Hill, Inc.
MIT P	The MIT Press
MLA	The Modern Language Association of America
NAL	The New American Library, Inc.
NEA	The National Education Association
Norton	W. W. Norton and Co., Inc.
Oxford UP	Oxford University Press
Penguin	Penguin Books, Inc.
Pocket	Pocket Books
Popular	The Popular Press
Prentice	Prentice-Hall, Inc.
Princeton UP	Princeton University Press
Putnam's	G. P. Putnam's Sons
Rand	Rand McNally and Co.
Random	Random House, Inc.
St. Martin's	St. Martin's Press, Inc.
Scott	Scott, Foresman and Co.
Scribner's	Charles Scribner's Sons
Simon	Simon and Schuster, Inc.
UMI	University Microfilms International
U of Chicago P	University of Chicago Press
U of Toronto P	University of Toronto Press
UP of Florida	The University Presses of Florida
Viking	The Viking Press, Inc.
Yale UP	Yale University Press

MLA also shortens the names of publishers' imprints (names given to groups of books within a company's publications) to one word, unless more are needed for accurate identification. To distinguish Laurel Editions from Laurel Leaf, both imprints of Dell, the second word should be included. In MLA style, the name of the imprint, followed by a hyphen without spacing on either side, precedes the name of the publisher.

Below is a partial list of well-known imprints.

CHICAGO MANUAL STYLE	MLA STYLE
(Words modifying the name of the imprint, such as *Books* and *Editions,* may be omitted unless they are required for accurate identification.)	
Dell, Laurel Editions	Laurel Editions-Dell
Dell, Laurel Leaf Classics	Laurel Leaf-Dell
Doubleday, Anchor Books	Anchor-Doubleday
Doubleday, Dial Press	Dial-Doubleday
Doubleday, Image Books	Image-Doubleday
Doubleday, Quantum Press	Quantum-Doubleday
Harcourt Brace Jovanovich, Harbinger Books	Harbinger-Harcourt
Harcourt Brace Jovanovich, Harvest Books	Harvest-Harcourt
Harper and Row, Colophon Books	Colophon-Harper
Harper and Row, Perennial Library	Perennial-Harper
Harper and Row, Torchbooks	Torchbooks-Harper
Holt, Rinehart and Winston, Owl Books	Owl-Holt
Houghton Mifflin, Clarion Books	Clarion-Houghton
Houghton Mifflin, Riverside Editions	Riverside-Houghton
Alfred A. Knopf, Dragonfly Books	Dragonfly-Knopf
William Morris, Reynal	Reynal-Morris
New American Library, Mentor Books	Mentor-NAL
New American Library, Plume Books	Plume-NAL
New American Library, Signet Books	Signet-NAL
Pocket Books, Poseidon Press	Poseidon-Pocket
Simon and Schuster, Touchstone Books	Touchstone-Simon

GLOSSARY

This glossary lists terms and abbreviations that occur in notes, parenthetical literary references, and bibliographic entries. Many of these terms, particularly those in Latin, are no longer recommended for current use, but because they are part of the tradition of scholarly research and writing, they appear frequently in the literature.

When you are deciding whether to use one of these terms or abbreviations, your first guide should be the requirements of the style you are following. Your second consideration should be brevity and clarity. If an abbreviation will save space and contribute to understanding, it should be used; if it will merely obfuscate or confuse, consider other phrasing.

Foreign words and phrases not yet Anglicized should be italicized (underlined in typing). Conclusions concerning which foreign words have become Anglicized vary among disciplines, institutions, and journals. The trend seems to be toward Anglicizing the abbreviations and terms listed in this glossary. Italicized words in parentheses are the Latin originals.

For terms and abbreviations not included here, consult a dictionary.

ABBREVIATION OR TERM — MEANING	EXAMPLE
anon. — anonymous	
ante — before	
art., arts. — article(s)	Art. 5 (but "art. V" in legal citation); the next 4 arts.
bk., bks. — book(s)	Bk. 1; Bks. 3–5
c., cc. — chapter(s) (used only in legal citations); copyright	
ca. or c. *(circa)* — about	ca. 1473 (an approximate date)
CD-ROM — compact disk read-only-memory	
cf. *(confer)* — compare	
ch. or chap., chaps. — chapter(s)	Ch. 2 of 6 chs. *or* Chap. 2 of 6 chaps.
col., cols. — column(s)	col. 6; cols. 3 and 4
comp. — compiled (by), compiler	

ABBREVIATION OR TERM—MEANING	EXAMPLE
diss. — dissertation	
div., divs. — division(s)	Div. 3; Divs. 4 and 5
ed. — edited (by)	
ed., eds. — editor(s) or edition(s)	
e.g. *(exempli gratia)* — for example	
et — and	et al.; et passim
et al. *(et alii)* — and others	
et seqq. *(et sequentes* or *et sequentia)* — and the one(s) that follow(s), and those that follow	pp. 17 et seqq.
et passim — and here and there	
ex., exs. — example(s)	
f., ff. — and the following page(s), line(s), etc.	pp. 5 f.; pp. 17 ff
fig., figs. — figure(s)	Fig. 7; figs. 8 and 10
fn. — footnote (cf. n.)	fn. 27
fol. or fo., fols. — folio(s)	fol. 3; fols. 2 and 4
ibid. *(ibidem)* — in the same place	
idem — the same (person)	
i.e. *(id est)* — that is	
illus. — illustrated (by), illustration(s), illustrator(s)	
infra — below	
introd. — introduction (by)	
l., ll. — line(s)	l. 8; ll. 10–12
loc. cit. *(loco citato)* — in the place cited (not recommended for current use)	
MS, MSS, ms, mss — manuscript(s)	
n., nn. — note(s), endnote(s), footnote(s)	n. 9; nn. 6 and 7
NB *(nota bene)* — take notice, mark well	
n.d. — no date (of publication)	
no., nos. — number(s)	no. 1; nos. 2–6

ABBREVIATION OR TERM— MEANING	EXAMPLE
n.p. — no place (of publication) or no publisher	
n.s. (also NS, N.S., ns) — New Series, New Style	n.s. vol. 13
op. cit. (*opere citato*) — in the work cited	
o.s. (also O.S., OS, os) — Old Series, Old Style	o.s. no. 7
p., pp. — page(s)	p. 5; pp. 5–7 (signifies pages 5 through 7 inclusive)
par., pars. — paragraphs	par. 6; pars. 7 and 12
passim — here and there	
PC-DOS — personal computer disk operating system	
pl., pls. — plate(s)	Pl. 3 of 6 pls.
post — after	
pseud. — pseudonym	
pt., pts. — part(s)	Pt. 2; Pts. 3–5
q.v. (*quod vide*) — which see	
rev. — revised (by), revision; reviewed (by)	
rpt. — reprint, reprinted	
sc. — scene	
sec., secs. — section(s)	sec. 4; secs. 6–9
ser. — series	4th ser.
sic — thus	
supra — above, earlier in text	
s.v. (*sub verbo* or *voce*) — under the word or heading	
trans. or tr. — translated (by), translation, translator	
v. (*vice*) — in the place of	
v. (*vide*) — see	
v. — versus (in legal citations)	
v.,. vv. or vs., vss. — verse(s)	
viz or viz. (*videlicet*) — namely	
vol., vols. — volume(s)	Vol. 1; 4 vols.
vs. (*versus*) — against	

INDEX

Numbers for sample pages are in italics. Entries of particular interest to typists are in boldface.

TO THE READER

Since *Form and Style* serves writers in many disciplines, it would be helpful to the authors to know how the book worked for you and how it might be improved in the next edition. We would appreciate your filling out this questionnaire and sending it to Campbell/Ballou/Slade, c/o Marketing Services, College Division, Houghton Mifflin Company, One Beacon Street, Boston, Massachusetts 02108-3166.

1. What type(s) of paper(s) have you written using this book? _____
   _____

2. Did you need any additional definitions or explanations? _____
   Please explain. _____
   _____
   _____
   _____

3. What features of the book were most helpful? facing pages with note and bibliography forms? index? table of contents? headings? sample pages? _____
   _____
   _____
   _____

4. Did you use *Chicago Manual* or Modern Language Association format? _____
   _____

5. If you used MLA format, did you find the instructions clear and complete?
   _____ If not, please explain. _____
   _____
   _____

6. Did you use the note-bibliography format or the parenthetical reference format?
   _____

7. Did you consult the Appendix on American Psychological Association format?
   _____ Did you use APA format for your paper? _____

8. Should note and bibliography forms be provided for any additional types of materials? Please be specific. _____
   _____
   _____
   _____
   _____

9. Did you write your paper on a word processor? _____ If yes, did you need any additional information? Please be specific. _____

_____

_____

_____

10. Did you conduct any of your research with computers or computer technology? _____ Please explain briefly. If yes, did you need any additional information? Please be specific. _____

_____

_____

_____

11. Did you find any inconsistencies or inaccuracies in this book? Please explain.

_____

_____

_____

12. If this book was either required or recommended for a course, we would appreciate knowing the name of your instructor and of your college or university.
Instructor   College or University

_____

13. Please add any further comments that you think might be useful. _____